Color Plate 1 (overleaf). The Gibson Girl, in 1901, the first universal pin-up—adored by men, imitated by women, an influence on the customs and fashion of her time, 1890–1914.

Color Plate 2. *Golden Dreams*, the 1951 calendar pin-up that introduced Marilyn Monroe's allure to a spellbound public. This famous pose helped launch Miss Monroe as the world's greatest sex-goddess. Photo: Tom Kelley Studio. First and exclusively published in Champion Calendars by John Baumgarth Co., Melrose Park, Ill.

the pin-up

a modest history
by Mark Gabor

A Universe Book
•
Bell Publishing Company • New York

Designed by Harry Chester Associates

Copyright © MCMLXXII by Universe Books
Library of Congress Catalog Card Number: 73-189116
All rights reserved.
This edition is published by Bell Publishing Company
a division of Crown Publishers, Inc.
by arrangement with Universe Books
381 Park Avenue South
New York, N.Y. 10016
        e f g h
Manufactured in the United States of America

Every effort has been made to locate the copyright
owners of the illustrations reproduced in this book.
Omissions brought to our attention will be corrected
in subsequent editions.

Lovingly dedicated
to my friend and wife
Nancy
and to our bright-eyed daughter
Julia

Contents

List of Color Plates

Foreword

The Packaging of Rape: A Feminist Indictment

To a woman, rape is the ultimate outrage. Rape symbolizes, in a primitive form, all the elements of the power relationship between males and females. Historically as well as psychologically, rape is the essence of male domination of the female. It is an act that subdues the female by crushing her will and violating her person. Embodied in the act is a sadistic hostility toward women. Milder expressions of this hostility are behind many sarcastic remarks, as well as in behavior that ridicules or humiliates the woman. More extreme forms might lead to the mutilation or murder of the victim. Rape falls somewhere in between.

Women do not, as a rule, fantasize their domination over men or their humiliation of them. If they participate in masochistic behavior with men it is, in most cases, because the men demand it and the women wish to please their men. Even in the most uninhibited sexual arena, the "swinger's" party, wives are frequently introduced as "nervous, but willing to try."

In James Thurber's familiar cartoons illustrating the "war between the sexes," women are shown overpowering tiny, frightened men. But these were a man's fantasies about women and should not be confused with a woman's very own imaginings. In fact, in most literature dealing with psychological topics, very little is written about women based on their reported experiences. Men write about women in terms of what *they* already believe and, therefore, reinforce the mythologies.

Young boys are taught that they are naturally superior to girls. The lesson is reinforced at every subsequent stage of their development. At play, at school, and in business and social activities, a man quickly learns that the place reserved for him in the world is unquestionably better than the one reserved for that other "class"—women. In his personal relationships with women, and later, in his singular relationship with his wife, all the patriarchal values will emerge and he will proceed to impose his will on his "inferiors."

Kate Millett, in *Sexual Politics,* explains that the "unacknowledged . . . birthright priority whereby males rule females" is an institutionalized part of our social system. She goes on to describe how the patriarchal mentality has created numerous rationales based upon women's inferiority to justify their treatment of them. Underlying much literature and openly expressed in many other forms, including psychoanalytic theory, is

the male fantasy that women desire to be dominated—raped—by men. A well-known authority on human aggression explains it this way: "The idea of being seized and borne off by a ruthless male who will wreak his sexual will upon his helpless victim has a universal appeal to the female sex." * This belief is frequently expressed by men writing about women.

Mark Gabor, the author of this history, feels that, in pin-ups, men are seeking what they do not have in real life, that is, a woman they can dominate. Implicit in this view is that males relate to a fantasized "mate" who will not "answer back, or demand reciprocation, compromise, or fair treatment." She will be subordinate to him. He will rule her. It is clear, then, that many men must find a way to reinforce their need to dominate. These fantasies, according to Mr. Gabor, may actually help a man "fulfill the rule imposed upon him by society," a society in which "a man is a man *only* if he can dominate women." This need appears to be so great that men project it onto women who they claim want to be dominated.

There are women who say they like big men, strong men; there are even a few women who write home about the size of a man's genitals—a few who may even be obsessed, as men are, with this dimension game. (Is it possible that these women have somehow been strung into the male's own machismo problem?) But most women relate to a total person, not an isolated aspect—the sexuality—of a person. Women feel insulted and demeaned when a relationship is reduced to detached sexuality. They object to men's sexist comments about them and about other women, to the "clucking noises" that men emit when they spot an attractive woman. Women complain that there is too much emphasis on bodies, too much exploitative use of women as passive objects (as in advertising). They continually ask, "Can't men relate to women as human beings?"

Even among homosexuals, lesbians tend to seek a total relationship with other human beings while male homosexuals tend more to objectify their sexual partners. Magazines for gay men feature males performing the same pictorial functions, for homosexual male readers, as the female model performs for the heterosexual male reader.

---

* Anthony Storr, *Human Aggression* (London: Penguin; New York: Atheneum, 1968).

Male sexuality contains elements of impersonality, brutality, sadism, and humiliation of the female as victim, as well as domination. Men are more frequently involved than are women in sexual acts with strangers (prostitutes); they gravitate toward pornography and toward gratification for its own sake. In homosexuality, also, male behavior often exaggerates all of these possibilities. Sex line-ups in isolated parks and parking lots are common. The buying of sex is almost exclusively a male act. Our paternalistic past and a long history during which men have owned women makes the exchange of money for sex almost a natural act.

Unlike women, who are expected to control their sexual urges—sometimes it is not recognized that they have any—men are permitted an almost constant source of tantalizing sexual outlets. It is embarrassing for a woman to go into some areas where men work because of the proliferation of erotic art on the walls. The source of the discomfort, to the woman, is the knowledge that the man is measuring her against the archetype hanging up there on the wall. She feels reduced to a similar status, that of a sex object.

From examinations of this phenomenon, it is not clear whether men deliberately keep themselves in a constant state of excitation for pleasure, or whether the continual exposure to eroticism diminishes or represses their constant excitation. Without evaluating them, Mr. Gabor reviews the two positions for us: that erotic fantasies might be considered healthy substitutes for promiscuity, extramarital sex, and fetishism or that unfulfilled fantasies might lead to greater emotional repression and intensify psychosexual problems. In a recent article on nudity, an anthropologist favored the former interpretation—that nudity can be a healthy sublimation for deviant psychosexual behavior such as voyeurism and exhibitionism.* As it becomes more erotic in intent, more an excuse for "swinging," nudism seems to be following a path parallel with the development of the pin-up. Many "new nudists" use polaroid snapshots to advertise for other couples. The photos are pornographic in that the women are frequently shown with their legs spread apart—clearly a sexual invitation, according to the author, although in primitive mythology, the presentation of the exposed vulva was believed to frighten the devil away. It is, it seems, another case of a technology (in this case, a camera) lending an assist to—perhaps creating—a social phenomenon. Just as the advent of printing ensured the distribution of pin-ups to a mass audience, the polaroid camera ensures the expansion of "swinging."

Inherent in all these extreme forms of male sexuality is the objectification of the female—and the extreme forms could not exist outside the process. In Mr. Gabor's words, she is "a man's object in a man's world."

The author has thoroughly traced the development of the pin-up from its earliest-known appearance in the

15th century, when, in 1491, an illustrated poster advertised a Belgian edition of *Histoire de la Belle Melusine.* Until the early 19th century, the image of women was used primarily as an accompaniment to products. A 1741 poster advertising parasols (A-16), although credited with "sex appeal," is austere compared to illustrations that appeared in the next century.

The use of sex appeal in advertising followed its own development, becoming one of the most exploitative mediums, in which the description "sex-for-the-sake-of-selling" could be reversed and stated, "selling-for-the-sake-of-sex," as in some recent airline advertisements that proclaim, "I'm Judy" (or Linda or Sherrill) and urge the reader, "Fly me." Many contemporary critics of the image of women in advertising claim that advertising (like the pin-up) reflects men's fantasies of how they would like women to be—empty-headed consumers, dedicated to serving men.

By the late Victorian era, the use of the female body to "suggest" sex was increasing. At that time, according to Mr. Gabor, the first real pin-ups were distributed *en masse.* More and more exploitatitive photographs were published. The theater was popular and show business magazines featured actresses in enticing poses and in various stages of dress and undress. It was not unusual to see semi-nude or "spicy" pin-ups, many of them from France, in the magazines. The semi-nude with the bicycle (A-21) could easily have been a forerunner of a modern erotic poster featuring fetishism. The high heels and stockings are typical of this form.

Near the turn of the century, the author notes, the Gibson Girl seemed to embody an elegance of her own. She was a personality, an ideal for other women, but still attractive to men. The Gibson Girl's outstanding characteristic was her self-confidence (A-35) and her sense of privacy. "For the first time in the evolution of the pin-up," the author tell us, "a woman was presented for her own sake outside the context of advertising, dance, theater, burlesque, and 'art.'" (Could the Gibson Girl actually have been pinned up—an act analogous to tossing Grace Kelly or Princess Margaret into a swimming pool? There is something in the eyes of women of this type that ensures their dignity.) In any case, the Gibson Girl vanished shortly after 1910, and the next symbol of womanhood was the angular, energetic flapper.

Leading up to the period of high-class cheesecake, the author noticed a trend—a change in the image of women—influenced by the advent of "confession" magazines, in which women were being presented in more depth, more as individuals than as "happy-go-lucky sex objects." Then, in the 1930s and the 1940s, the Petty Girl and the Varga Girl appeared in *Esquire,* which was the first men's magazine to publish pin-up material for a higher-class reader. The author likens the difference between *Esquire* and other girlie magazines of the time to the difference between call girls and street-walkers.

After the war, an era of increasingly sensational publications, the "Hollywood dream" apparently be-

---

* Sheila K. Johnson, "The New Nudism vs. The Old Nudism," *The New York Times Sunday Magazine,* June 4, 1972.

came "superfluous," and people seemed to need a raunchier form of entertainment. The 1950s saw a transition to the heavier side of sex—psychosexual themes illustrating fetishism, sadomasochism, masturbation, homosexuality, lesbianism, and exhibitionism. Movie fan magazines, which had been popular since the 1920s, also began a more exploitative presentation of Hollywood's sex goddesses.

During those years, which are within almost everyone's memory, examples of cheesecake, "girlie" photos, and nude "art" photos seemed to be everywhere. Children and women were exposed to the whole range of the genre—in mass magazines and at the movies—and took it all for granted as part of the culture. In the 1950s, when it was no longer considered obscene to bring the stuff home, *Playboy*, a "quality" magazine that came into being in 1953 as *Esquire* was in the process of eliminating pin-ups from its pages, was read openly by most members of sophisticated households. Children, both girls and boys, were fascinated, particularly by the sadomasochism of some of the *Playboy*-type magazines. Mothers, in many cases, were afraid of taking it away—afraid of *causing* a "complex" by seeming to disapprove of the content. They would wait until the child put down a magazine and then they would throw it away. So Dad would spend 75¢ one day on a magazine that would disappear the next day from the shelf in the bathroom.

To feminists, *Playboy*, as the author describes it, has "come to epitomize the worst features of male chauvinism" in its presentation and exploitation of women as "unreal," "demeaning," and representative of an "offensive image of femininity." The Penthouse Pet, he points out, however, is much less of a sexist idealization of a woman, and, although coming nowhere near the values of Women's Liberation, is less eager to serve a man, more tuned in to pop culture, and more natural in expressing herself than Playboy's Playmate.

In any case, in the 1960s and the early 1970s, psychosexual themes have proliferated in magazines and in pop posters. Some magazines now border on hardcore pornography. In Britain, "masturbatory" poses have been introduced into the quality magazines for men.

Another recent major change is evident. According to Mr. Gabor, the presentation of the female is "no longer limited to the cheesecake tradition," and "eroticism for its own sake is much in evidence." This is exemplified by the photograph of Ann, "A Whole Bunch of Woman" (*A-3*), in which the photographer has shot the woman from a low angle, thus exaggerating her genital area and breasts, and the placement of her hands is directly sexual. There is nothing coy about it.

In addition to the new sex, a second trend reflecting an image of women that began, perhaps, with the Gibson Girl has appeared. She is the independent woman—as defined by the author, "varied—complex, moody, lonely, dynamic, poetic, engaged in life—hence more

beautiful and appealing." This type is represented by Brigitte Bardot (*D-51* through *D-54, G-28*).

Mr. Gabor has made visible the evolution of the pin-up genre from a relatively innocent representation of a "sexually alluring woman"—one who evokes an image in which either the "expression or the attitude of the subject invites the viewer to participate vicariously in or fantasize about a personal involvement with the subject"—to a new type of image, which ultimately becomes pornography, in which sex is explicit. This was a process—a development of the past hundred years—whereby the female gradually shed her clothes while the panderers shed their "excuses for the display of female nudity." They just displayed it cold. Without trim. No themes, no products, no stories—just flesh.

Erotic fantasies now take the form of direct sexual encounters with the subject. The intention behind the presentation of these images defines them as cheesecake (which "suggests" an involvement) or pornography (which elicits a direct sexual response). The range of sexual images has been expanded from the "peekaboo" pin-ups of the Victorian era through today's "orgy"-oriented hip posters. One thing is clear: The pin-up is a continuum of titillation, an escalation of eroticism, which began when the first hint of flesh was shown.

Why discuss rape and the power relationship between men and women in a foreword to a history of pin-ups? Because if you accept the validity of a continuum through which the exploitation of women increased in all the mediums, you realize that the germs of rape are inherent in all these forms, from the first tentative pin-up to the last orgiastic poster. The development of social nudity has exhibited a similar evolution: The "old nudity" and today's open sexuality can be seen as the extreme forms of nudity representing opposite poles of the continuum in the same way that cheesecake and pornography represent both ends of a different scale.

Even in a genre as innocent looking as the pin-up, all the elements of patriarchal values are present in the exploitation of the woman as a sexual object and the objectification of the female as a piece of property to be owned and ruled by men.* Reflected in the pin-up is the masculine view of woman as passive—an object to be pinned up—and masochistic—existing for men's pleasure in whatever form it might take. (As Kate Millett says, it was ingenious for men to ascribe masochism to females, for it "justifies any conceivable domination or humiliation forced upon the female.")

Also reflected, subtly in the pin-up, more blatantly in the erotic poster, is masculine hostility toward

---

* "The image of women as a sexual object, or status symbol, emphasizes the physical attractiveness of the female body and face and de-emphasizes the other attributes of the woman such as intelligence, creativity, ideas, and so on." Jane Prather, "Why Can't Women Be Like Men?: A Summary of the Sociophysiological Factors Limiting Women's Advancement in the Professions," *American Behavioral Scientist*, November-December 1971, p. 173.

15

women. As restrictions of censorship are removed, pornography increasingly dehumanizes and insults women, and as Kate Millett notes, "it has become far easier to assess sexual antagonism in the male."

It becomes evident, then, that the same emotions—hostility, contempt, aggression, or hatred—are present in all forms of pornography as are present in the act of rape.

It is no accident that there is no similar form of erotic stimulation for women. Women don't generally respond to "beefcake"—they don't seem to objectify men. Even when they do collect pin-ups and posters, according to Mr. Gabor, the male's personality and talent are emphasized, not his sexual attributes. Visual presentations of males are not *"intended* [italics are mine] to stimulate sexual fantasies alone,"* as pin-ups of women are; they are intended to encourage "fuller, amorous glamorous associations." This difference is reflected in advertising also, where the woman is presented as a sex object for the male, while men are usually presented as potential husbands for women, and, therefore, symbolize a total environment.

The author reports that although movie fan magazines are read more by women than by men, women are not so "inclined" to relate exclusively to the male nude body. He notes that the stories feature the characteristics, styles, moods, and roles of the men—perhaps glamorized, but, at least, more than simple figure studies. The representations are not necessarily sexually evocative, but evoke "emotion" or "admiration" through the personality of the man.

Women responding to a male nude centerfold in *Cosmopolitan* (New York), March 1972, thought it was "a joke," and they "couldn't take it seriously." It seems that women are simply not "turned on" by male nudity. Most women report that it is "pleasant" to look at attractive, esthetic nude bodies, of *both* sexes. Some heterosexual women are reluctant to say they appreciate another woman's body esthetically; they fear charges of lesbianism. The more "artistic" a woman is, however, the easier it is for her to admit a pleasurable response to a nude female figure.

Cosmopolitan reported that a few men "sheepishly" came into the office and asked for a copy of the centerfold. The model, Burt Reynolds, has also been the object of some ridicule, not by women, but by men. On one television news program, the male reporters made fun of the fact that the model's hand covered the genital area. They put him down in the same manner in which they put down women as sex objects.

Most homosexual women laugh at or respond negatively to erotic pictures of women. "The sexuality is so exaggerated," they say. They assume that the pictures are published for men and think it "hysterically funny that men can be turned on by this." By way of "proof," they point out that these photos are published in men's magazines, not in magazines for women. You can be certain that if there were even a hint of a potential market, some enterprising businessman would supply the product—but the market simply doesn't exist.

Joan Nicholson

Recognizing the feeling of many people today that sexism is imbedded in layer upon layer of tradition and that the cheesecake tradition has been one of the most exploitative of all, the author and publishers felt it appropriate that this history be prefaced with that point of view. Thus, Joan Nicholson, who has chaired the "Image of Women in the Media" committee of the National Organization of Women (NOW), was invited to preview the galley proofs and illustrations for this volume and to discuss here the subject of women's attitudes toward pin-ups. Ms. Nicholson, a continuing student of psychology and other social sciences, is a free-lance writer on subjects of social interest. Active in the Women's Movement since 1968, she edits NOW's action newsletter, Do It Now, *and is a member of the board of directors of NOW's New York City Chapter.*

Acknowledgements

In a book encompassing such diverse fields as magazines, posters, calendars, postcards, photography, and show business, it is not easy to recall or thank everyone who contributed material, data, advice, and—most important—the boundaries of this vaguely defined, virtually undocumented subject.

I am indebted to the staff and facilities of the New York Public Library—to Diane Shaw O'Neal and Elizabeth Roth (Print Room), Robert Allen (Main Information Desk), Joseph C. Mask (Main Reading Room), Anthony Cardillo (Art and Architecture), Paul Goren and Perry O'Neil (Arents Collection).

For their valuable time and cooperation, I thank Eugene Baily; Dorothy Ryan, Ray Brand, and Maurie Eichers of Brown and Bigelow; Chris Watson, Captain Publications; Myron Davis, Esquire, Inc.; Mark Ricci, The Memory Shop; Martin Geisler, Personality Posters; Peg Tighe, Poster Prints; and Peter Wolf, Signal Publications.

Special thanks are due to Harry Chester, for his quick, efficient, and imaginative solutions and resolutions of the problems caused by my selection of hundreds of illustrations from widely different periods, sources, and mediums; to Dion McGregor, whose encyclopedic knowledge of Hollywood filled many gaps in my original script; to Jack Rennert of Darien House, Inc., for his guidance through the rich world of *fin de siècle* poster art; and to John Tebbel, for his cosmic overview in ferreting out the roots and highlights of pin-up history.

Deepest gratitude to Louis Barron of Universe Books for his diligence, humor, and encouragement through all phases of this project.

Some Notes on the Illustrations

The publishers and I have made every possible effort to locate and credit the original sources of illustrations used in this volume. Also, where the information has been accessible and relevant, we have incorporated in the captions the names of artists, photographers, and models. In many instances, information about sources and creators has proved difficult or impossible to come by, particularly when our only choice of material was from scrapbooks, walls, and other places where full bibliographic data is not normally preserved. In a number of cases, we have also had to contend with selections from publications that, perhaps deliberately, do not print information regarding proprietorship, copyright, address, even country of origin. Nonetheless, through internal clues, research in American, British and European archives, and voluminous correspondence with collectors, libraries, and other helpful parties around the world, we have been able to attribute most of the illustrations even when information was not immediately evident. I apologize to those persons whose proprietary or creative interests we have failed to determine and credit. Information brought to our attention will be included in future editions.

I am grateful to my publishers, to designer Harry Chester, and to the printers for the extraordinary time, effort, and expense that has gone into the reproduction of the illustrations I have chosen. To reproduce a recognizable image from clippings that can be found only pasted in scrapbooks, from faded postcards and tattered handbills, from under-the-counter pulps that were atrociously printed to begin with, or even from quality magazine tear-sheets when the original art or photographs no longer exist (as, for example, with most of the famous Petty and Varga pin-ups) is technically no easy matter. Yet the 550-odd illustrations in this work are not merely recognizable; they are in general amazingly accurate renditions of the art *as it was preserved*. In some cases our lithographers felt they could even spruce up colors, restore lines, eliminate fold marks, and do away with a variety of other blemishes. In most instances, however, we opted for less cosmetic treatment, feeling this course would best convey the "flavor" of pin-up art as it has been handled and handed down through the years and as we appreciate it today.

My publishers have been most cooperative in dealing with the problems of taste inherent in a retrospective of pin-up art. Even in an age when the portrayal of sex in novels, magazines, art, cinema, and advertising is far more blatant than the peekaboo titillation characterizing most of the history traced in this volume, the publication of such a work inevitably involves certain moral considerations for a legitimate publisher. The very nature of pin-up art places it on the peripheries of "respectability" in any given age. To explore the peripheries of the 1910s and '20s is now "safe"—some call it nostalgia; to extend the exploration to the peripheries of the 1970s is to tread the borderline between exposition and exploitation. Nonetheless, the publishers share my feeling that one can hardly illustrate the state of today's pin-up art (and even much of yesterday's) without dealing in some measure with such matters as full frontal nudity, homosexuality, both male and female, and interracial sex. And, although we have chosen a measure considerably smaller than that commonly available in the mass media, some readers are bound to be offended. I can only hope that our selection of illustrations, and our judicious sizing and cropping of them, will prove to have done justice to my subject without injustice to the sensibilities of most readers.

Foundations of the Cheesecake Tradition

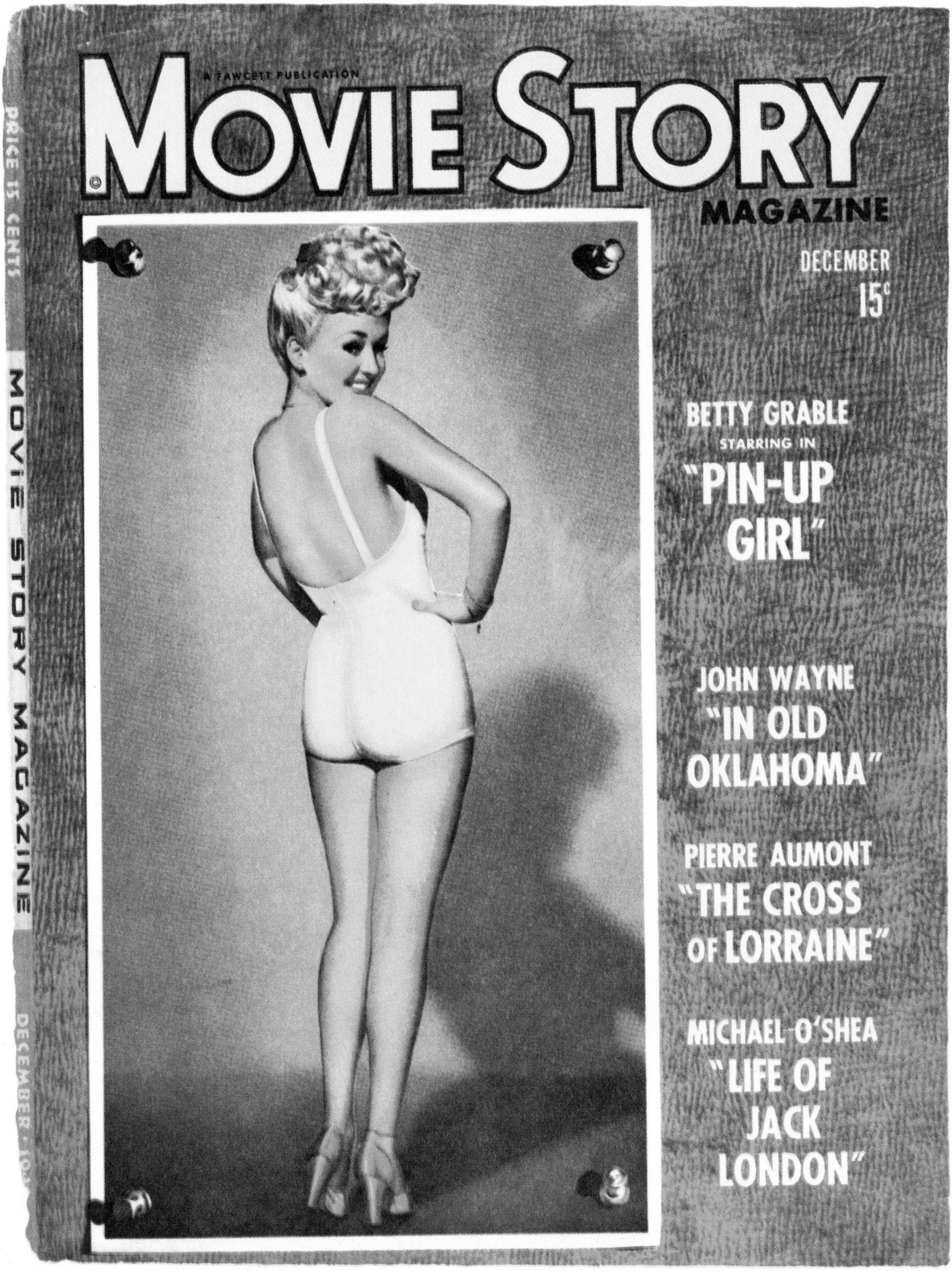

MOVIE STORY
MAGAZINE

DECEMBER
15c

PRICE 15 CENTS

MOVIE STORY MAGAZINE

DECEMBER · 1943

BETTY GRABLE
STARRING IN
"PIN-UP
GIRL"

JOHN WAYNE
"IN OLD
OKLAHOMA"

PIERRE AUMONT
"THE CROSS
OF LORRAINE"

MICHAEL O'SHEA
"LIFE OF
JACK
LONDON"

Color Plate 3. Betty Grable. This movie-studio publicity photo, which became one of the most famous pin-ups of all time, inaugurated the era when the term "pin-up" entered the world's vocabulary. The photograph was probably hand-colored for reproduction on this magazine cover. Note the pins, still a novelty in 1942, and the announcement of Grable's latest film, *Pin-up Girl*—a testament to her unquestioned reign as "Queen of the Pin-ups."

Color Plate 6 *Exhibition* was first issued in 1966 as a 12″ × 63″ poster calling for entries in the 46th annual art show of New York Art Directors Club. After the strikingly beautiful model, Wanda Embry, had been decorated in body paint by artist Tom Daly, she was photographed for the poster by Ken Harris. The sponsors reportedly found the initial rendition too revealing, so considerable retouching was required before the poster could be issued.

Color Plates 4 and 5
From modesty to mod—these illustrations epitomize attitudes, styles, and spirit in early and contemporary pin-ups.

September Morn (detail), subject of the first nude pin-up calendar (1913), reflects the sentimentalism and ideal of feminine purity characteristic of pin-ups in the early 20th century. As an oil painting, it was virtually unnoticed by the public; censored by the New York Society for the Suppression of Vice, it became a *cause célèbre* and was pirated as a reproduction on millions of calendars.

The *Soulmate Calendar* (1971), featuring chic black models, was refreshingly brash in its twelve satirical photographs on civil rights themes. Here, for July, is "Betsy Ross" making the American flag. Other subjects included soul food, the Civil War, minstrels, slavery, the Ku Klux Klan, and the Statue of Liberty. According to the publisher, this calendar did not sell well because it was too sophisticated for both blacks and whites; it was most appreciated by a radical minority who, unfortunately, were not interested in buying calendars. Published by Poster Prints, Norristown, Pa.

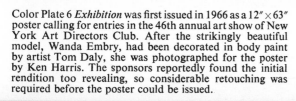

Foundations of the Cheesecake Tradition

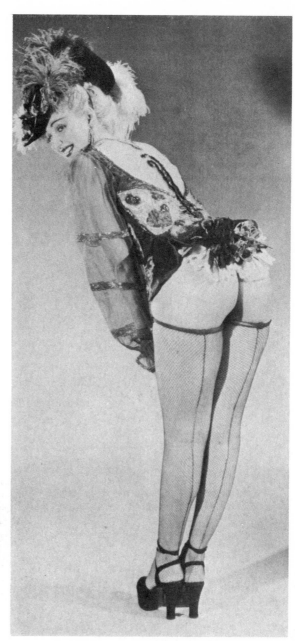

A-1. Lynne O'Neill, the original "garter girl." A typical pin-up of the cheesecake variety: dressed, but partly exposed, smiling and teasing the viewer with her body. (Picture Collection, New York Public Library.)

A pin-up can represent whatever we love, want to love, or want to have. Any printed image that can be hung on a wall could conceivably be regarded as a pin-up, and in common usage the term extends even further —to pin-up images, for example, on playing cards, key chains, drinking glasses, cigarette lighters, and other objects that never reach the wall. In World War II, pin-ups frequently adorned the sides of tanks and aircraft as mascots or good-luck talismans. Thus, despite the literal meaning of the term, it is clear that the essence of a pin-up is not so much its physical form as its quality of image, the image most commonly being that of a person—particularly a sexually alluring woman.

Our intention here is not to stretch this popular conception of the pin-up but to explore visually the scope and tradition of the classic pin-up types—cheesecake, movie stars, cult heroes, and other varieties. To avoid straying too far into the realm of the idiosyncratic and purely subjective, we have based our working definition of the pin-up on the intentions of the artist, photographer, or model: A pin-up is a sexually evocative image, reproduced in multiple copies, in which either the expression or the attitude of the subject invites the viewer to participate vicariously in or fantasize about a personal involvement with the subject. And, because of their overwhelming predominance, we will focus on printed pin-ups—those that can, literally, be pinned up.

The classic pin-up genre—cheesecake— fulfills our definition perfectly. Cheesecake (which Webster defines as "photography displaying especially female comeliness and shapeliness") is said to have gotten its name when, in September 1915, a newspaper photographer, George Miller, noticed a visiting Russian diva, Elvira Amazar, just as she was debarking from her ship in New York. Miller asked the opera singer to hike up her skirt a little for the sake of his picture. Later, the photographer's editor, something of a gourmet, is supposed to have exclaimed, "Why, this is better than cheesecake!" The story, apocryphal or not, dates from an era

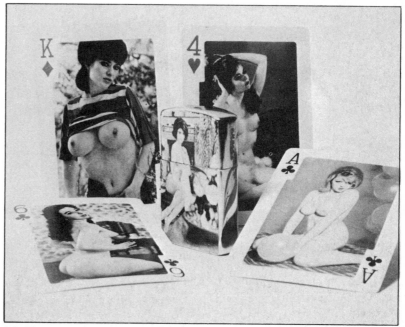

A-2. Pin-ups not for pinning up: cigarette lighter made in Japan and playing cards from England. (Photo: Victor Atkins.)

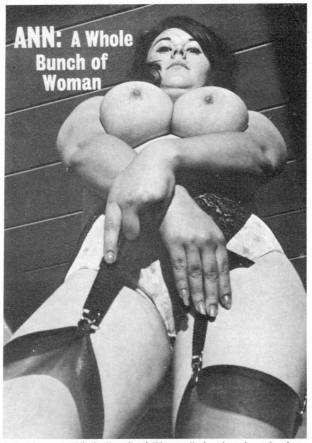

A-3. "Ann: A Whole Bunch of Woman," showing through photographic technique an exaggeration of body, suggestive expression, and direct sexuality. *Gent* (New York), June 1971.

that saw the birth of an international mode in illustration that still teases the eye, the libido, and the wallet of most men. It continues to thrive in the worlds of entertainment, publishing, and advertising and is used to sell almost everything, from ball bearings to ideas.

The cheesecake image is based on notions of teasing and allure—and frequently humor as well. But other styles of pin-ups have been used in association with a vast array of emotions, attitudes, pursuits, subjects, mediums: violence, satire, romance; eroticism, purity, fetishism, lesbianism, "softcore" eroticism (i.e., pictorial punning on erotic themes); dance, drama, burlesque, aspiring stardom, sports; cartoons, comic strips, advertisements; domesticity, nature, nationalism, pacifism. Yet overall, erotic fantasy is the key to understanding all styles of the pin-up.

Some men still dream about Marilyn Monroe (*Color Plate 2*) untouchable but eminently touchable; divine but earthy; strong but vulnerable. Others fantasize about Ann (*A-3*), presented as "a whole bunch of woman." There are doubtless as many kinds of fantasy desires as there are individuals who look at pin-ups.

The only overt sharing of pin-ups seems to exist in men's working or living quarters —on factory walls, in men's room, locker rooms, "back rooms," dens, clubhouses, dor-

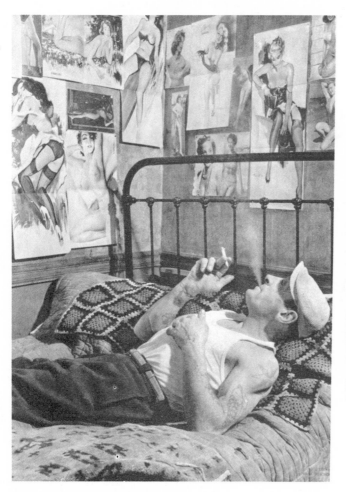

A-4. Characteristic settings for pin-ups that are pinned up. *Left*, a workingman's room (Photo: Robert Doisneau). *Above*, a machine shop (Photo: Victor Atkins).

mitories. Gathered around the wall plastered with pictures of "girlies," or "birds," men admire the women they crave the most and boast about how they would or could perform with their fantasy objects. Men may love their wives, but many would seem to have one affair after another with their pin-ups. They can treat the pin-ups as they wish they could treat their wives—buy them, seduce them, pamper them, rule them.

Many categories of image border on the pin-up: nude or erotic original art, pornography and obscenity, comic strips, candid photography, nude "art" photography, pictures of animals, athletes, and children, technological illustrations, and advertising. Many such images, to be sure, are pinned up—cinema stars ranging from Rin-Tin-Tin to Shirley Temple, athletes like Pele or Joe Namath, and racing cars, motorcycles, or the Boeing 747—but in these cases they are pinned up because of individual viewers' associations and inclinations, not because they were intended as pin-ups in terms of our definition.

Although the pin-up depends for its success on a sexually evocative image, it should not be confused, for instance, with original nude or erotic art. The pin-up is a *printed* form, intended for general distribution to a large audience. An erotic painting or drawing may be, and often is, reproduced, but in most cases the artist's intention would be thwarted if such a reproduction were regarded with the special state of mind normally applied to a pin-up. A reproduction of Botticelli's *Venus* could be construed as a pin-up, but in doing so, surely the viewer would limit not only his psychological perception but also his esthetic and historical appreciation of this great work of art. Why force *Venus* into such a narrow mold? You may pin her up, but she is not a pin-up.

Many pin-ups do originate as drawings or paintings—for example, the Gibson, Petty, and Varga girls and innumerable calendar subjects. These images are pin-ups simply because they are *intended* to be pin-ups—to be mass produced for the purpose of arousing sexual fantasy.

Candid photography does not normally convey the purposeful erotic evocation characteristic of the pin-up. Although many candid photographs can be described as sexy, they generally lack the tease or allure that pin-ups—through eyes or body—address to the viewer. In candid photography, by definition, the subject is unaware of the camera and hence of the audience.

In the case of a cartoon sex image—such as Al Capp's "Daisy Mae" or Britain's World War II darling, "Jane"—it is not the medium (drawing) that rules out these sex-kittens as pin-ups, but the fact that their semi-nudity or tease serves primarily the purposes of a story and only indirectly

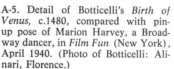

A-5. Detail of Botticelli's *Birth of Venus*, c.1480, compared with pin-up pose of Marion Harvey, a Broadway dancer, in *Film Fun* (New York), April 1940. (Photo of Botticelli: Alinari, Florence.)

A-6. Shirley Temple in publicity still for the film *Baby Takes a Bow* (1934). (Memory Shop, New York.)

A-7. Three photographs from "art photography" magazines showing the range from true art photography to pseudo-art photography to near obscenity. *Right:* Photo by André de Dienes. *Figure Photography Quarterly* (Hollywood, Calif.), 1971. *Center: Sprite* (Los Angeles) [undated]. *Below: Nouvelle Série de Studio* (Copenhagen) [undated]. According to *Sprite,* "artists will find help and inspiration in these pages." *Nouvelle Série de Studio* was "re-

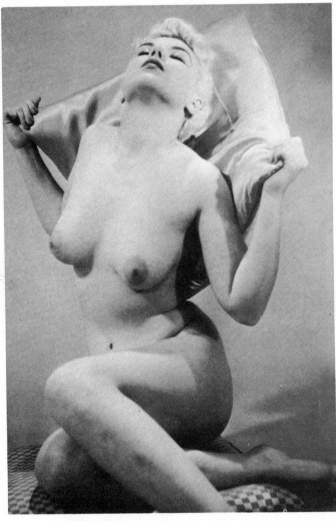

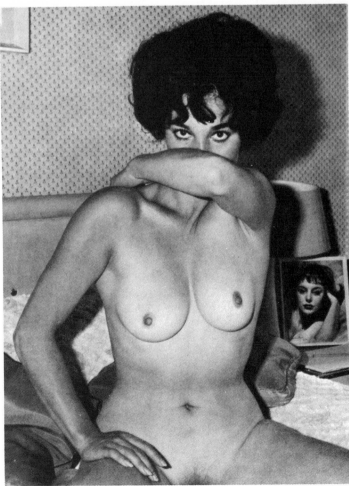

leased by the publishers exclusively to furnish serious artists and persons interested in art, who have some difficulty to find living models, with suitable photographs to be used as substitute for drawing, painting and sculpturing. Therefore the magazine will be sold only to adults who are serious-minded of problems of art and will look on our pictures solely from an aesthetical point of view."

arouses the viewer. To put it another way, they are unable to dislodge themselves from their frame-by-frame context so as to exist solely, specifically, and separately for the reader's delectation

One of the most common uses of the pin-up image is in advertising, and there are many well-known examples of sex-for-the-sake-of-selling—the White Rock girl (*A-28, right*) being among the most famous. Although at various points throughout this volume we will touch on the use of pin-ups in advertising, our attention will be directed mainly to advertising pin-ups that have transcended the sales pitch and are now esteemed for their artistic value, as with the French posters of the 1890s, or for their intrinsic sexual allure.

Pornography does not qualify as pin-up material because it accomplishes—and realizes—exactly what a pin-up must not do: Pornography is explicit, acting out the rituals that are only suggested by the pin-up and removing vital—and potentially more intoxicating—possibilities of imagination.

Most pin-ups are not even completely nude. The reasons may already be obvious: A fully exposed nude woman is not nearly as tantalizing as a partly clad lass who seems to be asking to be further undressed by the viewer. The traditional male preference for teasing rather than direct sexual confrontation is analogous to the relationship between cheesecake and a totally nude pin-up. Completely nude pin-ups do exist in special situations, however—usually outdoors, in natural surroundings.

The lack of clothing alone does not constitute nudity. There are, in fact, several important features of some "nude" pin-ups that traditionally indicate we are definitely not seeing art nudes. These features comprise jewelry, makeup, carefully arranged hair settings, and an endless assortment of props—ranging from sashes, belts, shawls, towels, and pillows to toys, sports equipment, and bric-a-brac—all carefully arranged to cover particular vital areas of the anatomy. True art nudes do not wear high heels and earrings.

In addition to this distinction between nude pin-ups and art nudes, there are several other indicators: the context of nudity —whether it is natural and esthetic or contrived and programmatic; the degree of erotic evocation—whether we are seeing beauty for its own sake or for its deliberately sexual suggestiveness; the printed vehicle of presentation—whether it is an art book, a photography magazine, or a "girlie" magazine.

The classic cheesecake pin-up shows a curvy woman, sumptuous breasts exposed (or nearly exposed), posing coquettishly in a predictable, stylized setting—a bedroom, perhaps, or a studio, beach, or theatrical environment. There are in cheesecake end-

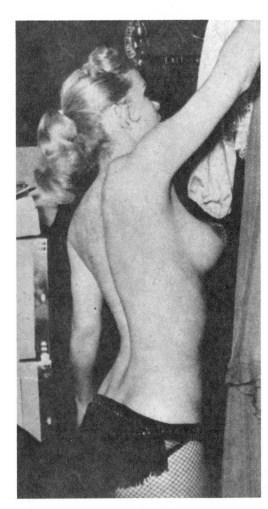

A-8. Candid photograph of burlesque actress. Not considered a true pin-up because there is no erotic appeal in this unposed situation. *Gala* (New York), November 1961.

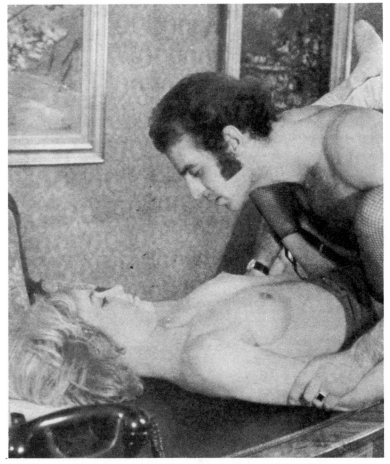

A-9. Pornographic subject, with explicit eroticism but no pin-up allure. *Sexy* (Hamburg).

27

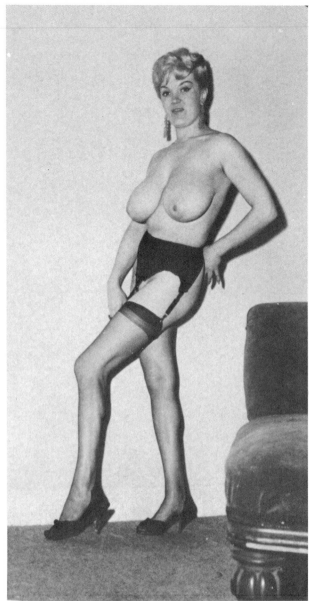

A-10. Four pin-up photos, showing atypical physical attributes, poor photographic technique, unconvincing expressions, or overstated sexual appeal. *Far left: Gala,*

less variations of setting, pose, and anatomical emphasis. Cheesecake is the type of pin-up found most frequently in girlie magazines, Hollywood magazines, calendars, and posters.

There is an equally large range of esthetic quality in cheesecake pin-ups. The best of the genre these days can be found in the centerfolds of such magazines as *Playboy* (Chicago), *Club, Mayfair,* and *Men Only* (London), *Penthouse* (London and New York, *ER* (Munich), *Lui* (Paris), *Playmen* (Rome), and *Aktuellt* (Stockholm)—all of which display attractive young women more or less tastefully posed in elegant and inviting surroundings.

But cheesecake can also be crude and

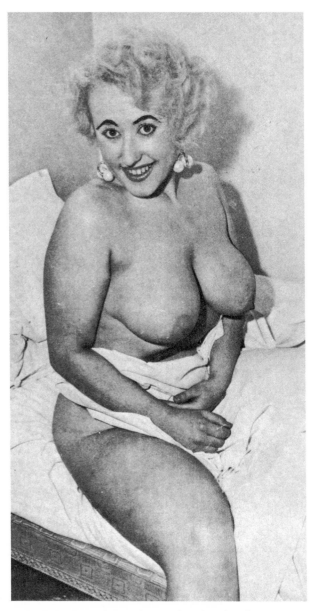

June 1966. *Two photos above: The Magazine for Artists and Photographers* [no place or date], c.1960. *Far right: Glamorama* [no place], c.1970.

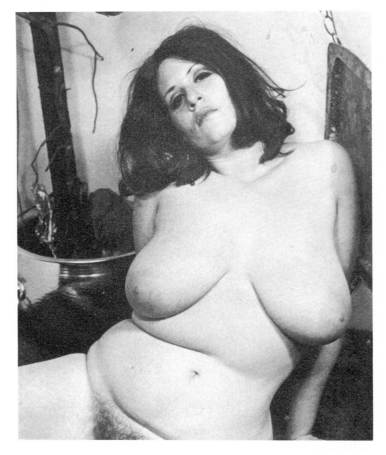

sometimes vulgar. The models may be aging women who pretend to be youthful; they may have grotesquely large breasts, be conspicuously overweight, or have bruised or blemished skin. The pose may be too obvious, too sexually exploitative; and the surroundings may be dingy, like a cheap hotel room. The only thing notable about these rather commonplace pin-ups is their pervasiveness and apparently enormous consumption by the public. Can it be that the Playgirl-of-the-Month is too "high class," too unattainable for the mass worshipper of cheesecake? Does the common man prefer an anomaly, an imperfect sexual object for what he intuitively feels are his imperfect sexual fantasies?

Mediums for pin-ups

Magazines

There are as many kinds of magazine pin-ups as there are magazine markets. Indeed, even as a magazine grows up with its readers, its use or non-use of pin-ups can reflect their change in age and taste. During the 1930s, for example, *Esquire* included pin-ups in each issue; but in the 1950s, as the magazine realized its literary aspirations, and as its college boy readers became young professionals and successful members of the upper-middle class, *Esquire* dispensed with pin-ups, presumably to reflect its cultural elitism. In addition, perhaps, *Esquire* wanted to attract potential advertisers who were shying away from the magazine's "girlie" image, or maybe *Esquire* preferred not to compete with the new magazine sensation, *Playboy* (which was first published in December 1953).

Playboy has always been overtly committed to the sensuous pleasures—gourmet food, high fidelity, romantic travel, and, of course, sex. With the gradual relaxation of censorship laws, *Playboy*'s pin-up presentation has become progressively bolder. The pubic areas of pin-up models can now be exposed without interference, or with relatively infrequent interference, from state or church, and without flak from advertisers or readers. (Actually, the London-based *Penthouse,* in its issue of April 1970, was the first of the "class" magazines to expose the pubic hair of its centerfold subjects.)

Esquire and *Playboy* were among the first magazines to dignify the cheesecake pin-up and elevate its hitherto low-class image. These pioneering monthlies recognized that their educated, cultured readers were susceptible to the same instincts that for decades had inspired the masses of men.

The widest range of pin-up images, the greatest variety in technique, style, and choice of subject—ranging from extreme mock-innocence to blatant suggestions of sexual arousal or the largest breasts a body can carry—appear in girlie magazines. Here one finds phallic, vaginal, homosexual, bestial, and sadomasochistic poses; surroundings that are traditional and contemporary; situations that are common and uncommon.

But what about those pin-up magazines that have page after page of peekaboo pictures? Must the pictures be taken out and pinned up to be considered pin-ups? Probably not. One supposes that these pin-ups mostly stay between the covers of the maga-

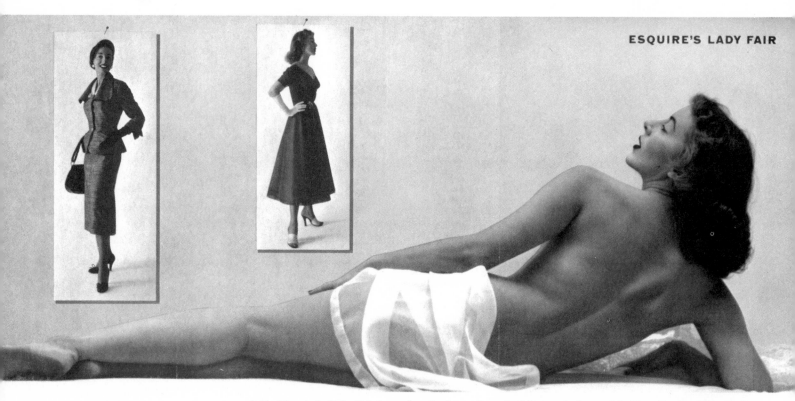

ESQUIRE'S LADY FAIR

A-11. "Esquire's Lady Fair," an elegant pin-up de-emphasizing sex in favor of fashion. *Esquire* (New York), March 1953. A late pin-up in *Esquire's* transition from Petty and Varga Girls to no pin-ups at all (1958). Note the conservative taste, with complete nonvisibility of breasts and buttocks.

zine and that the magazines themselves are kept in private places. Of perhaps twenty or thirty full-page cheesecake photographs, one or two may in some way "reach out" more strongly than others—and these few pages may be literally pinned up by the viewer.

In Hollywood fan magazines, a pin-up is a recognizable person, a motion picture star (female or male) or starlet with whom the viewer may wish to relate in a variety of ways—not necessarily sexually, perhaps just amorously or socially. Leading examples of this type of pin-up have been Marlene Dietrich (*D-33*). Betty Grable (*Color Plate 3*, and *D-39*), Marilyn Monroe (*Color Plate 2*, and *D-44*), and Rudolph Valentino (*E-1*).

Calendars

The use of calendars for the presentation of pin-ups has not added stylistically to the pin-up vocabulary; it has merely provided another mass outlet for the distribution of girlie images. On some calendars, there is one subject for the year, and on others, a subject for each month. Calendar pin-ups, ranging from pocket size to life size, are usually printed in full color of good quality.

There are two categories of calendar pin-ups: photographic and artist-rendered. Most of the models who appear in calendar photographs are the same girls who pose for girlie magazines. Generally large-breasted and large-hipped, they are photographed in standard cheesecake poses. Often the same photograph appears both in a magazine and in a calendar. The artist-rendered pin-ups are made specifically for calendars, although some of the artists, like Varga, gained their reputation mainly through magazine pin-ups.

The most famous calendar pin-up is the nude photograph of Marilyn Monroe (*Color Plate 2*), taken when Miss Monroe was badly in need of money, before she achieved prominence through her brief film role at the end of *The Asphalt Jungle*. Monroe's calendar appearance was followed by the somewhat lesser sex-queens Jayne Mansfield (*Color Plate 36*) and Diana Dors (*Color Plate 37*). Generally, however, film stars do not expose themselves to their fans through the calendar medium, and only by exception can one find nude calendar photographs of stage or screen stars. (Usually, the vehicle for nude exposure of a film star is a "class" magazine such as *Playboy*, in which the photography accompanies a feature article on the star—for example, Jane Fonda in *Playboy*, March 1968.)

A-12. This first exposure of pubic hair—albeit modest to the point of invisibility—in a major magazine's girl-of-the-month pictorial was considered a breakthrough in quality-magazine centerfold features; almost all other high-quality magazines followed suit within months. *Penthouse* (London and New York), April 1970.

Posters

Posters utilizing pin-up types evolved toward the latter part of the great age of art lithography in Paris, late in the 19th century. The objective of the poster was typically to announce a theatrical event, promote a café, or sell a product—even in those years of relatively primitive advertising techniques, sex was used as a means of attracting the public. Many early posters containing pin-up images to promote various products are now collectors' items, having been rendered by some of the finest artists of 19th-century Paris—most notably Toulouse-Lautrec.

Until recent years, the poster was intended more for public display than for private consumption. Today, the poster is still used in theaters and recruiting stations, on billboards and bulletin boards, and in other public places. The 1960s, however, gave birth to a new development—the contemporary poster, in which the emphasis is not on advertising an event or a product but on gaining attention for a social cause or movement, a culture hero, a political hero (Che or Fidel) or villain (Agnew or Tricky Dick). This type of poster is intended primarily for display in homes and offices—much as one hangs paintings and other graphics. Among the most popular of the contemporary posters are the so-called personality posters featuring, for example, Humphrey Bogart, W. C. Fields, and Mae West, Mahatma Gandhi, John F. Kennedy, and Martin Luther King.

Among the sex-oriented contemporary posters are some straightforward girlie pin-ups. But others fit into a variety of moods and styles—humor, satire, homosexuality, motherhood, old age, rock music, soft-core pornography, and "soul."

In contrast to traditional cheesecake pin-ups, contemporary posters represent sophistication, hipness, political awareness (usually on the left), identification with the drug scene, the sexual revolution, Women's Liberation, and movements to undermine the establishment. These posters tend to promote new spiritualities and life-styles that go considerably beyond the boundaries of the traditional pin-up. The chosen subjects are often not the individuals themselves but the styles and movements they symbolize.

These new kinds of posters have given rise to a unique structure for commercial distribution—the poster shop. There are perhaps only a handful in most cities of the United States and Western Europe, but New York, London, Paris, Rome, and Amsterdam, among others, support a great many. Poster shops may seem to be products of, and outlets for, the hippie generation, but probably as much or more money is spent in them by members of the so-called uncool generation.

Prehistory

Although the idea of using sex appeal to attract people to various ideas, activities, or products is probably as old as humankind, the pin-up is a modern invention. Nevertheless, it is possible to trace its prehistory by applying our modern definition of the pin-up to what may be termed "archaic coincidences"—situations in which sexually evocative illustrations were used to attract attention to a variety of themes.

Most of the first pictorial woodcuts, printed in Europe early in the 15th century, portrayed religious subjects, and their distribution was limited to members of the clerical orders and the aristocratic elite. In the following century their subject range expanded tremendously and provided pictorial information, for the first time, on machinery and inventions, armor, astronomy, botany, classical Greek and Roman mythology, and travel. Many panoramic views of cities were also produced.

The earliest known illustrated poster—a woodcut of 1491 advertising a Belgian edition of Jean d'Arras's *Histoire de la Belle Melusine*—may also have been the earliest use of sex appeal in the graphic arts to sell a product (in this case, the book). This relatively crude poster showed the heroine of the story, Melusine, taking a bath.

From the 15th to the 17th centuries many reproductions of paintings were made in print form. They were, in effect, printmakers' interpretations of paintings, and many showed nude figures from Greek and Roman mythology. During that period, a still wider range of subjects—archaeology, anatomy, animals, costumes, clothing, architecture, and engineering—appeared in prints or illustrated books. By the end of the 16th century thousands of books appeared containing wood engravings and etchings on hundreds of subjects.

William Hogarth (1697-1764), in the 18th century, broke from the tradition of official art by depicting the lower orders of society and the seamier kind of life that was typical of people of the street. Hogarth produced series of engravings, *A Harlot's Progress* and *A Rake's Progress* (which originated as paintings), showing human degeneration step by step. These and other works portray women as sexual beings, usually participating in ribaldry.

Een schoene ghenuechlicke eñ seer meede hyst
torie van eenre vrouwe gheheeten Meluzyne/
eñ van harer afcoemste eñ gheslachte vã haer
voert ghecomen synde.eñ van harer alre won
derlike eñ vrome wercke eñ septen die sy gedaē
eñ bedieuen hebben Ende es nu nyewelijc wt
den walsche ghetranslateert in dupcsche/ende
met schoonē personagen ende figueren na den
eysch der materien verciert Ende mē salse met
vele meer andere niewe boecken vinden te coo
pe ter plaetzen hier onder gheschreuen

A-13. Melusine. This first known illustrated advertising poster
—and the earliest known use of sex appeal in advertising—
is a woodcut produced in 1491 by a Belgian publisher to
promote a new translation of *Histoire de la Belle Melusine*
by Jean d'Arras. Melusine's bosom is exposed (she is bathing), and there is an intimation of auto-eroticism in the
gesture of her right hand. The text beneath the illustration
reads: "A beautiful, pleasing, and most marvelous story of a
lady named Melusine, of her ancestors and descendants, and
the wonderful and devout works and deeds they wrought
and performed. Lately translated from the French into Flem-
ish and adorned with fine personages and scenes as the text
demands. This story, as well as a great number of other new
books, can be purchased at the place written hereunder."
(Reserve Room, New York Public Library.)

A-14. *Venus à la Coquille*, c.1522, an engraving by Benoist,
after Titian's painting *Venere Anadiomene* (1520-22), showing the printmaker's interpretation of a fine-art nude subject.
(New York Public Library.)

Later in the 18th century and early in
the 19th, Thomas Rowlandson (1756-1827)
produced engraved caricatures of London's
"low life" and the decadent upper classes.
These satiric prints often showed semi-
garbed women embroiled in sensual, Brue-
gelesque escapades. Another important English caricaturist, James Gillray (1757-
1815), also treated sexual subjects with
broad humor.

No artist, however, had yet employed a
printed medium to portray a sexy female
inviting the viewer to fantasize about join-
ing her in sensual pleasures. Women continued to be used mainly to enhance products, from parasols to story books.

Early in the 19th century, several major
breakthroughs in visual communication contributed to the evolution of the true pin-up.
First had come the discovery, in 1796, of
lithography by Aloys Senefelder and of
color lithography soon thereafter. Next, c.
1830-35, came the invention or discovery of
various photographic processes by Joseph
Nicéphore Niepce, Louis Daguerre, and
William Henry Fox Talbot. The development of high-speed presses by 1850 permitted the wider dissemination of both written and pictorial information. With these
advances in communications came the tech-

A-15. "The Tavern Scene" from Hogarth's series, *A Rake's Progress*, 1735. Viewed in isolation, the female figure in the right foreground could easily be considered a pin-up. (Print Room, New York Public Library.)

A-16. Detail of poster, c.1741, advertising parasols. Subtle but unmistakable use of sex appeal. (New York Public Library.)

nology for reproducing photographs in quantity. The high-speed press, however, tended quickly to wear out the thin etched or engraved metal plates. But when it was discovered that images engraved on the endgrain of wood could be printed by the tens of thousands before a woodblock would wear out, woodblocks were reintroduced to printing. Wood engravings proved to be not only more durable than metal plates but also more capable of reproducing fine detail. Illustrations could at last be mass produced.

Early America: Dialogue leads to schism

Although the earliest sources of pin-ups evolved through the development of the printed illustration in Europe, the pin-up itself became essentially an American concept and product. Apart from the era of the great art lithograph in Paris (1825 to 1900) from which the pin-up *type*—but not the pin-up for its own sake—emerged, it was through magazines in America that the image of the true pin-up was most aggressively pursued and was subsequently developed in its modern forms.

European magazines had routinely treated young women as ornate accessories to men, and women had routinely accepted this treatment. But America was a young country, not steeped inextricably in European tradition. And while the magazines of Colonial America, from their inception in the mid-18th century, carried on the attitudes toward women that were common in Europe, even the earliest magazines contained articles crusading against discrimination and the subjugation of women to the man's way of looking at things. *Lady's Magazine* said in the preface to its first issue in 1792:

> The female patronesses of literature . . . give ease to the weary traveller, in the rough paths of science; and soften the rigor of intense study . . . it is the province of female excellence alone, with the beams of intellectual light, which illuminates the paths of literature, to diffuse the glowing warmth of genial affection, and by a lively combination of sweet perfections, add charms—even to the native beauties of the most brilliant production.

But the more prevalent attitude of the times was exemplified by an article entitled "An Address to the Ladies" in *American Magazine,* March 1788:

> To be *lovely* you must be content to be women; to be mild, social, and sentimental—to be acquainted with all that belongs to your department—and leave

the masculine virtues, and the profound researches of study to the province of the other sex.

Weekly Magazine, August 1798, presented a remarkable male-female dialogue, written by the American novelist Charles Brockden Brown. Dealing generally with the controversial subject of the relative merit of the sexes, Brown's dialogue focuses here on the woman's role in society. The woman speaks:

> While I am conscious of being an intelligent moral being; while I see myself denied . . . the exercise of my own direction . . . subject in all periods of my life to the will of another, on whose bounty I am made to depend for food and shelter; . . . I see myself, in relation to society, regarded merely as a beast, as an insect, passed over . . . as absolutely nothing . . .

The dialogue continues. On the question of woman's role in politics, the man states:

> It would be hard to restrain a smile to see a woman rise in a popular assembly and discuss some weighty problem! . . . If this innovation be just, the period for making it has not yet arrived. You, madam, are singular. Women, in general, do not reason in this manner. They are contented with the post assigned them.

Finally, on the subject of the separation of the sexes in education, the woman deplores the double standard. She believes that

> the sullen imaginations of some men are disturbed, lest improving female education should introduce insubordination. . . . Tyrants of all descriptions look toward the progress of knowledge as the downfall of their power.

Despite this kind of continuing debate between the man's world and that of the feminist woman—as articulated primarily in magazines—the exploitative image of women prevailed. Those women who fought for equal rights were invariably the privileged rich and the highly educated. But the mass of women in 19th-century America, many of them semi-literate, were unable to identify with their superior crusaders. And since the female population was not organized as such, and was directed by the power structure of the man's world, a schism inevitably resulted among the women. The average woman rejected the minority crusaders, and continued to see her functions as secondary to those of the man. Thus, rather than compete with men, American women in general were more willing than even their European counterparts to accept exaggeration of their female roles.

The rejection of the feminists was in two forms. One was the open exploitation of women as sexual objects. Paris may have been considered "naughty" in the second half of the 19th century, but every American city and pioneer town, throughout the century, also contained prostitutes, dancing girls, bar girls, and traveling troupes of "actresses." The other was, of course, the tendency of most women to remain at home. Their duty was to raise a family, to cook, to sew, and to satisfy the desires of their husbands. For the majority of American men, however, something was lacking from the domestic scene. They needed diversion, escape, frivolity. Along with sports, drinking, and gambling, the dance halls helped fill the gap. Burlesque came from England to America, and "spicy" magazines achieved enormous circulations.

National Police Gazette and "vulgar seductions"

Perhaps the earliest American magazine to synthesize the sexual, moral, and social problems of mid-19th-century America was the *National Police Gazette*, a New York weekly established in 1845. ("Synthesize" in this context should not be interpreted to mean "attempt to solve" or "present objectively.") The *National Police Gazette* reported the feelings of the time by exposing the sins of America, with an attitude of stiff moral judgment. Sports and crime were its main features at first. (Later on, it referred to itself as "the leading illustrated sporting journal in the world" and concentrated on boxing, wrestling, and other forms of athletics.) It gathered its readership through the lure of "a most interesting record of horrid murders, outrageous robberies . . . hideous rapes, vulgar seductions."

Sensational stories dealing with scandal and sex appeared in other mid-19th-century magazines, but were largely fictionalized if not totally fictitious. In the *National Police Gazette,* however, real crime and real scandals were reported, and by the end of the Civil War these stories were fully illustrated. From 1878 on, sex pictures and sex advertising appeared regularly, as did exposés on New York's most unsavory brothels. The front pages of the *Police Gazette* showed pictures of prostitutes—and they were always voluptuous and well fed, not at all like the slender, svelte women seen in the fashion magazines. Naturally, the *Police Gazette* claimed to be protecting the innocent; its articles, stories, and editorials always conveyed moral guidance to its presumably unblemished but vulnerable readers.*

The *National Police Gazette* became especially easy to recognize after 1878, when it began to be printed on pink paper. It was widely distributed to saloons and cheap hotels, but its greatest distribution was in barbershops, where it became known as the "barbershop bible" until 1922, when women began having their hair bobbed and the magazines were consequently removed.

In 1880, the *Police Gazette* began covering theater in New York, particularly to exploit popular actresses displaying their talents in tights. In the 1890s, bawdy pictures and "spicy" stories of burlesque queens and actresses were standard features of the magazine. Around that time, too, it began publishing picture supplements of actresses and champion athletes, and successfully sold "cabinet size, exquisitely finished photographs" of actresses, dancers, sports figures, race horses, fighting dogs, and fighting cocks. The photographs of women

A-17. *Godey's Lady's Book* (Philadelphia), 1852. Begun as *Ladies' Magazine* in 1828 by Sarah Josepha Buell Hale, this magazine, aimed at women, provided them with a "beaconlight of refined taste, pure morals, and practical wisdom" —obviously reflecting one side of the dilemma of woman's role during the mid-19th century. Despite allegorical wings on this cover, and despite the magazine's stated declaration, this "cover girl" is nonetheless an exploitation of the female form to attract buyers.

_____
* A modern counterpart to the *National Police Gazette* might be the *National Enquirer* (New York) of the early 1960s—a "gruesome tabloid" (according to *Time,* February 21, 1972) containing features on "cannibalism, sadism, and sick sex," with banner headlines such as "I Cut Out His Heart and Stomped on It."

were advertised as the "snappiest of all girl pictures."

After World War I, the magazine's circulation declined sharply. Newspapers virtually had taken over the coverage of crime, achieving a faster, far more accurate picture of the criminal world. The *Gazette* reacted by turning even more to sensationalism and sex. But the moral climate had become looser, and the discussion of sex was more open by the 1920s. The *Police Gazette* became less credible and certainly less shocking. Playful "girlie" magazines and "confession" magazines proliferated, and these newer publications were far more abandoned than the *Police Gazette* in exposing women's bodies and, for the first time, their emotions. Its circulation gradually declined, and it reached bankruptcy in 1932.*

Many magazines imitated the *National Police Gazette* in its early years, but none surpassed it in circulation. In 1868, for example, *Day's Doings, Last Sensation,* and *Stetson's Dime Illustrated* appeared. In 1883, *Fox's Illustrated Week's Doings,* which claimed to be "the spiciest dramatic and best story paper in America," published a picture supplement of "The Prettiest Women in Paris." In 1885, the *Illustrated Day's Doings and Sporting World* offered "frisky females" and "fly Gothamites."

The rise of burlesque: Dazzle —not sizzle

Unlike the mid-20th-century forms, burlesque in its earliest years in Europe was not bump-and-grind striptease or a grotesque display of silicone-inflated breasts, and it was not presented in hot, smoky, musty, out-of-the-way theaters. Growing out of traditional farce, early burlesque in Europe was a popular art form of the legitimate theater in which classical and other serious dramas were parodied or travestied. Although it always trod the borderline of social scandal, and was usually spoken and sung in the common man's vernacular, its early flavor was that of mischief rather than vulgarity, of dazzle rather than sizzle.

New York received burlesque with surprise and delight. There had been little or nothing like it in the American musical

---

* Revived under new management in 1934, the *National Police Gazette,* as a monthly, continued to carry sensational sports features and "hot" girlie pictures. It built up a fair circulation, but never again became a magazine of major importance. The magazine's editorial offices are not given in the masthead. The Manhattan telephone directory lists only a mailing address and telephone service under "Police Gazette," but no telephone messages are taken, and the only possible contact is by mail.

A-18. Wood engraving from *National Police Gazette* (New York) in the 1870s, showing linked themes of sex, sin, crime, scandal, and moralism (in caption) in a single picture. Note before-and-after effect, through use of inset at upper right.

A-19. *National Police Gazette,* November 15, 1879, showing tattooing of high-class prostitute.

A-20. Four typical engravings from *National Police Gazette* in the 1880s. *Upper left:* "Favorites of the Footlights Miss Emma Rose, Variety and Burlesque Actress." *Upper right:* "Training for the Ballet . . . How the Prospective High-kickers Teach the Supple Limb to Elevate." *Lower left:* "Scene in a Bicycle Hall—Tempting Providence on a Narrow Guage [*sic*] Route." *Lower right:* Scene in a New York brothel, with caption referring to the "Spider [of prostitution] Spreading Her Webs for the Flies Who Make Her Loathsome Trade Profitable."

theater tradition. Young women in tights were its chief enticement; and Adah Isaacs Menken, dressed in tights while strapped to a horse in a play based on Byron's *Mazeppa,* was the first of a series of Mazeppas "whose one object was the exploitation of the female figure." In the ensuing years, various other "tights plays," most notably *The Black Crook,* delighted American men from New York to San Francisco. Critical reactions were mixed—even those from some of the "better" publications of the period. In 1869, for example, *Appletons' Journal* reported:

> Burlesque presents women garbed or semi-garbed in the most luxurious and seductive dresses possible, and makes them play the fool to the topmost bent of the spectator. One is dazzled with . . . beautiful faces and startled at the coarse songs, the vile jargon, the low wit, and the abandoned manners of the characters.

That same year, before the Women's Suffrage Convention, Olive Logan complained:

> No decent woman can now look to the stage as a career. Clothed in the dress of an honest woman, she is worth nothing to a manager. Stripped as naked as she dare, and it seems there is little left when so much is done, she becomes a prize to her manager, who knows that crowds will rush to see her.

And rush they did. This denunciation, and others, caused box office receipts to rise and "quickened the managers in the purchase of tights and the duplication of ideas." *

The best known "lady with tights" of the time was Lydia Thompson, a British burlesque queen who, with her troupe of British Blondes, was imported by P. T. Barnum to appear in F. C. Burnand's *Ixion, or The Man at the Wheel* at the Woods Museum and Theatre, New York, in September 1869. They grossed $40,000 in their first month, and subsequently launched a coast-to-coast American tour that yielded a half-million-dollar profit. In 1870, *Punchinello Magazine* reported of Miss Thompson:

> Legs have heretofore been inseparable in the public mind from Lydia Thompson. Her successes have varied inversely as the length of her trunk hose.

And she was described as "offering up her fatted calves at the shrine of a prodigal New York audience." After ten successful seasons in America, she appeared in England as a legitimate actress as late as 1895.

---

* Bernard Sobel, *Burleycue: An Underground History of Burlesque Days* (New York: Farrar & Rinehart, 1931).

A-21. Five typical late-19th-century "frisky" or "spicy" pin-ups. Many of the photographs came from France but were more widely distributed in America than in Europe.

A-22. Apart from having been the first burlesque queen seen in America, Lydia Thompson was credited with having first peroxided her hair and worn tights on stage. (Picture Collection, New York Public Library.)

A-23. Chorus from the original 1866 production of *The Black Crook,* first of the "tights shows" in America, which had a long, successful run at Niblo's Garden, New York. The use of tights by the chorus in 1866 was as controversial as the use of nudity in the 1969 production of *Oh! Calcutta!* (Picture Collection, New York Public Library.)

Indigenous American burlesque was originated by M. B. Leavitt of New York. In 1869, he produced *Mme. Rentz's Female Minstrels,* a combination of songs, choruses, and gags adapted from the minstrel show form, plus a section of variety and another section reminiscent of the English type of burlesque. Leavitt took over the minstrel device of placing the performers in a "circle" (actually a semi-circle) on the stage, except that, following the English custom, he presented girls rather than black-face men. The girls at the ends of the semi-circle, the "boy-girls," wore tights, while those in the center, the "girl-girls," wore gowns slashed to show their legs. Featured in Leavitt's company was Mabel Santley, whose name became synonymous with American burlesque. Another popular burlesque queen was May Howard.

In 1879, *The Black Crook* was revived, and the *National Police Gazette* offered the following advice:

> There can be no excuse for young men spending their time in low barrooms, in billiard saloons . . . since the grand, gorgeous, resplendent, bang-up, utterly incomprehensible "Black Crook" is in town again.

For the rest of the 19th century, and on into the 20th, pictures of burlesque actresses, dancers, and singers, dressed in tights or short pants or low-cut dresses, appeared on playing cards, cigarette cards, cut plug tobacco cards, and magazines.

Magazines: Early varieties of pin-up experience

Historians regard the decade of the 1870s as a time of changing morality in America. The influence of burlesque, and its concomitant discovery of calves and other carefully exposed parts of women's bodies, are not to be underestimated in their effect on a fairly naive, puritanical culture. In the late 1880s, legs, tights, and lingerie took precedence over the satirical "art" aspects of burlesque. The exploitation of the female figure steadily increased. And whatever was happening on the stage was echoed and re-echoed in the "spicy" illustrations of weekly and monthly magazines throughout the country. These early pictures of unidentified or little-known show girls, dancers, and actresses are the first true pin-ups.

Lillie Langtry and Lillian Russell were two of the reigning beauties in 1893, when *Munsey's* reported, "This is the period and ours is the country of the Stage Beauty." A general-interest magazine, *Munsey's* (1889-1929) published articles on picturesque personalities, places, and institutions ("The German Student Duel," "American Illustrators," "Famous Artists and Their Work"), poems, and stories by Frank A. Munsey himself. It also described and photographed "Plays and Players of the Day," "Stage Favorites," and "Types of Beauty," and, particularly during the mid-1890s, it specialized in nude and semi-nude pictures. Later, *Munsey's* toned down its pictorials in favor of reproductions of nudes in works of art, theatrical pictures, and famous actors and actresses. *Munsey's* regularly carried illustrated features on "Types of Fair Women" and "Artists Models." After several years, however, it turned away from them and toward such subjects as "Modern Astronomy," "Chinese Festivals," "Honey Bees and Honey," "French Palaces," and "Indian Types."

Nickell Magazine (1894-1905) contained critical articles on the theater, as well as "Gossip of the Playhouse," with photographs of leading actresses. It also displayed "nude art" and carried "snappy stories" with accompanying artist-rendered illustrations. Its bicycling column, "The Wheel," showed mainly women bicyclists.

During its first few years, *Metropolitan Magazine* (1895-1911) printed many pictures of dancers, prima donnas, the nude in art, artists models, bathing beauties, "Paris Beauties," "naughty" French music-hall singers, and "English music-hall women who have just come to this country and who sing topical songs in classical costumes." Also pictured were New York society women—such as one who "takes a pardonable pride in her shoulders" and another "who is noted for her beautiful neck and shoulders." In 1898, however, *Metropolitan* abruptly changed direction and became a more respectable literary and dramatic magazine, with Theodore Dreiser as one of its principal contributors.

In its early issues, *Metropolitan* published elaborately illustrated articles about "the living-picture craze"—performances in which nude or near-nude models posed for re-creations of famous or newly created "classical" paintings and sculptures. Justifying its own proclivities, *Metropolitan* stated:

The older civilizations of the world have long since decreed that only prurient and bestial minds see suggestions and wickedness in classical studies of the nude. Hence pictures in which the feminine figure is treated clearly and plainly, as Nature designed it, are so numerous everywhere that children grow up to accept such pictures as a matter of course, and do not discover that they have been looking at anything shocking or demoralizing until some rabid reformer calls their attention to

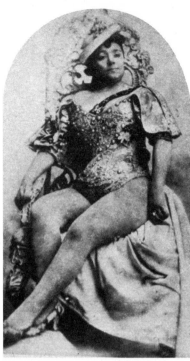

A-24. *Left:* Mabel Santley, c.1875, America's first native-born burlesque queen. *Right:* May Howard, c.1885, whose peak years in burlesque during the 1890s made her as popular as Lydia Thompson and her British Blondes had been, thirty years earlier.

A-25. Two pin-ups of the 1890s, one of an unknown "Continental Actress" in lingerie and gartered stockings, the other of an unidentified "French Actress."

Foundations of the Cheesecake Tradition

A-26. Lillie Langtry, the famous "Jersey Lily," an English actress of the 1880s and 1890s, was renowned for her "exquisitely symmetrical" figure. In *The Westerner,* a film of 1940 starring Gary Cooper and Walter Brennan, Miss Langtry appears in poster pin-ups that embellish the saloon in which much of the action takes place. An unfortunate cowpoke who shoots a hole in Lillie's tooth (in the poster) gets plugged on the spot by the overzealous Langtry-worshipper (Brennan), who, later in the film, dying from a fatal gunshot (fired by Cooper), finally meets the "live" Lillie Langtry.

A-27. Lillian Russell, American stage actress, epitomized "the lusty, boisterous, flamboyant, carefree nation that was the U.S.A. in the 1890s. She was deep-bosomed and big-hipped and gorgeous to look at. She loved steaks and platters of corn on the cob. Cigars were named after her. She had a gold-plated bicycle trimmed with mother-of-pearl and sapphires . . . and a $3,900 corset with gold ribs and diamond trimmings. She was married four times, divorced twice. And is remembered by many as the most glamorous woman in all American theatrical history" (*Life,* May 20, 1940).

it. In America . . . [an] enlightened contingent is a very small proportion of a very tempestuous and violent whole.

Lithographs of women in tights have been suppressed in various parts of the country by reformatory societies, and newsdealers have been prohibited from selling art publications on the ground that they corrupted the morals of the community.*

Metropolitan somehow managed to avoid such suppression despite the fact that it contained many photographs of living-picture performances as well as of living-picture models "waiting to go on." *Saroni's Living Pictures* (1894-95), a New York monthly, carried ten or twelve full pages of such pictures in each issue.

Broadway Magazine (1898-1911)—later called *Hampton's Broadway Magazine*—picked up in 1898 where *Metropolitan* left off. Until 1902 *Broadway* presented "risky" pictures of burlesque queens in tights, art reproductions emphasizing the nude female figure, bathing girls in bloomers, "Types of Metropolitan Loveliness," "Beautiful Women of New York Society," and living pictures. Each of its early issues contained a page entitled "Broadway Magazine Calendar," which pictured an attractively undressed, well-busted young woman. *Broad-*

---

* J. Malcolm Tenney, "The Living-Picture Craze," *Metropolitan Magazine* (New York), February 1895, pp. 2–15.

A-28. *Left:* "Psyche at Nature's Mirror—From the Painting by Paul Thumann," a semi-nude "art" subject, as it appeared in *Munsey's* (New York), December 1893. Earlier that year, when the original was displayed at the Chicago World's Fair, White Rock Beverages adopted the Psyche theme as their trademark of "true purity and quality" (*right*).

way's advertisers knew the pulling power of the ungarbed female form. Not untypical was an advertisement for Ditman's Sea Salt, featuring a naked long-haired beauty, breasting the waves. *Broadway Magazine* was regarded as shocking, but the size of its circulation indicated that the public was highly attracted to shock of that sort. In 1902, toning down its illustrations, the magazine gave more space to articles on art, drama, and New York life, with rather more respectable portraits of actresses. By 1904, burlesque queens were no longer to be found in *Broadway,* and in 1906 the magazine was thoroughly revamped and dignified under Theodore Dreiser's direction.

Truth Magazine (1886-1902) featured "bathing girls" but refused to print photographs actually taken at the beach. It preferred to idealize the bathing beauty through studio photography, because "in the water she is a fright."

Of all the general-interest magazines, *Peterson's* (1842-98), according to an eminent historian of the subject, "out-Heroded Herod in presenting nude pictures." * But that was for only a brief period, and *Peterson's* was better known for the relatively genteel fiction of Gertrude Atherton, Edgar Fawcett, and Julian Hawthorne, for its dress designs, illustrations of glove cases, linen trays, Java canvas, and crocheting,

* Frank Luther Mott, *A History of American Magazines, 1885–1905* (Cambridge, Mass.: Belknap Press of Harvard University Press, 1957), p. 152.

A-29. Madge Lessing, an actress, "From a photograph by Pickering, Boston," *Nickell Magazine* (New York), June 1898.

A-30. Four illustrations from *Metropolitan Magazine* (New York). From left to right: Bathing beauty superimposed on hand-drawn "natural" background (August 1895). Bloomer girl against another artificial backdrop (October 1895). Semi-nude art statue, with crude retouching of original photograph to veil the statue's nudity—or perhaps tease the viewer? (August 1896). Semi-nude art painting, probably retouched (December 1897).

A-31. *Broadway Magazine* (New York) tended to favour stage beauties in its presentation of pin-ups. *Above*: Cérise Bastien of France (June 1899), an exploitation of the Frenchwoman typical of many American magazines of the time, captioned: "From a photograph by Reutlinger, Paris, and published here for the first time in America." *Below:* Possibly the first double-page centerspread in an American magazine, captioned: "Have you ever before seen a center page in a magazine? Here's one." The photographs are of Isadora Duncan in 1899; the caption at the top of the spread states: "Snap-shots at Isadora Duncan, New York's Society Dancer. Showing some of the poses in which she indulges during her dances."

and articles on such exciting subjects as "Our Women Violinists."

Of the better magazines, *Cosmopolitan* (first published in 1886) perhaps best typifies the more tasteful presentation of pin-ups toward the turn of the century. *Cosmopolitan* presented pictures of actresses, dancers, and "beauties"—with an international flavor.

Paralleling these American magazines in time, if not in spirit, were various French periodicals—*La Vie Parisienne* (which began publication as early as 1863), *La Fétard, La Rigolade,* and *La Vie en Rose*—of which *Rabelais* was perhaps most typical. *Rabelais* was a boisterous comic magazine, with page after page of pin-up-type cartoons. Almost without exception, the cartoons were based on humorous sexual situations, with special emphasis on prostitution, promiscuity, and the boudoir. What was most noteworthy, however, was *Rabelais's* consistent sense of fun-and-games—no crime associated with the prostitutes, no guilt with the promiscuous, no shame in the boudoir. What a contrast to most of the American magazines! *Joie de vivre,* sophistication, and relaxation seem to be the keynotes to the French pin-ups of the time —and of various other Continental magazines such as the German *Das kleine Witzblatt* and the Italian *La Sigaretta,* which presented well-endowed pin-up girls in an easygoing ambiance—while in America there was an evident need for a veil of Puritan morality. Some American publications carried humorous pin-ups, indeed, but most were felt to be quite scandalous, bordering on sin—from the point of view of the reader, if not the publisher. America depended a great deal on nonsexual themes— crime, art, theater, photography—in order to present sexual objects. Those few magazines that had dared to start out with the same kind of amoral freedom as *Rabelais* were invariably compelled to tone down their presentation of sex in order to remain in business.

Life—and the first universal pin-up

The earlier *Life* (1883-1936) was nothing like the weekly magazine that appears today. Started by John Ames Mitchell and a group of Harvard men, it observed American life satirically and humorously, but it is perhaps best remembered for introducing Charles Dana Gibson's image of the ideal American woman. Although *Life* could be shared by the entire family, its articles, pictorial features, and general tone were geared toward men. Magazines for ladies —*Ladies' Home Journal, McCall's, Vogue, Woman's Home Companion,* and others— carried innumerable pictures of women but emphasized fashion, coiffure, manners,

HAD AN EXCUSE.

"I hear Jack Dashing's going to be married. Are you going to the wedding?"
"Yes, I think I will."
"Pooh! I'm not."
"Well, I wouldn't, except for the reason that he is going to marry me."

A-32. Three carefully posed bathing beauties, rendered by Lucien Rossi. *Truth* (New York), July 1893.

A-33. *Cosmopolitan* (New York) was less "spicy" than some of the other American magazines. Here (April 1886) the model is somewhat orientalized by her garb, and not much of her anatomy is shown, but the pin-up appeal is clearly visible. The photograph seems to be of a wood engraving made after a painting by W. Gay.

A-34. *Rabelais* (Paris), in 1902, showed candor, social acceptance, and sophisticated humor in connection with *la vie sexuelle. Left,* a *Rabelais* cover, showing a well-endowed bathing beauty. *Center,* a cartoon, captioned: "He: I don't mean to make you uncomfortable . . . but it seems to me you are somewhat underdressed. She: You haven't looked very hard, I'm covered with two boxes of powder." *Right,* a pretty, voluptuous *fille de boudoir* looks invitingly at the reader. (Darien House, New York.)

A-35. The Gibson Girl, in *Life* (New York). *Above:* "Of Course There Are Mermaids," 1902. *Left:* Uncaptioned, 1901. *Right:* "Picturesque America Anywhere Along the Coast," 1901. (Picture Collection, New York Public Library.)

46

needlework, and similar subjects. Increasingly, they were influenced by the Gibson Girl, who had been created by a man for other men.

In 1887, Charles Dana Gibson (then 20 years of age) began a long-term contract with *Life*. As a young man, Gibson

> dipped his pen in the cosmic urge and tried to draw a girl so alluring that other young men would want to climb into the picture and sit beside her.*

By the early 1890s, his Gibson Girl was well established, and she kept the spotlight for two full decades. In 1903, Gibson signed a $100,000 contract with *Collier's* (1886-1957) to render a series of double-page "cartoons" over four years' time, yielding even further exposure for his historic creation.

The Gibson Girl was not simply a model but represented a way of life. Young women gazed intently at the drawings and "did their best to use them as mirrors." The illustrations "were their book of etiquette and the model for their graceful, stately bearing." The fair sex looked to Gibson to tell them "how to dress, stand, eat, walk, shake hands, enter vehicles or eat." Shop windows, counters, and advertisements were filled with Gibson Girl corsets, shirtwaists, skirts, shoes, hats, pompadours, riding sticks, handkerchiefs, china plaques, porcelain plates, and spoons; composers wrote Gibson Girl waltzes, two-steps, and polkas.

And for the first time in the evolution of the pin-up, a woman was presented for her own sake outside the context of advertising, dance, theater, burlesque, and "art." True, the Gibson Girl was sometimes shown as a bathing beauty, but such poses were no more than direct extensions of her gentle breeding, refinement, inspiration, conservatism, and general way of life. No matter where, the Gibson Girl carried the radiance and sweet confidence of a bride. Although some critics found her monotonous, they were vastly outnumbered by worshippers who admired her subtle variations—the Flirt, the Athlete, the Sentimentalist, the Ambitious Woman, and of course the Beauty.

Imitated by artist-illustrators around the world, the Gibson Girl was an inspiration to American students of fine art who were not yet aware of the existence of Degas, Manet, Renoir, and Lautrec.

The Gibson Girl was, of course, not a real person. She was born on Gibson's sketch pad in black and white, and was reproduced in wood engravings. This was the period when the photo-engraving process

---

* Fairfax Downey, *Portrait of an Era as Drawn by C. D. Gibson: A Biography* (New York and London: Scribner, 1936), p. 184.

A-36. This derivative of the Gibson Girl, one of many, is by M. Greiner, c.1908. (Picture Collection, New York Public Library.)

was just beginning to succeed wood engraving in magazine illustration—well before the color processes made possible the reproduction of seductive pin-ups in their natural hues.

When the Gibson era ended—shortly after 1910—there was no new pin-up form to replace her until after World War 1, when there emerged what many critics still regard as the most unladylike, angular, underdressed, short-haired image of womanhood—the Flapper.

Britain: Victorian overground and pornographic underground

There is doubtless a parallel between 19th-century America and Great Britain during the Victorian Era, with respect to the social and moral conditions providing a climate for popular, large-scale sexual exploitation. Feminist movements, strong in Britain, provided the same schism between upper- and lower-class women as in the United States. There were dancing girls, prostitutes, and burlesque troupes, some of which were exported to America. And there was Britain's mass of domestic women—serving, sewing, cooking, and bearing children.

Why, then, since British culture was longer and more deeply imbued than America's with the moral conflicts of Victorianism, did America rather than Great Britain spawn the pin-up and become the leader in publishing pin-ups? Perhaps the answer, at least in part, is that men in 19th-century Britain already had another source of popular stimulation—pornography. Indeed, as early as the 17th century, for example, playing cards had existed in England that showed various forms of erotic experience. Books and magazines on pornographic themes circulated throughout the country, with heavy emphasis on bondage and flagellation. All these publications, however, flourished in an underground movement unconnected with the established world of British publishing, which was staunchly conservative and in no way interested in the popularization of sex through the exploitation of a semi-literate mass market. Meanwhile, upper-class Englishmen could privately partake of the expensive illicit pornography.

There was no *National Police Gazette* or its equivalent for the workingman in Victorian England, no *Broadway* or *Metropolitan* magazine to give an "artistic" or even moral sanction or status to sexual imagery. Before the turn of the century, in Britain, there were in fact no significant publications that spanned the gap between por-

nography and Victorian novels. In America, however, little, if any, pornography circulated. There was no real need for it, since risqué over-the-counter publications were sanctioning sexuality in one form or another. However naive or devious we today regard these early American publications, they nonetheless pre-empted a potentially mass market for pornography.

The gap in America between the popular press and the literary-political press could be spanned within the life experience of most individuals, given the accepted notion that John Doe could go from "rags to riches," culturally as well as financially, in relatively few years. This was not the case in Great Britain, where society was more stratified.

The American publishing industry in the late 19th century was in a period of extremely rapid growth. The spirit was speculative and entrepreneurial; all parties were trying to lasso the great untapped market. Popular magazines came and went by the dozens. Many of them were highly successful, breeding more successful imitators and offshoots. In Britain, however, the official publishing world, stable and conservative, made its profits on specialized, rather more literate markets. There were weak attempts at cheap mass publishing in Britain by mid-century—"penny dreadfuls," generally of poor quality, focusing on "lurid tales of violence, crime, and mystery," with little illustration, less than little relating to sex, and nothing at all relating to pin-ups.

Britain's first step toward a significant popular press came in 1881, with George Newnes's *Tit-bits,* a weekly paper.* *Tit-bits* was an accidental discovery of Newnes, who originally owned a London eating house frequented by cab drivers. To entertain the cabbies, Newnes put together a number of scrapbook albums containing pictures, articles, and jokes, cut out of a wide range of publications, some from America and France as well as from England. The scrapbooks became so popular that Newnes decided to start his own publishing business; and from *Tit-bits* he built a publishing empire. *Tit-bits* featured comic cartoons, clean farce, line drawings, and rather corny jokes, usually spelled out beyond the worth of the humor —but no pin-ups.

(It is interesting to note that an American publication called *Tid-bits* was begun in August 1884. Describing itself as "An illustrated Weekly for These Times," *Tid-bits* was a cheap miscellany featuring many jokes, with accompanying woodcuts—and with no emphasis on pin-ups or sexy girls. In 1886 it became a higher-quality political and humorous paper. The magazine ceased publication in February 1890, when it was

---

* "Tit," in 19th-century England, was the short form for tittle-tattle (idle chatter).

merged with *Munsey's Weekly,* which later became *Munsey's.*)

Alfred Harmsworth (the later Lord Northcliffe), another pioneer in British publishing, followed in 1888 with *Answers to Correspondents,* much like *Tit-bits* but featuring a lively exchange of questions from readers, answered by Harmsworth and his staff. Also included were short stories and jokes. This approach to popular publishing was, incidentally, already standard fare in Sunday editions of American newspapers. An admirer of the American popular press, young Harmsworth is quoted as having said, before 1888, that he was prone "especially to watching the development of publications in America, ever the leader in the publishing industry." Harmsworth contended that British newspapers were for "high-brow classes," and "periodicals much the same." The monthlies, he claimed, were old fashioned, and the "cheap weeklies, such as story papers and humorous sheets were far behind the times . . . and had comparatively small circulations." Finally, he is quoted as having said that American newspapers and magazines were far ahead of anything Europe had ever produced.

Not until 1903, in Harmsworth's newspaper *The Mirror,* were beauty contests publicized and the contestants illustrated. That was the same year in which French postcards showing bathing beauties were first issued in Great Britain.

The only significant turn-of-the-century British publication that followed the American magazines in carrying a wide selection of girlie pictures was *Photo Bits,* which was started in 1898. (By that time in America, there were, as we have seen, at least a dozen comparable magazines, with substantial circulations, that showed bathing beauties, actresses, burlesque stars, and other related pin-up themes.) *Photo Bits* went through several changes of name in the early 1900s (*Photo Fun, New Photo Fun, New Fun,* and *Fun*), expiring as *Bits of Fun* in 1920. It was an illustrated weekly boasting "more than sixty pictures" in each issue, many of them in the pin-up vein. Its original aim was to break away from the dullness of other English weeklies through its "Bright, Sketchy . . . Witty . . . Pithy . . . Spicy" pictures and features—an already familiar formula in many American publications of the 1880s and 1890s. In 1906, when *Photo Bits* became *Photo Fun,* it showed drawings of semi-nude chorus girls and actresses in bathing suits, and only later included photographs on the "nude-in-art" theme in its Art Gallery feature.

To summarize, it was not until the Edwardian period that British popular magazines appeared in a substantial way, while in America a comparable popular press was well-established by 1895.

A-37. Jules Chéret: *Loie Fuller,* 1897. Miss Fuller, the toast of Paris night life, may have been the first person ever to perform a psychedelic dance-and-light show. For her debut at the Folies Bergère in 1893 (see *Color Plate 42*) Miss Fuller chose Chéret to design the poster. Better than any other posterist, Chéret could suggest the swirling play of contrast and color, rhythm, and excitement that was synonymous with the name Loie Fuller. She was later rendered by almost every important Parisian poster artist. (Darien House, New York.)

French posters: Chéret creates the pin-up type

Although 1825 to 1900 constituted the age of the great art lithograph in Paris, the earliest pin-up posters did not appear until the final decades of the 19th century. Central to the introduction of the pin-up type in the poster, was Jules Chéret (1836-1932). A lesser-known Impressionist when he set up his own printing establishment in 1866, Chéret made at least two major contributions to the art of his time: He established the basic principles of the successful art poster, and he created some of the outstanding individual posters of all time—on a par with those of his more famous contemporaries, Daumier, Toulouse-Lautrec, Mucha, and Beardsley.

Letters and figures dominated Chéret's posters; background and detail were minimized. Chéret used large masses of color, brilliantly and rhythmically juxtaposed. His work conveys an almost dizzying energy, an energy that seems to push his subject, or his product, right off the two-dimensional plane into the lap of the viewer. No wonder, then, that his use of vivacious women to present a variety of products gained Chéret's posters tremendous attention and acclaim. In addition, they really got the advertising message across.

The key to Chéret's lively poster art is curiously akin to the secret of a successful pin-up. It draws in the onlooker as a participant and lets his imagination supply the missing elements. It suggests a continuing enjoyment of the subject beyond the confines of the printed image. It offers not only the subject or product itself but also extends vicarious pleasures to the viewer.

Fuller treatment of pin-up poster art begins on page 201.

Picture postcards: Pin-ups go international

Although many people believe that pin-ups first appeared on "French postcards" as early as the 1870s, it is, in fact, unlikely that a picture of a woman in any form was reproduced on a postcard before 1895, and possibly not before 1900. Until 1889, relatively few picture postcards, as we know them, were produced at all. Publishers and stationers designed cards only for special occasions, and the printed images comprised mostly decorative linecuts.

Léon Besnardeau, a French bookseller, is credited with having created the first picture postcard in 1870, during the Franco-Prussian War. The design, a line drawing, showed stacked weapons and ornamental wreaths and contained the inscription *"Souvenir de la Guerre de 1870—Camp de Conlie—Défense Nationale, Familie, Honneur, Patrie, Liberté."* There was a little space left in the middle of the design for name and address of delivery and for listing the battles in which the sender had fought. The Prussians also issued field postcards in that year, and a series exists with humorous designs bearing somewhat suggestive verses.*

Postcards without pictures had existed since the 1860s, but not until 1875 did most countries pass a uniform postal law for the handling of postcards. By 1889, the picture postcard was being sold mainly on the basis of its pictures. In that year, *Le Figaro*, the Paris newspaper, issued a card depicting the Eiffel Tower that tourists were encouraged to mail directly from the Tower. It was a "raging success" and made the postcard world-famous.† In 1889, also, came the first use of color on postcards. Color was sometimes printed by chromolithography on a machine press, but quite often, especially when several colors were required, the cards were tinted by hand.

In the 1890s, many new categories of illustrations were developed, among the earliest of which were "views" (of cities, rivers, etc.) and historic events (such as the visit of the Tsar's fleet to Toulon in 1893). The first picture postcards in America were published in early 1893, in color, and were sold at the World Columbian Exhibition in Chicago in May of that year. The cards showed views of various city buildings.

Also in the 1890s, encouraged by the success of their posters, many artists in Paris began rendering postcards of exquisite beauty. Among them were Chéret, Toulouse-Lautrec, Bonnard, Boutet, and Mucha. M. F. Champennois, the publisher of their posters, anticipated the value of reproducing these poster works on postcards. Thus, one could often find on postcards the same de-

A-38. The first known picture postcard, 1870—made by a Frenchman, Léon Besnardeau, during the Franco-Prussian War.

GUERRE DE 1870   CAMP DE CONLIE

SOUVENIR DEL   DEFENSE NATIONALE

ARMÉE DE BRETAGNE

* Frank Staff, *The Picture Postcard and Its Origins* (London: Lutterworth; New York: Praeger, 1966).

† Richard Carline, *Pictures in the Post,* 2d ed. (Bedford: Fraser, 1971).

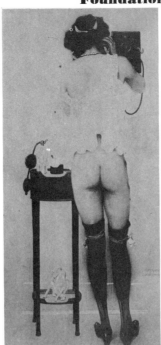

A-39. Raphaël Kirchner postcards. *Left:* From the "Sun-Ray" series, 1902. *Center and right:* Two delicately rendered seminudes, c.1905. (Collection Eugene Baily.)

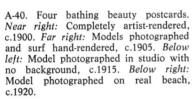

A-40. Four bathing beauty postcards. *Near right:* Completely artist-rendered, c.1900. *Far right:* Models photographed and surf hand-rendered, c.1905. *Below left:* Model photographed in studio with no background, c.1915. *Below right:* Model photographed on real beach, c.1920.

A-41. Four famous "English Actresses," from a postcard series, c.1905-9. *Top:* Camille Clifford and Phyllis Dare. *Bottom:* Marie Studholme and Gabrielle Ray.

signs that were on the huge street posters of Paris.

Perhaps the strongest artist to emerge on the basis of his postcard art alone was Austrian-born Raphaël Kirchner (1875-1917), whose artistic treatment of women was so unique that his provocative women were referred to as Kirchner Girls. Soon after arriving in Paris around 1901, Kirchner created several series of suggestive postcards that became instantly successful—among them "Sun-Ray," in which girls were shown against a background of swirling patterns, and "Marionettes," showing amorous couples dangling from strings held by Venus. His "modern" style was characterized by a freer treatment of subject and design than had been seen during the Victorian period, yet he depicted women "partially clothed or coyly showing their charms," but without vulgarity, "as the average man liked to see it pictured."

The earliest postcards of bathing beauties came from France around 1900, and soon thereafter such cards were also made available in England. The first bathing scenes were rendered by artists. Later, when the camera was used, the model was usually photographed in a studio, posing against a hand-drawn beach background.

Postcard series in the early 1900s featured "French Actresses," "Japanese Beauties" dressed in traditional costume, "Actresses" in color, and ballet dancers and bathers posing in tights. Some card manufacturers glued silk, oilcloth, or spangles on their pin-up cards.

These series, and scores of others on pin-up themes, led the public beyond the mere buying and sending of postcards. Collecting became a major hobby, particularly in the United States, Great Britain, and France. Certain postcard series soon were valued at many times their original cost. Cartophiles, as the dedicated collectors called

CARTES POSTALES SUGGESTIVES
Pour Amateurs et Collectionneurs

Éditions artistiques et photographiques en noir et en couleurs

			Prix					Prix
5001	Ardents baisers,	8 cartes en noir	1 25	5012	Danseuse parisienne,	8 Cartes	noir	1 50
5002	Bacchante,	6 — couleurs	1 25	5013	Danseuse mauresque,	6 —	couleurs	1 25
5003	Bain de la demi-mondaine,	12 — —	2 50	5014	Danses aériennes,	10 —	noir	1 85
5004	Bain de la favorite,	10 — noir	1 85	5015	Danses antiques,	6 —	couleurs	1 00
5005	Belle pêche,	6 — couleurs	1 25	5016	Danse du sabre,	6 —	—	1 25
5006	Bord de l'eau,	6 — —	1 25	5017	Danse du Ventre,	12 —	—	2 50
5007	Chambre nuptiale,	12 — —	2 50	5018	Danse au harem,	10 —	noir	1 85
5008	Chasse aux papillons,	12 — —	2 50	5019	Droit du Seigneur,	12 —	couleurs	2 50
5009	La Cigarette,	12 — —	2 50	5020	Enfin seuls,	12 —	—	2 50
5010	Cocotte et Charbonnier,	10 — noir	1 85	5021	L'Epuisette,	6 —	—	1 25
5011	Dans les blés,	6 — couleurs	1 25	5022	Equitation fin de siècle,	6 —	—	1 25

Envoi franco contre toute commande, accompagnée de son montant en mandat ou timbres-poste, adressée à la Librairie du "Rabelais", 5, rue du Croissant, Paris.

A-42. Advertisement from *Rabelais,* 1902, showing how postcard series could be ordered and at what cost. Note various names of series relating to sex-oriented themes. (Darien House, New York.)

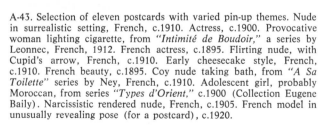

A-43. Selection of eleven postcards with varied pin-up themes. Nude in surrealistic setting, French, c.1910. Actress, c.1900. Provocative woman lighting cigarette, from *"Intimité de Boudoir,"* a series by Leonnec, French, 1912. French actress, c.1895. Flirting nude, with Cupid's arrow, French, c.1910. Early cheesecake style, French, c.1910. French beauty, c.1895. Coy nude taking bath, from *"A Sa Toilette"* series by Ney, French, c.1910. Adolescent girl, probably Moroccan, from series *"Types d'Orient,"* c.1900 (Collection Eugene Baily). Narcissistic rendered nude, French, c.1905. French model in unusually revealing pose (for a postcard), c.1920.

A-44. Eight cigarette cards, showing range of pin-up subjects. May Yohê, actress, from "Actors and Actresses," a series of 25 cards, English, c.1885. (Back of card reads: "Miss May Yohê (Lady Pelham-Clinton-Hope) who comes from America gained distinction by her clever interpretation of what are known as coon songs. Her music abilities and sprightliness made her a welcome acquisition to the English stage.") Miss Woodford, actress, in standard profile pose, emphasis on neckline, English, c.1895. Miss Rosie Heath, actress-dancer, English, c.1895. Mlle Théo, actress, French, c.1900. Miss Kitty Mara, acrobatic dancer in leading Parisian musicals, notably at the Folies Bergère, from a series of 50 cards on entertainers, Irish, c.1920. From "En Casa del fotógrafo," a series of 19 cards showing various stages of undress in a photographic studio, Mexican, c.1900. From series of 10 cards showing fully clothed, sophisticated models, Chinese, c.1915. (Pictures of women smoking were regarded as in doubtful taste at that time, even on cigarette cards.) From "Morning Glory Maidens," a series of 15 cards produced by Victory Tobacco Company, American, c.1890. (Arents Collection, New York Public Library; also private collections.)

themselves, began publishing comprehensive catalogues of series, along with new prices of postcards, as they appreciated in value. Cartophilic clubs were formed for trading, discussing, and sharing postcards.

In 1903, Gibson Girls first appeared on postcards, and in the following year, actresses began to be identified by name on postcards. This was still before the era of the Hollywood movie magazine, so that postcards offered actresses the best possible publicity—given the fact that cards were being mass produced and mass circulated. By 1910, in France alone, 123 million picture postcards were printed, and the industry employed 33,000 workers.

The picture postcard seems to have reached its peak during World War I. By then, the great variety of pin-up or pin-up-related themes that appeared on postcards included bathing beauties, cheesecake and peekaboo poses, sequential "amour" stories, risqué cartoons, cute or embarrassing situations, women in surrealistic situations, nude art photography, kissing, courtship, seduction, motion pictures, theater, cabaret, and music hall. The Kirchner Girl, at the very top, delighted and amused thousands of fighting men.

By 1925, the "Golden Age of the postcard," as Ado Kyrou calls it, was at an end.* For all its world-wide popularity, the picture postcard ceased to be a continuing force in the evolution of the pin-up. Perhaps more than any other medium, it contributed, during its heyday, to the establishment of woman as a separate, independent erotic object, not necessarily connected to profession or product.

Cigarette cards: A chapter in the evolution of pin-ups

The international mania for cigarette cards started in the 1880s and lasted through World War I. Collecting was a major pastime during those years, and many series of cigarette cards became famous solely on the basis of their high value in the marketplace.

The original function of the cigarette card was as a stiffening to protect the contents of a cigarette package. The first cards contained no pictures or text. The earliest known illustrated cigarette card, issued in the United States around 1878, contained the picture of an actress. (Unfortunately this card is no longer extant.) Shortly thereafter, cigarette manufacturers in several countries saw the promotional possibilities of illustrated cards and started issuing series based on themes ranging from royalty and weaponry to pin-ups.

By 1890, cigarette card series were pour-

* Ado Kyrou, *L'Age d'or de la carte postale* (Paris: Balland, 1966).

ing out of the United States, Great Britain, Germany, Italy, Spain, Portugal, France, Belgium, Norway, Holland, Switzerland, China, Siam, Egypt, Argentina, Chile, Cuba, Mexico, Peru, the West Indies, and South Africa.

The following pin-up cigarette-card series have become collectors items: Actors and Actresses, Beauties, Actresses, Character Sketches, Eminent Actresses, Gallery of Beauty, Worlds Beauties, Continental Actresses, and Miniatures. In addition, many publishers issued series in which alluring women were combined with other subjects such as girls with flowers and girls with flags.

Writing in 1937, I. O. Evans observed:

[Certain cards] illustrate the complete change in masculine taste during the last half-century. They . . . consisted of those studies, so dear to the light-minded of our grandfathers, of lightly-clad ladies in frills, bloomers, or inadequate kilts, with preposterous wasp-like waists and hour-glass figures, and carrying various incongruous implements. In a series of "Sporting Girls," the girl who represents the swimmer is in an ill-fitting one-piece garment, girded by a belt; her hair flows free, and is adorned with a bow of ribbon, and she wears high-heeled shoes, while to complete the picture, a number of pieces of cork are tied at intervals round her! . . . Such pictures may have been very thrilling to the males of the time, but to-day it is doubtful whether many men would regard them with more than distaste.*

---

* I. O. Evans, *Cigarette Cards and How to Collect Them* (London: Jenkins, 1937).

A-46. Two unusually early examples of pin-ups in calendars. *Left: Broadway Magazine,* featuring actress Beatrice Morgan. *Below:* German magazine supplement, c.1900.

A-45. American-issued cigarette card depicting bather with cork "life preservers," c.1905.

Cosa sono 1000 Km.
con una super come questa.

BP

Un viaggio lungo,
lungo quanto vuoi,
finisce per sembrare
meno lungo quando
nel motore c'è la nuova
Super BP con Enertron.
Perché è la Super
che brucia tutta e lascia
il carburatore sempre pulito.
Nuova SUPER BP,
l'unica con ENERTRON.

**Scappa
con Superissima.**

A-47. Sex in advertising. The model gazes provocatively at viewer, and the gasoline nozzle suggests phallic symbolism. July 1971.

Evans's viewpoint was quite liberated in 1937, if one considers what a writer for *The Times* (London) wrote in the 1880s—that cigarette cards were "placing licensed sex on a pedestal."

Calendar pin-ups: Sex in monthly installments

Pin-up calendars were, and to a great extent still are, advertising tools—either as extensions of a magazine or as business gifts, displaying the sponsor's name and address. The earliest girlie calendars were published at the end of the 19th century and at the beginning of the 20th. Only relatively recently has the pin-up calendar been published for non-promotional reasons and made available to the general public through retail stores.

A full discussion of calendar pin-ups begins on page 175.

Modern pin-ups — stripped of excuses as well as clothes

The pin-up, as we have defined it, evolved as a concept from many different sources. It is a combination of elements that produce a particular quality of image based on titillation and allure. Whether from prints, posters, magazines, calendars, postcards, or from cigarette cards, the earliest pin-ups were almost all tied to themes, commercial products, stories, and professions.

In large part, this trend continues up to the present, as with sex in advertising and the contemporary poster with its political and social content. But what is also apparent is the increasing trend toward the pin-up for its own sake, the presentation of the body solely for the visual delectation of the onlooker. This process has been gradual. The Gibson Girl was never just a body; she was Love, Fashion, Integrity, and Refinement. But in the 1930s and 1940s the Petty Girl and the Varga Girl, as we shall see, were no more or less than sexual objects—vivid, yet unreal, functioning in their own world, the fantasies of men. The pin-up, therefore, evolved through the process of shedding excuses for the display of female anatomy.

Another shedding process that can be observed through the years is the literal undressing of the pin-up: the emergence of naked breasts and buttocks and, today, the unabashed exposure of pubic hair and vulva —no longer presented in a context of "artistic models" or "nudists."

Thus, freed from strategically placed clothing, needing no excuse but herself, today's pin-up reveals with refreshing directness the motive that was often obscured by the modesty or pretensions of her predecessors: sexual enticement. Be she in a soldier's foot locker, in a barbershop magazine, on a calendar at the filling station, on the walls of a student dorm, or in a bachelor's posh apartment, there is no denying the pleasure of her summons. At the very least, she submits her charms to our judgment. At her best, she allows us to escape into her private and gratifying world.

Erotic fantasy: Variations on a theme

It is well recognized that everyone has, and must deal with, erotic fantasies. Although most of these derive from social experiences, especially in childhood, many other stimuli condition our thoughts and feelings. Without question, pin-up images are a strong source of erotic fantasy. The basic one is that of direct sexual liaison with the pin-up subject. The subtlest shifts in the model's pose or attitude can suggest many varied erotic possibilities, ranging from the most refined seduction to the crudest fetishism or orgy.

The viewer can find—through the endless variety of available materials—whatever images best suit his appetites. Obviously men seek out most of all what they do not have in real life. Typically, the adolescent, lacking experience, looks for mature, uninhibited sexual partners; the adult bachelor searches for the girl he cannot find in his little black address book (that is, an idealized image that can satisfy him more than the real people in his life); the married adult, bored with domestic humdrum and fidelity, seeks escape through vicarious exoticism, promiscuity, or other life styles.

Just as there are many kinds and degrees of fantasy and escape, there are many different responses to pin-up images. A common example is masturbation with the use of pin-ups as stimulation. And, as discussed below, pin-ups may function as personally acceptable diversions of socially unacceptable inclinations. For some men, pin-ups reinforce feelings of male domination. The married man looks for a fantasy mate who will not "answer back" or demand reciprocation, compromise, or fair treatment. The man is the unchallenged ruler of his chosen pin-up.

In erotic fantasy we see two general directions: idealization, by which a man seeks to associate with the "beautiful people" (film stars, jet setters, Playmates); and vulgarization, by which he safely indulges in "lower-class" sex objects (prostitutes, women with grotesque or exaggerated bodies, tawdry burlesque queens, and fetishists). These kinds of erotic fantasy do not

A-48. Three fairly direct, exploitative pin-ups. *Above:* Low-neckline toilet scene, 1901. *Center:* "Good morning, have you seen my maid?" *Broadway Magazine,* June 1899. *Below:* Noticeably unplayful bathing beauty, German, c.1905.

necessarily reflect abnormal tastes; nor can we say that it is more "normal" to idealize than to vulgarize. Either type of fantasy can be valid for a given man with his own unique set of sexual responses.

Since fantasizing about pin-ups is socially acceptable, it might be considered a healthy substitute for actual promiscuity, extramarital relations, or fetishism. On the other hand, many studies indicate that fantasies *not acted out* lead to greater emotional repression, and this in turn may intensify the psychosexual problems of the individual. Fantasies that are realized tend to evaporate. So one cannot generalize about the therapeutic value of pin-ups.

Pin-ups in several ways may dissipate insecurities about one's masculinity. A man may try to impress his peers by sharing a collection of pin-ups. This can be a gesture of camaraderie, as in an army barracks, or a mask for sexual insecurity or latent homosexuality. In this respect, pin-ups certainly can limit man's sexual latitude. They buttress the notion that a man is a man only if he can dominate women. Thus, a man uncertain of the potential range or limits of his own sexuality may seek in his relationship with pin-ups fulfillment of the role imposed on him by society. But by staring at picture after picture of barely clad women in provocative poses, he actually narrows his sexual potential.

Another role of the pin-up is as hedonistic stand-in for one's wife or mother. Most men probably would dislike their wives (or mothers) being featured as pin-ups. Their immediate response might well be, "I don't want the whole world to see her half-naked." There are at least two possible reasons: first, the embarrassment associated with public exposure of one's intimate relations, a carry-over from the repressive conditioning of Puritanism and other religious creeds; second, the presumed vulnerability and potential loss of a loved one's exposed body. The fear of losing a love object to another man—unknown, impersonal, perhaps more virile and desirable—heightens one's feelings of sexual inadequacy. The pin-up is opposite in principle and theme to wifedom or motherhood. She is neither for marrying nor for child-bearing. She is pure escape.

A man's object in a man's world

The pin-up for its own sake did not begin to emerge until the latter part of the 19th century. It took two major forms: magazine photographs of renowned, even notorious, actresses and dancing girls; and the Gibson Girl, who represented the first conscious effort to create a popular ideal of femininity. Thus, even in the early period, one discerns different social levels of pin-ups.

The Gibson Girl at the turn of the century was the world's image of the American Beauty. Although she had universal appeal —to the educated and uneducated, rich and poor, young and old, male and female— she was distinctly "high class." "Gentility" and "breeding" were frequently used to describe not only her physical attributes but her conduct and demeanor as well. Fairfax Downey saw the morality of the Gibson Girl as related to "Youth and beauty. Honor and decency and dignity. Love conquers all. Money isn't everything." She was a status symbol for the masses. And, ironically, she helped set the stage for today's Women's Liberation movement. For the Gibson Girl, in establishing an idealization of femininity, also created a false concept of womanhood —a dishonest romanticism and sentimentality against which Women's Lib now raises its voice.

The other general class of pin-ups has been equally objectionable to feminist movements. It has presented women exclusively as sex objects, to be exploited massively through girlie magazines, movie fan magazines, calendars, posters, and other vehicles. Actresses and dancing girls, as well as burlesque queens, "show girls," chorus girls, and movie starlets, came to represent the promiscuous image of women, relished in the main by men of lower socio-economic standing. One recalls pin-ups like Lillie Langtry and Lillian Russell and Little Egypt, who, at the 1893 Chicago World's Fair, drove crowds of men mad by gyrating in a new dance called the cooch. Dancing girls, and reproductions of them, were part of man's barroom domain. From this world women were, or chose to be, excluded.

In subsequent years, intermediate classes of female pin-ups developed, and no one level has been representative of a given period. Rather, one finds high-, middle-, and low-level pin-ups in peaceful, mutually exclusive coexistence.

The caliber of a pin-up usually reflects the social caste of those who appreciate it. It is unlikely that the same person reads both *Penthouse* and *Topper*. No moral judgment is implied by such an observation, for one might argue that higher-class magazines are hypocritical in presenting pin-ups in literary and other cultural contexts and that lower-class magazines are at least honest in offering their pin-ups without pretensions.

In their most prevalent forms, pin-ups have been traditionally disseminated among, and supported by, lower-class men. We think of the pin-up as a "backroom" phenomenon, not for display in the home and certainly not for women to share. This

A-49. Little Egypt introduced the "cooch" in Chicago in 1893. By 1904, at least five "Little Egypts," gyrating across the United States, were accumulating scandals and box office receipts. (Picture Collection, New York Public Library.)

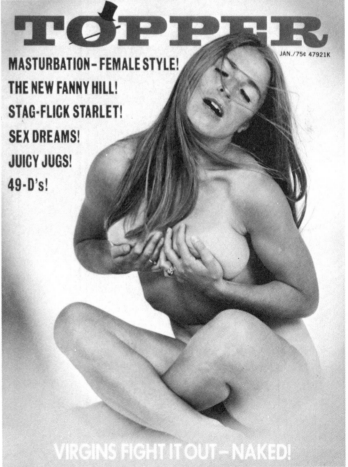

A-50. Covers from two contemporary magazines showing contrasting appeals for different markets. *Left:* Subdued, elegant model with emphasis on face and direct gaze. *Penthouse*, December 1971. *Right:* Model in ecstasy from auto-erotic stimulation. *Topper*, January 1971. Note also the articles advertised by each magazine.

A-51. The first Petty Girl to appear in *Esquire* (Autumn 1933) set a new trend by establishing the pin-up on an "upper-class" level.

perhaps reflects the sexual repression and attendant guilt that grew out of the Puritanical attitudes of the late 19th century. Sociological studies reveal a greater incidence of sex-associated guilt among the lower classes than among middle and upper classes. Conceivably this guilt dissipates more easily when men, as a group, *share* a wall covered with pin-ups or a stack of girlie magazines in a barbershop.

Interest in pin-ups obviously is not restricted to particular classes or age groups. Hardly a teenage boy from any socio-economic background has not at some point shared with his friends a copy of a "dirty" book of fiction or a girlie magazine. Does the adolescent share his fantasy life with Dad? No more than Dad is likely to share *his* with Mom. The experience does not normally go outside the boy's peer group.

The traditional exclusion of women from appreciation of the social aspects of the pin-up has been one facet of male chauvinism. (The pin-up is, by definition, a sexist concept.) But women, particularly young women, have their own forms of pin-ups: movie idols (from Rudolph Valentino to Peter Fonda) and singing stars (from Rudy Vallee to Paul McCartney). However, the presentation of these idols as pin-ups—through magazines, posters, and record-album inserts—is not intended to stimulate sexual fantasies alone, but permits fuller amorous and glamorous associations. There is an important distinction between this type of male pin-up (personality and talent as well as body) and the traditional female pin-up (usually body only).

Only recently have women gained a type of male pin-up analogous to the traditional girlie images. The first widely circulated examples occurred in April 1972, when *Cosmopolitan* (New York) featured a centerfold illustration of the actor Burt Reynolds, completely nude though not frontally exposed, and its London counterpart *Cosmopolitan* simultaneously featured Paul de Feu in a similar state. Many commentators saw some irony in the fact that de Feu had been married to Britain's foremost women's liberationist, Germaine Greer. The first pin-up issues of *Cosmopolitan* were reportedly sold out almost immediately after appearing on the newsstands, but one may speculate as to whether most of the purchasers were women.

Over the years, as we have seen, girlie magazines took on various guises—"studio" photography, burlesque, theater—in order to present pin-ups. Only by exception, in the first thirty years of the 20th century, were any of these magazines not aimed at a mass audience on the lowest socio-economic levels. Not until *Esquire* began (1933) was the pin-up aimed exclusively at readers of a higher social status. *Esquire* featured, from the start, articles and pictorials in the finest tradition of literary and esthetic magazines. Its pin-ups by Petty, Varga, and other artists maintained the aura of "good taste." The pin-ups, many of which were two- and three-page foldouts, showed comic, sex-oriented situations reflecting the sophistication of the urban upper classes. One could say that *Esquire* ranked above a mass market girlie magazine as a call girl did to a prostitute. By the time *Playboy* appeared in 1953, *Esquire* had all but dropped the pin-up from its features. And while *Playboy* has a number of poor imitators, it has offered a consistently high-class pin-up to a full generation of Americans. Thus, the audience for pin-ups expanded qualitatively as well as quantitatively. Subscribing to the magazines from their homes, the readers of *Esquire* and *Playboy* exposed their women and children to the risqué world of the pin-up.

Still another expansion of the pin-up audience has come by way of the contemporary poster, through which today's younger generation has *its* particular brand of pin-up, based on themes of today's sexual revolution. Many of these posters go beyond the simple presentation of the women as sex object and portray, instead, heterosexuality (male and female together), nude groups, homosexuality, interracial couples, mothers, the aged, overweight nudes, and so on.

Today, there are pin-ups that appeal to virtually every echelon of society; they are more socially acceptable than ever before; and although they still tend to exploit women as sex objects, they offer more physical variety, a wider range of insights, and greater encouragement of self-awareness than ever before.

A-52. Four contemporary posters showing themes of sexual liberation. *Above left: The Naked Truth* reminds us that nudes come in all ages. *Above right: Mother and Child,* in which the child gives the mother's nudity an air of innocence or purity. *Right: Heavy* demonstrates that overweight does not preclude attractiveness. (For contrast, see the obesity shown on page 29.) *Below: Back-anal-ia,* an uncommon view of nude women, although essentially nonsexual, may suggest to some viewers an interracial lesbian orgy. (Personality Posters, New York.)

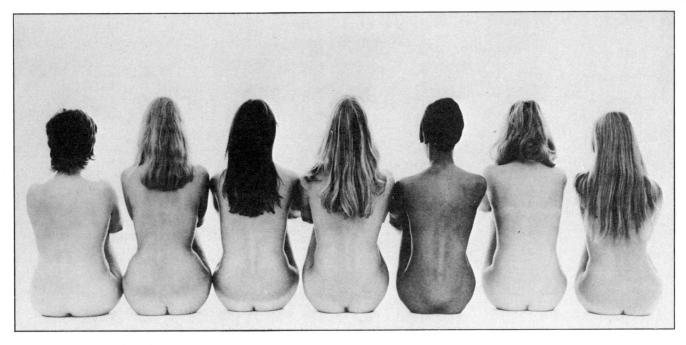

Magazines: "Artistic" Pin-ups

B-1. Gladys Phillips, an actress in topless production of *Earl Carroll's Vanities. Art Inspirations: Magazine of Photographic Art* (New York), December 1926.

Magazines: "Artistic" Pin-ups

During the first decade of the 20th century, girlie pictures appeared only in popular magazines of general interest, and not until around World War I were several types of specialized publications issued—"art" magazines, girlie magazines, and Hollywood fan magazines—each of which presented pin-up images in its own way. By then, America had indisputably taken the commanding lead in the publication of such magazines, with France as the nearest competitor. In their girlie features, however, American magazines constantly alluded to French women, and some American publications were given such names as *French Follies, French Frills, Gay Parisienne, Les Dames, Paris by Night, Paris Life,* and *Paris Nights.* (Indeed America was perhaps more responsible than France itself for promoting and establishing Paris as the universal mecca of amour and sex.) * Americans seemed to regard French women as sexually exotic and more sophisticated than American women; consequently, they found pin-ups of French models and actresses to be both more authentic and more appealing. (Undeniably, American publishers made more money on French pin-ups than French publishers did.) Only when French or quasi-French pin-ups were well established and accepted by the public in the United States were American publishers confident enough to create and promote American pin-up images.

Early pin-up magazines can be appreciated today—if at all—mainly for their naiveté and deviousness. Throughout this century, publishers of girlie magazines have probed the extremes of what is legally permissible. They have used such themes as nudism, physical fitness, sports, and party games to expose female bodies. Today, shrewd publishers of girlie magazines have observed and exploited the finest technicalities: the fact that sexual organs may be exposed but that the depiction of sexual penetration is illegal; that a penis may be shown, but not erect; that a vulva may appear in full view, but only if the *theme* of the illustration is stockings, girdles, legs, hose, or the like. Recently, some magazine publishers have based entire issues on "blue movies," or "art cinema." Overall, perhaps, "art" has been the single most exploited guise for the presentation of full nudes.

Until relatively recently, complete nudes in frontal poses could not be printed in girlie magazines. Before the legal rulings were changed, therefore, publishers had to either distribute their publications illegally or use the protective umbrellas of "art photography" or "art studies." To gain as large an audience as possible for photographs of fully nude women, and to do so legally, some publishers—especially before the liberalization of censorship in the 1960s and 1970s—issued magazines presumably intended for art students but actually, if not openly, directed to pin-up fanciers. The "art" approach was meant not so much to mislead the reader as to avoid conflict with censorship regulations or postal laws.

Although nude art photography can be a valid, meaningful form of creative expression, and most good figure photography contains elements of eroticism, nude art photographs do not ordinarily reach the point of *intentional* sexual evocation characteristic of pin-ups. Publishers therefore have used various devices to "spice up" their photographs. The pictures in these pseudo-art magazines—examples of which are illustrated on the following pages—violate the formal, esthetic, and academic principles of bona fide art photography—work represented, for example, by the body landscapes of Edward Weston or the distortions of Bill Brandt. Almost always, the publications in which they appear contain copy stating that the pictures are intended for use by students of art and photography. The texts and captions stress drawing, painting, or photographic techniques, but the pictures, the subjects, the styles—and the lack of artistry or creativity in the photography—make it evident that serious study of this material for artistic purposes is most unlikely.

Evolving from the more general magazines of the early 1900s, the earliest "art" magazines contained pictorials on the nude in art, nude photography, semi-nude actresses, and so on. *Art Inspirations,* a monthly that was among the earliest magazines of its kind, was first issued in 1926 (*B-1, B-3*). From then until the present day, hundreds of "art" magazines have been published, with innumerable themes and variations on the nude and semi-nude figure. The following selection is intended to show a wide range of such pin-ups, over many years, from this peculiar sub-genre of girlie magazines.

---

* English attitudes antedate American by centuries. "Among other good old British prejudices, we have inherited their traditional estimate of the French people and of French society, and are obstinately wedded to it . . . It may be said, that . . . all good Americans 'expect to go to Paris when they die' . . ."—"French Morals and Manners," by a Roving American, *Appletons' Journal* (New York), April 24, 1869, pp. 114-16.

B-2. Lee Byrne, an actress in the *Vanities,* c.1925. Although some New York theaters were giving topless productions, nudity of this kind was publishable only in "art" magazines.

B-3. Captioned: "Soft tones and careful retouching make this study one both of character and beauty." *Art Inspirations,* 1926. Both this plate and B-1 demonstrate the mixing (or mixing up) of stage and art themes that was common in the early years of photography magazines.

B-4. "Suzanne." *Artists and Models Magazine* (Wilmington, Del.), January 1927. Presumably a photograph of a "classical" painting, this is a fine example of the nude-in-art theme that began in general magazines in the 1890s. Is this a photograph of a painting or of a studio model, subsequently retouched and given a classical backdrop?

B-5. Rama-Tahé, c.1928. Dance was another popular theme of the art magazine; and it was almost exclusively in connection with dance that black, Indian, Oriental, or other exotic models were photographed.

B-6. "Coquetry." *Artists and Models Magazine,* March 1928. Pure cheesecake.

B-2

B-3

B-4

B-5

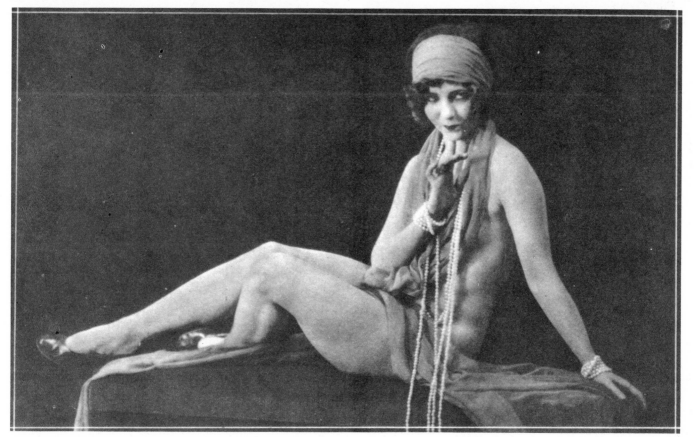

B-6

Magazines: "Artistic" Pin-ups

B-7

"A MODERN EVE"—From the Art composition by the Alta Studios.

B-9

B-8

B-10

B-11

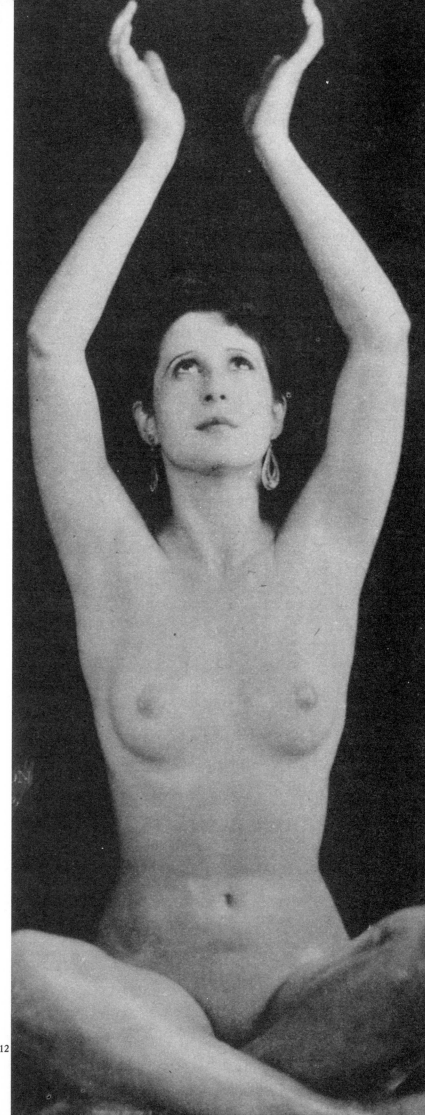

B-7. Mary Higgin, dancer and singer. *Camera Art* (New York), May 1929. Captioned: "Interesting pose and lighting treatment shown here." The model's direct gaze at the viewer, her makeup, jewelry, and high-heel shoes give a pin-up rather than art quality to this picture.

B-8. "A Modern Eve," 1929, a characteristic nature pose, linked here with the Garden of Eden. Retouching to eliminate exposure of pubic hair—a common practice even in recent years—may have been done to avoid censorship, but even more so to present the model in "good taste."

B-9. c.1929. The use of a prop, or "gimmick," to cover portions of the model adds an element of tease and eliminates the necessity for retouching the pubic area.

B-10. A cellophane-wrapped model in a pose of dubious interest to art students. *Students Art Manual* [no place], c.1930.

B-11. *Spotlight* (New York), c.1935, professed to be for "the artist who turns photographer," and, like hundreds of other "art" magazines through the years, offers "a photographic text of form, lighting, style, anatomy, and composition," serving an "instructional and illustrative purpose."

B-12. "Figure for Pagan Adoration," c.1935, showing retouched pubic area and modern earrings.

B-12

B-13

B-14

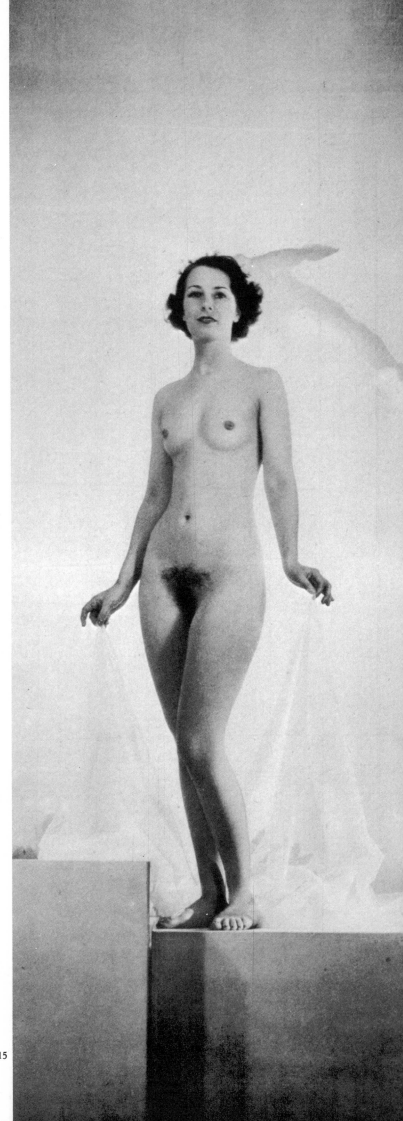

B-15

B-13. "Upper Torso Study," c.1935, an unmistakable pin-up pose. Note eye makeup and lipstick.

B-14. "The Odalisque," c.1935, an exotic dancer, wistfully posed.

B-15. *The Body Beautiful* (New York), 1936. This photograph with its "artistic" backdrop is unusual for its unabashed exposure of pubic hair.

B-16. *"La Femme au Chale,"* c.1938. Apparently from a French "studio" magazine, this photograph shows a black (possibly Moroccan) model in a cheesecake-type pose.

B-17. Model in communion with nature, an esthetic pose that leaves something to be desired. *Girl Beautiful* (Chicago), 1939.

B-18. This picture is not from a magazine but was sold in a package of 18 "original pictures." *Nude Art Studies* [no place], c.1945, "for Artists, Art Students, Collectors, Photographers, and Studio Directors." Note model's props and nail polish, and slight retouching of nipples, navel, and pubic hair.

B-16

B-17

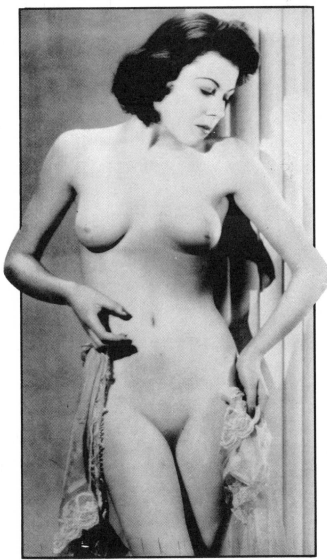

B-18

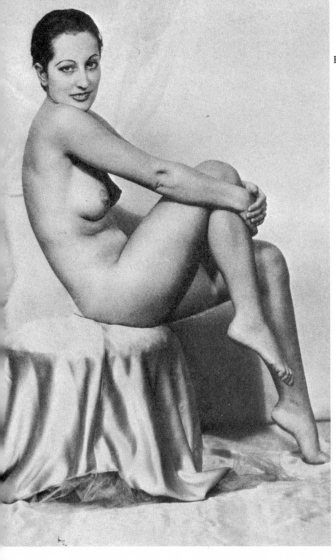

B-19

B-20

B-19. *Girl Picture Album* (Chicago), c.1945. An obvious pin-up pose in a boudoir setting. In this magazine, pencil drawings accompanied some of the photographs to demonstrate to art students how the photographs could be best utilized.

B-20. *La Femme: Art of the Camera* [no place, "Printed in the U.S.A."], c.1945. Detail of nipples on this "art photograph" has been retouched beyond visibility, yet facial makeup almost leaps off the page.

B-21. *Amateur Screen and Photography* (Chicago), June 1951. According to the caption, this photograph was used to demonstrate the "unimportance" of background.

B-22. *Presenting the Fabulous Zorita* (New York), c.1955. This is an "art" magazine only by virtue of the clear black type on the front cover reading "For Artists and Photographers" and the paragraphs on the back cover containing the standard artist-photographer-student blurb.

B-23. This photograph, from an incomplete (damaged) photography magazine, c.1950, is accompanied by a caption describing various "lighting effects." The pose resembles the famous Monroe calendar pin-up (see *Color Plate 2*, page 2).

B-24. Unnatural pose, makeup, and hairdo are the only "art" qualities of this photograph. *Sprite* (Los Angeles), late 1950s.

B-25. Captioned: "A pensive mood is projected in this shot of a mediatating [*sic*] model in a semi-relaxed pose. The design on the hip and the lace of the bra invite added attention and interest. The forms are sharp." *Contours: Anatomy Studies for Artist, Sculptor, Photographers* (New York), c.1955.

B-21

B-22

B-23

B-24

B-25

73

B-27. *Nouvelle Série de Studio* (Copenhagen), late 1960s. Printed in Denmark, this polylingual publication was also distributed in France and the United States. The unmistakable pin-up-style poses are not only pseudo-artistic but also resemble those of the raunchier girlie magazines of the 1960s. (See *A-7.*)

B-26. *Etudes Académiques* (Paris), c.1960. Like its American counterparts, this Parisian publication used props, makeup, and direct gazes that rendered the pictures true pin-ups.

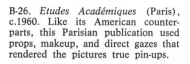

Girlie Magazines

Playgirl der Woche

»Sie sind der erste Reiseleiter, dem mein Badeanzug nicht gefällt!«

Girlie Magazines

Girlie magazines (or what have come to be called "men's magazines") are the most widely disseminated medium for pin-ups. Intended largely for servicemen in World War I, the earliest girlie magazines were founded on jokes and cartoons. The humor, of the unsophisticated "farmer's daughter" variety, came in earthy stories and racy line drawings, but occasionally there were photographs of starlets and bathing beauties. The leading magazine of this type was *Captain Billy's Whiz Bang* (C-2), published by William H. Fawcett, who later headed the Fawcett Publications empire. Like George Newnes' *Tit-bits* of 1881 (see page 48), *Whiz Bang* originated almost accidentally through Fawcett's noncommercial practice of mimeographing and distributing sheets of bawdy jokes and verses to servicemen. The humor became so popular that Fawcett decided to publish it as a pocket-sized magazine, priced at 25 cents. The printed version contained many spicy line drawings; one issue, in fact, was banned from the mails. A regular feature concerned the escapades of Pedro the bull. In 1923, *Whiz Bang's* circulation peaked at 425,000; by 1930, the magazine was floundering, and it ceased publication in 1932.

Rival publishers issued imitations, among them *Ballyhoo, Honey, Jim Jam Jems,* and *Calgary Eye Opener* (which reached a newsstand sale of 2 million copies in 1931). Fawcett later issued his own imitation, *Smokehouse Monthly.*

In Britain, there was virtually no equivalent of these publications. *Blighty* (1918-20) was published to boost the morale of soldiers through the use of humor, and, strangely, some people still claim to remember its pin-ups. In fact, it contained no hint of pin-ups and no photographs at all. *Tit-bits* (see page 48) also found a wartime purpose, but its pictures focused on war heroes—conservative fare for the lonely men in tents and barracks and on the front line. Not until World War II did a British armed forces magazine, *Reveille,* include pictures of girls in bathing suits.

The German public had access to pin ups—typically "actresses" at the beginning of the 20th century; "bathing beauties" in the 1920s; outdoor, recreation types during the Nazi period—only through general newsmagazines. German pin-ups of a given decade usually appeared dated when compared with those in American or French magazines; and it might even be argued that they were not pin-ups at all, but rather embellishments of women in various activities, hobbies, or careers.

In America, around 1920, the first "confession" magazines began to influence the concept of women. *True Story* (1919), *True Confessions* (1922), and *Modern Romances* (1930) helped to advance the notions that there is no universal code of morals, that sex is one of the strongest motivational forces among human beings, and that good sex can mean a happy life. The effect of such thinking on pin-up publishing gradually modified the traditional view of women as happy-go-lucky sexual objects for men. By the 1930s, some pin-ups were showing a more serious side of female sexuality—women were being viewed as more complex, more formidable sexual objects. Nevertheless, most pin-ups of the 1930s and even of the 1940s were presented in a context of entertainment and merriment, using themes such as frolicking, burlesque (humor), stripping, show biz, sports, and humorous flirtation.

In the 1930s, the public having become more attuned to the pin-up concept, girlie magazines moved more confidently toward photographic rather than rendered pin-ups. Printed on pulp paper and designed specifically for workingmen, magazines such as *Wild Cherries* (*Color Plate 8*), *Love's Revels* (*Color Plate 9*), *and High Heel* (*C-11, C-13*) typified the cheaper variety of girlie magazines.

Esquire and the pin-up in "good taste"

In the 1930s, *Esquire* stood alone. Its publisher's decision to carry pin-up cartoons in a magazine that appealed to the fashionable, elite male was bold and innovative. The men's clothing trade originally inspired the publication of *Esquire,* which began, essentially, as a men's fashion magazine. Its first issue had a printing of 105,000 copies, 5,000 of which were to be distributed to newsstands and 100,000 to clothing stores throughout the United States. The popular demand was so great, however, that 95,000 copies were recalled from clothiers and redistributed to newsstands. *Esquire* became a monthly with its second issue in January 1934.

George Petty's famous pin-up girl (*A-51, C6*) appeared in *Esquire's* first issue, more as a cartoon than a pin-up, but the allure of her figure led rather quickly to her development as a singular female type (*C-10; Color Plate 12*) that was destined to become almost as much of a legend as the Gibson Girl had been thirty years earlier. Although the Petty Girl was always accompanied by a humorous caption, she stood by herself for a vast following of gentlemen. Her themes dealt fundamentally with marital infidelity, promiscuity, money, and flirtation. The general feeling was that of high society sophistication, and the level of humor was consistently upper class.

In early 1941, the Petty Girl began to appear regularly in *Esquire's* first foldout pages—a testimonial to her great popularity. In a subsequent issue, *Esquire* printed a tribute that conveyed all the flavor and snob appeal of the high-class pin-up:

> "Life," said the arch-cynic Baudelaire, "is a hospital, in which every patient is possessed by the desire of changing his bed."
>
> Now, it would seem that men are consumed by this unnamed and unnamable restlessness, a nostalgia for the unknown, a feverish curiosity about the Sumatras of the soul, those lands of Cockaigne where the air is voluptuously laden with jasmine and frangi-pani, where languorous, long-limbed women lean against the heaving flanks of the Hippogriff, watching him champ his gilded oats.
>
> For it is in the curious nature of life that night is more seductive than day, and the daughters of the night more seductive than milkmaids. It has

been that way since " 'Omer smote 'is bloomin' lyre," and probably ever will be.

But the Petty girl, like the hypnotic Manon—and the Helens, Circes, Loreleis, Clairamondes, is caprice itself; tender, tentative, and evanescent.

Every hour she is different. Her demands, her form, the movements of her rippling limbs, the spasmodic play of her wayward moods, give an infinite variety to her spanking beauty. When you tire of her, you tire of life.

Then, for reasons unknown, the Petty Girl made her final appearance in the December 1941 issue. But she has never been forgotten by *Esquire* readers of the 1930s. Later, in 1950, Columbia Pictures released *The Petty Girl,* a film starring Joan Caulfield (*Color Plate 10*).

In the October 1940 issue of *Esquire,* the Petty Girl began keeping company with her first and only rival —the Varga Girl—created by Alberto Vargas, an artist with imaginative gifts comparable to those of George Petty.* No longer in cartoon format, this new, rendered pin-up (*Color Plate 13*) was accompanied by Phil Stack's adulatory verses. In 1942 the Varga Girl found herself without competition from Petty, and Vargas continued to create his beauties for *Esquire* until March 1946 (*see C-21*). In December 1940, *Esquire* published its first Varga Girl Calendar (*C-14*) as part of the magazine and filled orders for more than 300,000 copies. Two years later, 1 million orders were received for the 1943 Varga Calendar.

Early in the 1940s, the Varga Girl was the subject of court action by the U.S. Post Office. The magazine was challenged to explain why—given the sexual nature of the Varga Girl—the second-class mailing privilege, granting cheap rates to publications of a "literary, artistic, or scientific nature," should not be revoked. At a series of hearings in Washington, D.C., *Esquire* sought to prove that it was fulfilling a public service. Witnesses—public figures, clergymen, psychiatrists, and Harvard professors—assembled to give evidence. The Post Office, for its case, called upon heads of several women's organizations for their opinions. After a lengthy legal struggle, *Esquire* was acquitted of the charge of publishing "lewd and lascivious" pictures.

Despite *Esquire*'s urbane image, its role in furnishing pin-ups to the battle-torn, bleary-eyed GI's during World War II should not be underestimated; indeed, a number of the Varga Girls sported the Stars and Stripes (and other patriotic-military accoutrements) on or in what little attire they wore. These pin-ups circulated widely among U.S. fighting men.

> Crews of the U.S.A.A.F. often plaster the centre sections of Flying Fortresses with drawings and photographs clipped from the pages of *Esquire, Men Only, Look,* and similar publications. One navigator had most of the film stars, including Gypsy Rose Lee, accompanying him on day trips to Berlin, and, in his enthusiasm, had pasted his pin ups on both the inside and the outside of his Fortress. On each flight down the "Kraut Run", the Navigator's skipper swore that their particular plane was singled out for special attention by the

German fighter pilots who "wondered what all the queer pictures were about." *

Following the demise of the Varga Girl in 1946, *Esquire* attempted to carry other types of pin-ups: the Esquire Girls (starting April 1946), showing renderings of seductive beauties, and the Esquire Gallery (begun September 1946), featuring show-girl types in various settings. The caption writers evidently regarded these rendered, sketchy, unrealistic pin-up illustrations as "art" and described them as such. In the early 1950s, *Esquire* began its Lady Fair series, which featured, at first, unknown photographers' models, usually in fashion settings; later, the Lady Fair pictorial carried well-known actresses, such as Leslie Caron (January 1954) and Betsy Palmer (November 1956). Appearing in December 1956, the final Lady Fair, actress Maria Felix, represented *Esquire*'s last published pin-up in a regular series.

With so much attention focused on the Petty and Varga Girls in *Esquire*'s early years, one tends to overlook the regularly featured pin-up photography by Hurrell, a well-known Hollywood camera artist. Starting in November 1936, and for a full decade, Hurrell's photographic portraits of actresses—for a time called "American Beauties"—provided many topnotch pin-ups of Hollywood stars (Jane Russell, for instance; *Color Plate 14*). In 1957-58, *Esquire* attempted pin-up pictorials by various photographers, much like those of *Playboy* (which was well established by then). But *Esquire* chose finally not to compete in the pin-up field; thus, its last notable pin-up feature appeared in October 1958—Bert Stern's multipage photographic spread of Hollywood beauties.

The 1940s

In the early 1940s, the term "pin-up" was commonly used to describe girlie illustrations. How it came into common parlance is uncertain, but the most tenable theory would seem to be that servicemen during World War II who avidly read and collected magazines in their barracks would then cut out their favorite pictures and paste or pin them up in their lockers or mess rooms and on their tanks or airplanes. Perhaps the single most famous wartime pin-up was of Betty Grable, with her "million dollar legs" (*Color Plate 3*; *D-39*).

Subsequently, Miss Grable starred in the film entitled *Pin-up Girl* (1944). Many photographers' models became known as "pin-up models." Hollywood stars posed for "pin-up publicity stills." Magazines published pin-up features and series of pin-ups called "pin-up parades" or "pin-up revues" (*C-11, C-15*). As a consequence, the pin-up came to be enjoyed more freely for its own sake and as a valid pictorial form. Esthetic standards developed—the beauty of the model's face and body, the tastefulness of the pose, and the varying degrees of cuteness, allure, and tawdriness of the model and her pose.

Most girlie magazines of the 1940s carried a blend of straightforward pin-ups, as described above, and thematic girlie pictorials—those that harked back to

---

* Only in connection with his work for *Esquire* was Vargas's name spelled without the *s*.

* "The 'pin up' craze among G.I.s," *Paper and Print* (London), Vol. 18 (1945), p. 99.

the humor of the 1930s. American magazines such as *Glamorous Models* (C-19) and *Tid Bits of Beauty* (C-18, C-20) showed nothing else but pin-ups, but others like *Click*, *Grin* (C-15), *Pic* (D-30, D-33), *See* (C-16), *Snap*, and *Spot* also covered sports, crime, and major current events, as well as "entertainment" (in which pin-ups regularly appeared). In England *Lilliput* (C-28) is fondly recalled for its pin-ups of screen stars and fashion models.

The 1950s: Playboy starts a tradition

By the 1950s, pin-ups, as a mature form, reflected some of the more modern attitudes toward sex. Magazines gradually infused their pictorials with psychosexual themes, leaning—at first tentatively, later more explicitly—toward fetishism, sadomasochism, masturbation, homosexuality (especially lesbianism), and exhibitionism. Most of all, girlie magazines began to dwell on fully exposed breasts and buttocks.

An outstanding development in the years following World War II was the rapid growth of men's adventure magazines, such as *Argosy, Saga, True,* and *True Adventure,* which, unlike girlie magazines, appealed to men through stories of adventure, rugged sports, travel, and the outdoors.

When *Esquire* began revamping its format and content in the early 1950s, de-emphasizing pin-ups and re-emphasizing the literary, social, and cultural purposes, a gap was left for a particular market—college-educated men of above-average income, climbing the ladder of success, and living chiefly in urban centers. *Playboy* began at that time.

From the start, in December 1953, *Playboy* was aimed at the indoor, sophisticated, city-bred man. The *Playboy* reader had some of the literary interests of the *Esquire* man and few of the interests of the rugged *Argosy* man. As stated in its first anniversary issue, *Playboy*'s intention was to be

> welcome by that select group of urbane fellows who were less concerned with hunting, fishing, and climbing mountains than with good food, drink, proper dress, and the pleasure of female company.

Hugh Hefner, *Playboy*'s founder (who had previously worked in *Esquire*'s promotion department) wanted his magazine to revive what *Esquire* had been before it de-emphasized sex.

Playboy's first issue was undated because Hefner was not sure there would be a second issue. The magazine's success was immediate, however. It became known for its girlie features rather than for its literary merits, and this approach was highly successful. By 1955, its written content improved in quality, and its girlie features were toned down. Among *Playboy*'s literary lights at that time were Jack Kerouac, Alberto Moravia, Carl Sandburg, and Evelyn Waugh.

The magazine's unique contribution to the pin-up vocabulary was the Playmate of the Month, a centerfold pictorial, featuring some of the most beautiful young women ever photographed. The first Playmate was Marilyn Monroe in a Tom Kelley photograph reputed to have been taken during the same sequence that yielded the famous Monroe calendar shot. "Playmate" became a household word in the 1950s, and the magazine thus set a precedent that was to be imitated to the present day.

For the first year and a half, only one picture of each Playmate was presented. From September 1955 on, however, *Playboy,* further exploiting the value of tease, printed clusters of Playmate pictures, usually clothed or semi-clothed, as a kind of foreplay, or warm-up, before the centerfold main event. Playmates in recent years have been paid a basic modeling fee of approximately $3,000.

For exponents of Women's Liberation, *Playboy*'s image of women has come to epitomize the worst features of male chauvinism. The Playmate is a sexist idealization. And surely no one doubts that, beyond the very stringent standards of age and measurements, the Playmate's body is "purified" through the magic of makeup and deft retouching (and even air conditioning, to stiffen the nipples) to remove skin blemishes, scars, veins, body hair, freckles, birthmarks—hence the unreal, the demeaning, the offensive image of femininity.*

Playboy's early imitators in the 1950s—*Cabaret* (*Color Plate 15*), *Duke* (C-36), *Jem* (C-43; *Color Plate 18*), *Jaguar* (C-53), *Dude, Escapade, Nugget,* and others—were, on the whole, patently inferior in both literary content and pictorials; but they found themselves a tremendous market, one characterized by more interest in girlie features than in contemporary literature and politics.

On a somewhat lower stratum were magazines with little, if any, emphasis on literature and general-interest features but stress on girlies, especially those with exaggerated breasts and buttocks—in the United States, *Ace, Bachelor* (C-71), *Cavalier, Cocktail, Dapper, Flame, Follies, Frolic* (C-26), *Fury, Gala* (A-8, C-44), *Gent, Lark, Man, Rogue* (C-56, C-57, C-68), *Spree*—the list seems endless—and in Great Britain, *Cutie, Droop, Fresh, Harem, Hush, Rosalinda's Album, Silky, Sir, Slinky,* and *Tinkle,* among others.

In Britain, by and large, there was little during the 1950s that was not already current or even slightly passé in America. There were pocket-sized publications like *Spick* (C-39), which began in 1953, and its adjunct, *Span,* which started in the following year and represented the poorer brand of pin-ups aimed for the workingman. They were comparable to *Foto-rama* (C-38) and other U.S. digest-sized magazines that had started some years earlier. And there was *Kamera,* begun in 1958, with photographic nude "studies," ostensibly for photographers. From its publisher, George Harrison Marks (who in the 1960s was to become a major figure in pin-up publishing) came *Solo,* also in 1958, a higher-quality, pocket-sized photographic magazine, each issue of which was devoted to only one model. Marks later converted *Kamera* into two magazines; he also published expensive hardcover pin-up photography books and later issued the Harrison Marks Calendar with great success.

---

* However, several of Playboy's newer rivals, notably *Penthouse,* have a firm policy not to obscure the natural "occurrences" on their Pets' bodies.

From the 1960s to the present: More shedding, more spreading

Playboy-type magazines have sprung up all over the world. They are not merely imitators but international counterparts. Their format, design and content vary somewhat from one to another, but they belong basically to the same family. All have centerfold subjects-of-the-month: in France, *Lui* (*Color Plate 27*); in Germany, *ER* (*Color Plate 26*); in Italy, *Playmen* (*C-63*); in Great Britain, *Club* (*C-62*), *Mayfair* (*Color Plate 29*), and *Men Only* (*Color Plate 31*); and, with both U.S. and British editions, *Penthouse* (*A-12*; *Color Plate 24*; *Color Plate 28*), among the fastest growing British quality magazines.

Penthouse, the first of Britain's *Playboy* counterparts, was founded in 1965. It was followed by *Mayfair* in 1966 and by *Men Only,* in a new format, in 1971. All three magazines—slick, high priced, and of high quality—contain literary, political, and cultural articles, and all are competing for the *Playboy*-type market in Great Britain. Aimed at the nostalgic, well-bred man, *Mayfair,* more escapist than the other two, emphasizes sports, sports cars, fashion, and status. Its pin-ups are not as bold as those of *Penthouse* or *Men Only*. *Penthouse* is published for a slightly older, less conventional, more liberal, intellectual man. Its pin-ups are more daring, and it has the widest range of fiction. Slightly larger in format than the other two, with a stiffer cover, *Men Only* "feels" like a better-quality printed vehicle; its production standards are among the highest in the world, and its price is slightly higher than the others. By 1971-72, it had become the world's boldest quality pin-up magazine, stressing masturbatory poses (which the other two magazines began cautiously to imitate) and Sapphism. Its readership is relatively younger and "hipper," and early in 1972 it had the largest British circulation of the three.

Penthouse, however, has a much larger international audience. It was started in London in 1965 by Bob Guccione, an energetic Italo-American photographer. Within five years, Guccione, photographing most of the *Penthouse* Pets-of-the-Month himself, had achieved major recognition for his magazine in the *Playboy* class. He added the U.S. edition in 1969 and injected an international flavor to its images by using models from Austria, Czechoslovakia, Denmark, France, Germany, Ireland, Italy, the Netherlands, Scotland, Switzerland, and Wales—as well as England and America.

Penthouse was the first quality magazine, technically, to expose the pubic hair of one of its centerfold subjects (*A-12*), and it tended consciously to avoid the *Playboy* cliché of "fixing up" its subjects-of-the-month. Thus, Pets seem more "natural." But far more important than *Penthouse*'s admission of blemishes is the character of the Pet. She is less servile than the Playmate, not so ready to please her man. She is generally more spirited looking, unconventional, and independent. Finally, she seems more oriented to pop culture than to cabaret life, to natural womanhood (but not yet to Women's Liberation) than to idealized femininity—distinctions that suggest the beginnings of a generation gap between Playmate and Pet.

Among middle-level magazines, *Fiesta* and *Knave* represent British equivalents of *Ace, Rogue,* and *Top-per* in the United States, and they contain pin-ups, erotic photographs, and articles about sex in films and varieties of sexual experience. Both magazines are issued by the same publisher, but the editors of *Knave* regard it as slightly more sophisticated. Each of *Knave*'s first issues (1968-70) was devoted to one sexual theme, but in 1971 the magazine began to carry articles and pictures on lesbianism, orgy, the history of sex, and a varied range of other sexual subjects (*C-74*). On a more popular level are general magazines such as *Parade* (*C-46*), whose pin-ups are provocative but not bold.

Some London newspapers, like the *Daily Mirror* (which started the practice in 1936) and *The Sun* (founded in 1969), carry traditional cheesecake pin-ups on their front pages as circulation builders (*C-76*). Somewhat related to this phenomenon are *Titbits, Reveille* (*C-77*), and certain other weekly tabloids that resemble in format the Sunday magazine supplements of American newspapers. "Popular" pin-ups continually appear on their covers, but seldom on the inside pages.

The newest British pin-up medium is the "sex-education" magazine—*Climax, Forum, Open, Relate, Search* (*C-72*), and others. In the question-and-answer columns of these digest-sized publications, one finds a lively exchange of readers' letters that detail supposedly personal sexual experience or raise questions about "normal" sexual behavior that invariably allow the writer to dwell on the abnormal. Along with the letters, articles, and columns, there are dozens of highly erotic photographs, mostly outside the traditional range of pin-ups.

In Germany, there were no girlie magazines of consequence until after 1945. During both World Wars, however, the German army had issued pin-up pictures, usually linked with propagandistic themes, for soldiers in the armed ser s. Currently, German girlie magazines range from the *Playboy* counterpart, *ER* (*Color Plate 26*), to those that contain near-pornographic pin-ups. Titles include *Girls aus Schweden, Girls Illustrated, Gondel, Daily Girls,* and *Spontan*. Mostly, however, German pin-ups are widely distributed through highly popular general-interest weekly publications and not through girlie magazines. Of the four largest general magazines today—*Bunte Illustrierte, Neue Revue, Quick,* and *Stern*—*Neue Revue* is regarded as the most daring (*C-23*). Its covers, like those of the other magazines, contain the main, sometimes the only, pin-up picture, but usually, there are one or two more inside—sometimes topless, always tastefully presented. *Bunte Illustrierte* is the most conservative of these German weeklies.

Neue Revue, started in 1965 as a merger of *Neue* and *Revue,* uses cover pin-ups purely and simply to attract readers. When no pin-up appears, sales drop, predictably, by 50,000 copies. From the same publisher comes *Praline,* a smaller quasi-girlie magazine, which emphasizes mild scandal, gossip, and crime, and likes to print sex stories. *Praline*'s cover, like that of its parent magazine, contains its best pin-up; the pictures inside are more general and are always associated with editorial features.

Although *Stern,* founded in 1948, has never been a girlie magazine—it is perhaps comparable to *Life*—its pin-up covers are its best-known features (*C-22*).

Today *Stern* is gradually de-emphasizing its cover pin-ups, but more than half the covers still contain provocative, often topless models. Inside the magazine, there are few pin-ups. Instead, there are many illustrated articles on politics, history, fashion, science, and various other topical subjects. *Jasmin,* related to *Stern* as *Praline* is to *Neue Revue,* is more sex-oriented in its pictures and stories; but all of these magazines use pin-ups chiefly to build circulation. Many other German general magazines, as well as smaller left-wing political magazines like *Konkret, Pardon,* and *Spontan,* use the same device.

Twen, a slick-paper girlie magazine of rather high quality, presumably was too modern, too high class for the German market, or, as some critics claimed, was "designed mostly for art directors." Consequently, it did not receive enough support, and it ceased publication early in 1972.

ER, Germany's *Playboy* counterpart, with a circulation of about 80,000 at the beginning of 1972, is not as significant in Germany as, say, *Penthouse, Mayfair,* or *Men Only* in Great Britain, *Lui* in France, or *Playboy* in the United States. Like *Twen,* it is considered expensive for the German market and its features seem not to be as attractive to German readers as those of the weekly picture magazines.

Sexy (C-69), printed in tabloid format on pulp paper, like many other contemporary German magazines, resembles and feels like a Sunday newspaper supplement. Its cheap appearance as much as its contents may have caused it to be banned early in 1972. Since it can no longer be displayed at newsstands, purchasers must specifically request it from newsdealers. Stylistically, *Sexy*'s pin-ups are about five years behind the times.

Die Nachrichten (first issued as *St. Pauli Nachrichten*) is, like *Sexy,* a pin-up and erotica tabloid, from St. Pauli, Hamburg's sex center; and also like *Sexy,* it was banned (under its original title) within a few months of its first publication. Finding a loophole in the law, however, its publishers simply re-named the paper and are again distributing it legally. It contains many near-pornographic pictures of heterosexual and homosexual couples and trios, as well as bold, modern pin-ups—beaver poses and the like (*C-70*). It also contains sensational articles on violent crime, prostitution, pornographic films, and "personal" sexual experiences.

In the wake of *Playboy,* its imitators, and its international counterparts, magazines that lean toward specialized erotic interests have been published more openly. The gradual infusion of psychosexual themes that began in the late 1950s has already been mentioned. But in the 1960s, such publications were everywhere to be found—*Black Stocking Parade (C-52),* *Gammla Blue (C-55), Heels and Hose (C-49, C-50), Hippy, Stocking Parade (C-42), Striperama (C-48),* and *Ultra (C-54),* as well as *Purr, Sextet, Stare, Thigh High, Tip Top,* and others. These magazines, to be sure, still relied on thematic disguises, but not like those of the 1940s, and not for the same reasons. Typical features are based on stockings, high heels, legs, and the "art" of stripping. By seeming to focus on these apparently harmless themes, the publishers can print photographs that many regard as tasteless and obscene yet that nonetheless get by the censors. There is, for instance, nothing technically illegal about displaying hose, although in the process of doing so, the photographs inevitably expose the model's buttocks.

Further, some magazines now openly elaborate on specific fetishes—bondage, sadism, leather and rubber clothing, and devices for sexual pleasure and pain. Their pictures are informational, at least for some readers, and voyeuristic rather than seductive or alluring. Other magazines are approaching hard-core pornography, just short of displaying erections or sexual penetration. Poor-quality, pandering magazines live on and probably always will.

C-1

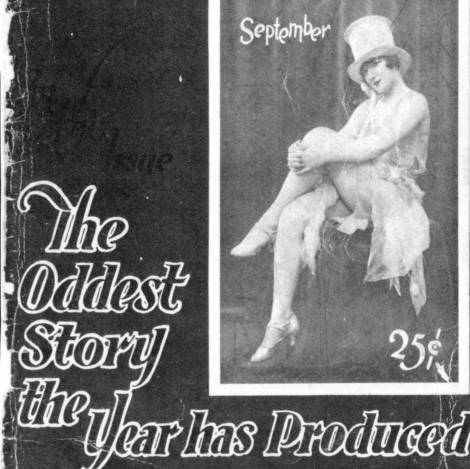

C-3

C-2

C-1. Gilda Gray. c.1920. Exponent of a dance called the Shimmy Shewabble (popularly, the Shimmy), Miss Gray grossed $45,000 in one week of "exhibition" dancing. When the Shimmy arrived in New York in 1918, the police threatened to close down any dance hall or club where it was performed, because, according to *Variety*, the dance could be done decently "only with much difficulty." (Picture Collection, New York Public Library.)

C-2. Lois Byrd, of Mack Sennett comedies, in bathing beauty pose typical of the period. *Captain Billy's Whiz Bang* (New York), May 1926.

C-3. Cheesecake pin-up cover with the statement "Girl Pictures too!!" *10 Story Book: "A Magazine for Iconoclasts"* (Chicago), September 1926.

College Humor

APRIL
35c

City Wed by Faith Baldwin

FORTY PAGE FEATURE COMIC SECTION

C-4. Very popular in the 1920s, the covers of *College Humor* (New York) featured rendered beauties in an elegant pin-up style, sophisticated for their day and appropriate to the magazine's pre-*Esquire* audience. Art work for this cover (April 1930) was by Rolf Armstrong, who is better known for his calendar art (see *Color Plate 33* and *F-6*).

C-5. A cover girl rendered in the French style. *Pictorial Weekly* (London), August 20, 1927. This magazine, founded about 1900, included few pin-ups inside, but each issue usually had one portrait-style picture of a prominent actress as well as articles ranging in subject matter from show business to sporting fads.

HOLLYWOOD TO-DAY! By MARGARET CHUTE.

PICTORIAL Weekly

2ᵈ

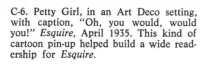

C-6. Petty Girl, in an Art Deco setting, with caption, "Oh, you would, would you!" *Esquire,* April 1935. This kind of cartoon pin-up helped build a wide readership for *Esquire.*

C-7. Posed pin-up, characteristic of late 1930s but rather unusual for its seriousness. *Candid Confessions* (Philadelphia), October 1937.

C-8. Three contest winners in a "Seaside Undress Wear Competition." *London Life* (London), October 5, 1935. Beauty competitions and printed photographs of contestants have been popular in British magazines and newspapers since the 1930s. This weekly magazine of "fiction, films, and future fashions," which enjoyed a wide readership during the 1930s (it ceased publication in 1942), included pin-ups of bathing beauties, known and unknown actresses, and female athletes and "physiculturalists," line drawings of coquettish models in negligées, and "camera studies."

C-7
C-8

C-9. Cover, by popular pin-up artist George Quintana. *Ginger* (New York), Vol. 2, No. 6, c.1939. During this period, artists took more liberty than photographers in exposing the body.

C-10. Petty Girl, with caption, "You might as well turn the page— I'm not turning around." *Esquire,* February 1938.

C-11. Double-page spread with a barrel as the gimmick for showing legs in hose and high heels. *The High Heel Annual* (New York), 1939. Later, in the 1960s, entire magazines were to be devoted to hose and heels as a fetish rather than as part of frolicking pictorials.

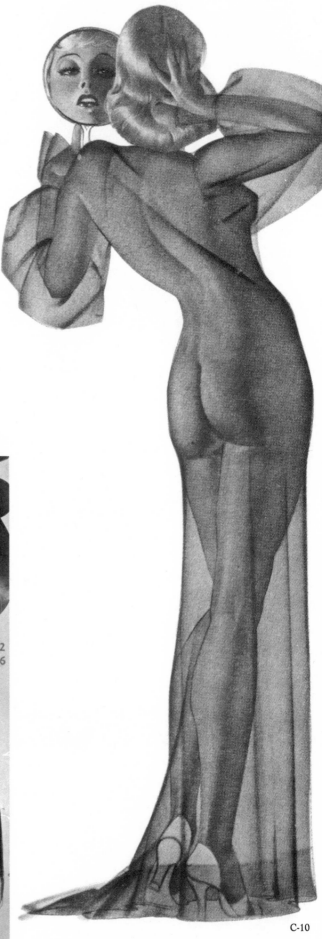

C-10

C-9

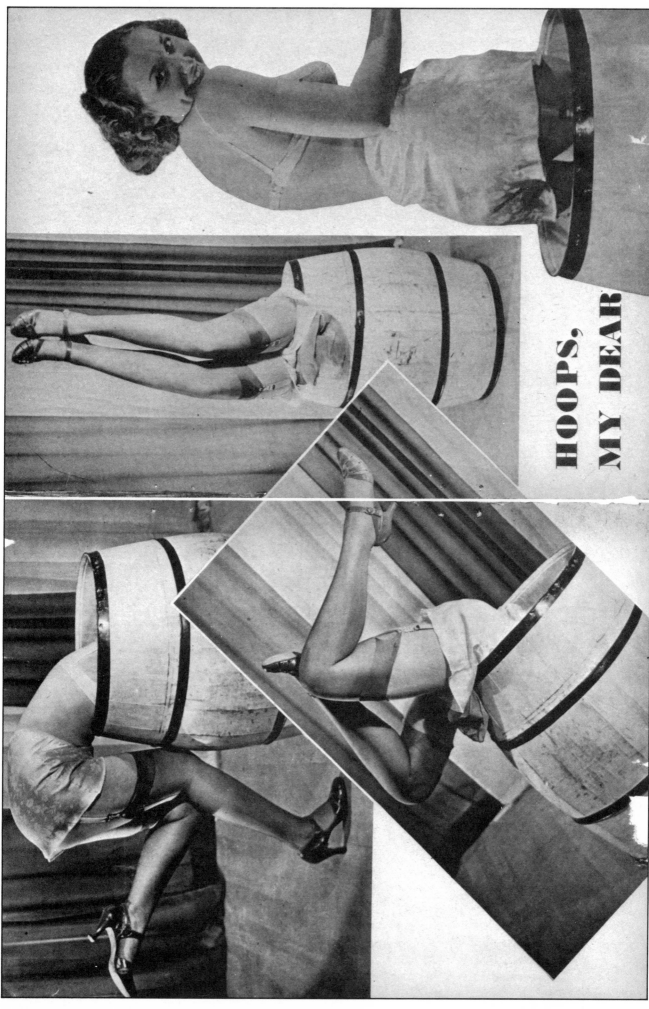

HOOPS,
MY DEAR

C-12

C-13

C-14

C-12. The first pin-up to appear on a cover of *Tit-Bits* (London), October 18, 1939. Founded in 1881, this weekly family magazine, in tabloid size, balances general-interest articles of amusement, entertainment, and "sheer escapism" with pin-up pictures of bathing beauties, "art" nudes, and screen stars. Today, as *Titbits,* it invariably features a full-color, fairly conservative pin-up on its cover.

C-13. A pin-up advertisement from *The High Heel Annual,* 1939, emphasizing not the sexual but the "art model" aspect of the pictures.

C-14. "September [1941]," from the first in a long line of Varga calendars; it appeared in *Esquire,* December 1940.

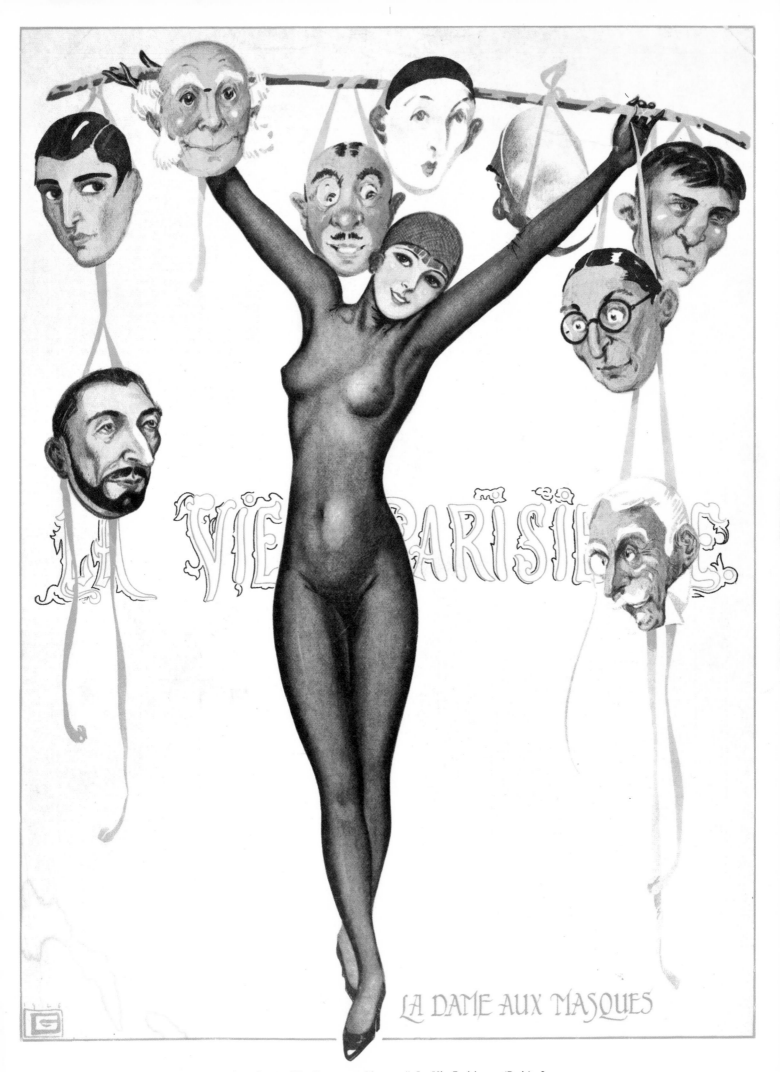

Color Plate 7. "La Dame aux Masques." La Vie Parisienne *(Paris), January 22, 1927. This magazine, founded in 1863, was famous for its risqué covers.*

Color Plate 9. Frolicking lass, nearly cross-eyed in her beer-toting revelry. *Love's Revels* (New York), December 1933.

Color Plate 8. "Naughty" spread-legged girl fondling cherries. *Wild Cherries* (New York), Summer 1933. The words "spicy," "snappy," and "peppy" on cover are euphemisms for "sexy."

Color Plate 11. Ann Corio, famous burlesque star. *Spot* (New York), 1941. Gaudy design, atrocious color reproduction, and melodramatic subject matter were characteristic of many girlie magazines of this period.

Color Plate 10. Publicity still of Joan Caulfield, starring in *The Petty Girl*, a Columbia Pictures film, 1950.

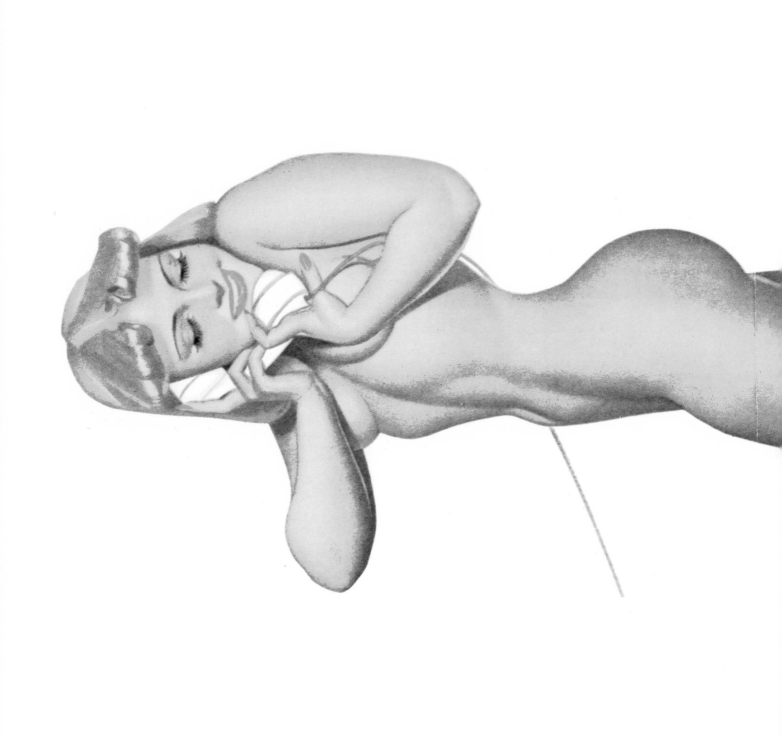

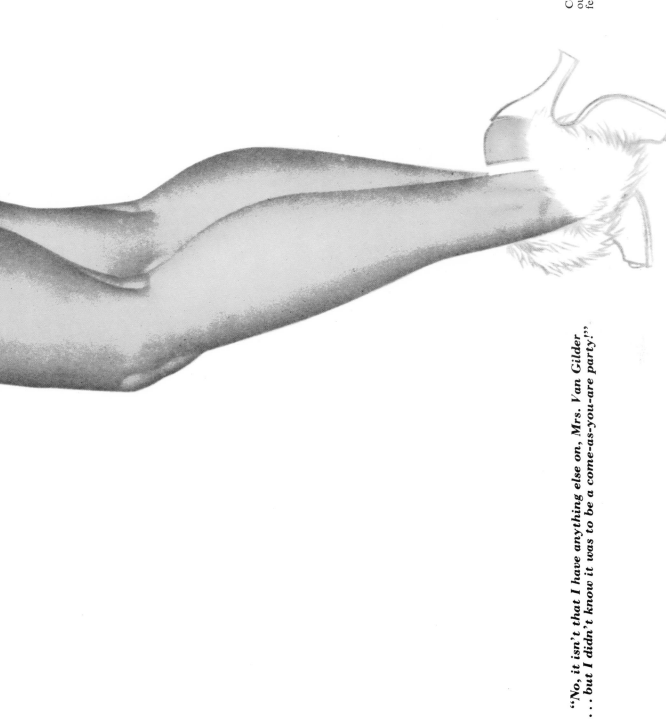

"No, it isn't that I have anything else on, Mrs. Van Gilder ...but I didn't know it was to be a come-as-you-are party!"

Color Plate 12. One of the first fold-out pages in *Esquire* (March 1941), featuring a bashful Petty Girl.

LOVE AT SECOND SIGHT

Irene, I just called up to let you know
That I am signing off that guy from Butte,
Though his intentions may be pure as snow
The way that cowboy rhumbas isn't cute!
He says it's pretty lonely in New York
And here is one for Ripley to endorse—
The other night when we were at the Stork
He called up home and asked about his HORSE!

What's that you say . . . for me to hold on tight?
Speak louder! This connection isn't clear . . .
Oh, Boy! You're sure that Winchell has it right?
SIX SILVER MINES! How interesting, my Dear!
As RICH AS THAT? He surely doesn't show it . . . .
MY GOD! I've been in love and didn't know it!

Color Plate 13. This first Varga Girl to appear in *Esquire* (October 1940) competed
with (or perhaps bolstered) the well-established Petty Girl.

Color Plate 14. *Esquire* foldout (June 1942) of the famous Jane Russell pose from *The Outlaw*, a film which was not publicly shown until 1946. The four-year promotion campaign for the film cost Howard Hughes $1.5 million. By the time the film appeared, Miss Russell's bosom was better known to Americans than that of the Venus de Milo. Her publicity agent mailed to all newspapers 5-foot-high pin-ups of Russell, and when a skywriter flew over San Francisco and made two circles with a dot in the middle of each, everyone knew what and who was meant *The Outlaw* eventually grossed more than $6 million.

C-15. Double-page spread showing women in assorted pugilistic positions. *Grin* (Dunellen, N.J.), August 1941. The gimmick is boxing, but the theme might well be regarded as a precursor of the sadomasochistic magazines of the 1960s.

PRETTY PUGS

Imagine If They

A fine state of affairs—the gals are learning how to protect themselves! Not only how to protect themselves, but how to belt the b'jeezus out of other people. It's getting so that a fellow can't insult a girl with impunity any more. Take these two rugged damsels, for instance. In a past generation they would have been staying at home, learning how to crochet doilies or play the piano or something equally practical. But not these present-day babes. Instead of dropping stitches, they drop left hooks and right crosses. Instead of banging a keyboard, they bang each other. Instead of learning how to sew and knit, they learn how to bob and weave. They never faint any more. But, boy, how they can feint!

Were Really Mad!

Kid Gwendolyn comes tearing out of her corner like a raging tornado. She throws a terrific right at her opponent's chin. Battling Betty comes back with a hurt look. And now the girls are in the center of the ring, saying mean things. Oops, pardon my glove! Gwen is wild with a right. She's wild with a left. She's wild about Harry, but so is Betty and that's what they're fighting about. "Ooooh, I could smash you! And I would, too, if I didn't have these pillows tied to my hands. I'd scratch your eyes out!" The pace is terrific. They're standing in the center of the ring and swapping secrets. And never once do they go into clinch, which is the one thing we'd do if we were in there. But we aren't, more's the pity!

Mash notes by the hundred overwhelmed Ingrid when small picture of her appeared in New York newspaper. Instant acclaim of soldiers caused paper to reprint full-page blow-up in subsequent edition. This is exclusive SEE photo.

C-16

GO CAMPING! WITH OUR PIN-UP CAMPER pages 14-15

Paris-Hollywood ENGLISH EDITION 2/6

C-17

LUCILLE Page

21

C-18

Cassie Evans

HEIGHT, 5' 7"   WEIGHT, 119

BUST, 36"   WAIST, 24   HIPS, 35"

NAVY PIN-UP GIRL

Cassie Evans is the Memphis belle who charmed the Navy Blue Jackets then came on to New York to win new laurels as a photographers model. She has soft-as-silk chestnut hair and sparkling green eyes; a modern Scarlett O'Hara.

C-19

C-20

Jean Harlowe? "I'm sorry you'r wrong;" it's Myrna Dean

C-16. "Ingrid." The caption in *See* (New York), September 1942, explains: "Instant acclaim of soldiers caused the paper to reprint full-page blow-up in subsequent edition. This is exclusive SEE photo."

C-17. "Betty, the Girl who sold apples in Brooklyn." *Paris-Hollywood* (London), c.1948. This fortnightly magazine, originating and co-published in Paris, contained "art" photography, pictures of burlesque strippers, pseudo-nudist snapshots, standard cheesecake pin-ups, and a full-color centerfold of an artist-rendered nude—but virtually no material on Hollywood.

C-18. Dancer Lucille Page. *Tid Bits of Beauty* (New York). Spring 1944. Body contortionists are popular pin-up subjects.

C-19. Cassie Evans. *Glamorous Models* (Dunellen, N.J.), Summer 1944. This magazine presented "models," page after page, each accompanied by her dimensions—height, weight, bust, waist, hips. In this case, an extra heading, "Navy Pin-Up Girl," was added.

C-20. "Jean Harlowe? 'I'm sorry you're wrong'; it's Myrna Dean" *Tid Bits of Beauty,* Spring 1944. The look-alike is a favorite gimmick of girlie magazines.

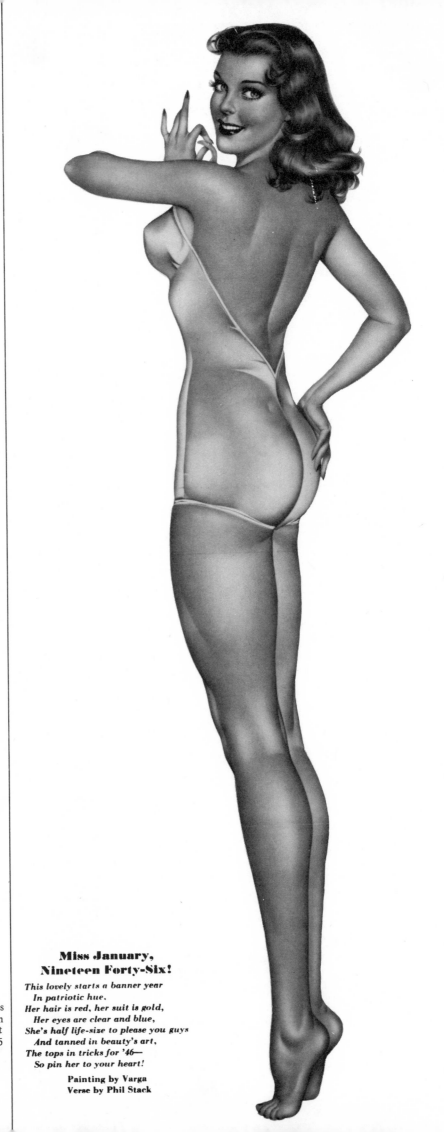

C-21. The largest foldout yet—four pages featuring one of the last Varga Girls in *Esquire* (January 1946). The very last Varga Girl appeared in the March 1946 issue.

Miss January, Nineteen Forty-Six!

This lovely starts a banner year
In patriotic hue.
Her hair is red, her suit is gold,
Her eyes are clear and blue,
She's half life-size to please you guys
And tanned in beauty's art,
The tops in tricks for '46—
So pin her to your heart!

Painting by Varga
Verse by Phil Stack

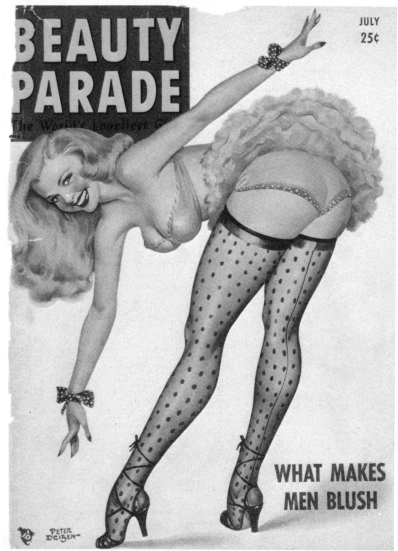

C-22. Ida Lupino, described as "a Swedish [*sic*]
film actress, of whom it is said she is the Greta
Garbo of the future." *Der Stern* (Hamburg),
November 7, 1948. A German general magazine
comparable to the American *Life* or the French
Paris Match, Stern is well known for its pin-up
covers, of which this was the first.

C-23. *Neue Revue* (Hamburg), April 1, 1972. The
cover of this German magazine, like those of its
somewhat less daring competitors *Stern, Quick,*
and *Bunte Illustrierte,* contains its main pin-up.
When such magazines do not put a pin-up on their
covers, sales drop by about 50,000 copies.

C-24. A peekaboo pose, a variation of cheesecake.
Beauty Parade (New York), July 1951.

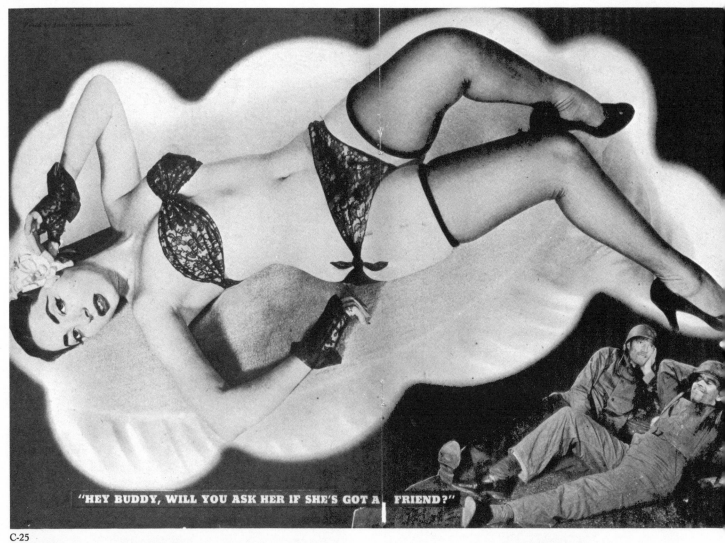

"HEY BUDDY, WILL YOU ASK HER IF SHE'S GOT A FRIEND?"

C-25

and so to bed

Lovely Mara Corday, a Frolic favorite, coyly faces the camera before her twenty winks. Mara was a raving beauty as a blonde, and is even more striking with her long, brunette tresses, that seem to caress her shoulders.

C-26

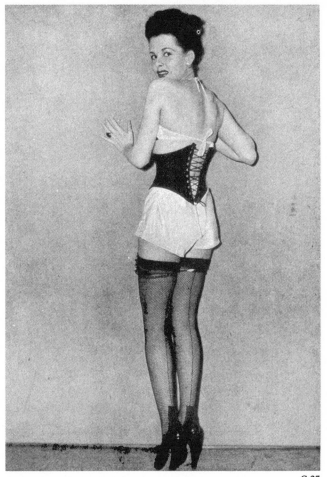

C-27

C-25. Centerfold illustrating a prime application of pin-up pictures—two G.I.'s fantasizing about the reclining model, Joan Stevens, a movie starlet. *Beauty Parade,* July 1951.

C-26. Mara Corday posing on a bed—somewhat bolder and more serious than most pin-ups of the early 1950s. *Frolic* (New York), 1952.

C-27. The title-page of this special issue of *C'est Paris* (Paris), April 1951, a magazine distributed in France, Britain, Germany, and Denmark, lists illustrated articles devoted to panties and hose and shows a rather modern pin-up for 1951.

C-28. "Sweater Girl," an art photograph by André de Dienes. *Lilliput* (London), April 1950. British readers, especially of the World War II period, remember *Lilliput* (founded 1937) for its pin-ups of fashion models and screen stars (usually two or three in each issue), as well as for art photos, caricatures, fiction, serious and humorous articles, and other forms of stimulation, entertainment, and sheer escape.

C-29. Foldout. *Latin Interlude* (London), 1950. Co-published in Paris and New York, each issue of *Latin Interlude* contained half-a-dozen badly printed, stylistically dated, photographic pin-ups and articles—"The Mistaken Caress," "The Passionate Sister," "He Didn't Come for Love"—of the cheap sex variety.

C-29

C-28

C-30

C-31

Three pictures of Marguerite Empey (see *Color Plate* 15). C-30: *Art Photography* (Skokie, Ill.), November 1955, in a pose reminiscent of that used by *Playboy*. C-31: *Jem* (Union City, N.J.), March 1957, under the assumed name Diana Webber. (Models often use pseudonyms when appearing in several types of magazines, and Miss Empey also appeared elsewhere as Diana Webber.) C-32: Calendar, c.1955.

C-32

C-34. Two pages of concentrated cheese-cake, about as gauche as this style ever gets. *Wink* (New York), August 1953.

C-35. Unidentified burlesque stripper, an unusually bold picture for the mid-1950s. *Playgirl* (San Francisco), c.1955. An early exploitation of the name Playboy, this magazine evidently irritated *Playboy* magazine so much that the publisher of the West Coast publication editorialized as follows: "A group of Chicago attorneys with the usual improbable names like Lipschultz, Hommengranite and Opkopostopolous sent us a chiding letter, taking us to task and even threatening us. They claim that the title *Playgirl* is prejudicial to the rights of their client, *Playboy* magazine. We had our attorney . . . reply and his missive was both witty and to the point. 'There is,' his letter states, 'certainly a difference between boys and girls which is known to the general public. Therefore, no similarity or confliction between the two magazines can possibly exist.' He could have added, but he didn't know it, that there is a kids' magazine called *Playmate* and that we are considering publishing another one calling it *Plaything*. What about all of the Playlands?"

cosetta white

C-36. Cosetta White, "Duchess of the Month." *Duke* (Chicago), August 1957. A *Playboy*-type magazine for the black man, *Duke* carried a wide variety of features—fiction, fashion, humor, poetry, and pictorials.

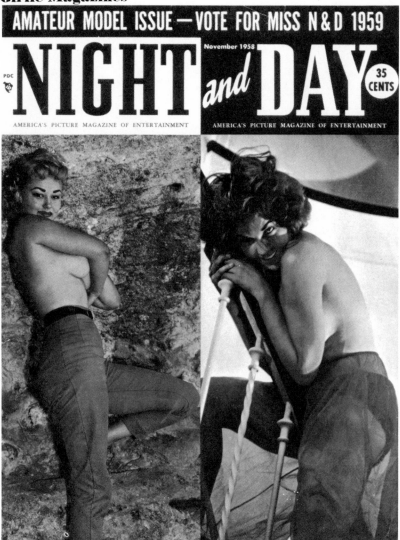

C-37

C-38

C-39

C-40

C-37. Topless but unexposed pin-ups of Donalda Jordan (*left*), who raises Siamese cats "for love and money," and Colleen Tyler (*right*), who is "'Miss Denmark' and a lot of other things." *Night and Day* (New York), November 1958. This "picture magazine of entertainment" carried features on modeling, travel, and fiction but attracted most of its readers through its girlie pictorials.

C-38. "Melanie." *Foto-Rama* (New York), November 1958. A digest-sized magazine, containing mostly pin-ups in features such as "Italians like 'em plump," "Cynthia is loaded," and "Are College Girls Best at Sex?"

C-39. "Bikini Twosome." *Spick* (Croydon, Surrey), April 1958. A digest-sized magazine, *Spick* started in December 1953 (the same date as *Playboy's* first issue); its counterpart, *Span,* followed in September 1954.

C-40. "Lorraine Burnett!" *Carnival* (Birkenhead, Cheshire), July 1958. Another digest-sized magazine, *Carnival* contained pin-ups, cover to cover. The drawn-in outlines around the figures and the rough silhouetting of hair and feet give the model a synthetic if not cheap appearance.

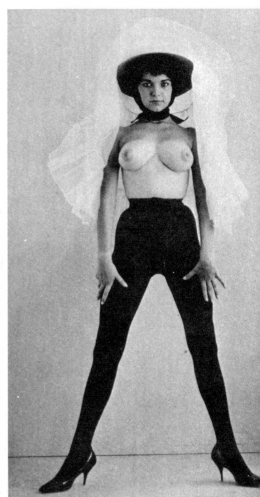

Free (
Tin

Once again w
of our sensa
gain gift offer
have to do is s
copies of this
a postal c
twenty-eight
and fourpenc
our office
wonderful, su
ity, Hindu c
will be rushe
home addres:
CHARGE. T
date for thi
Jan. 31st, 1960

*Photo shows love
KIM FOSTER pr
displaying her g*

C-41   C-42   C-43

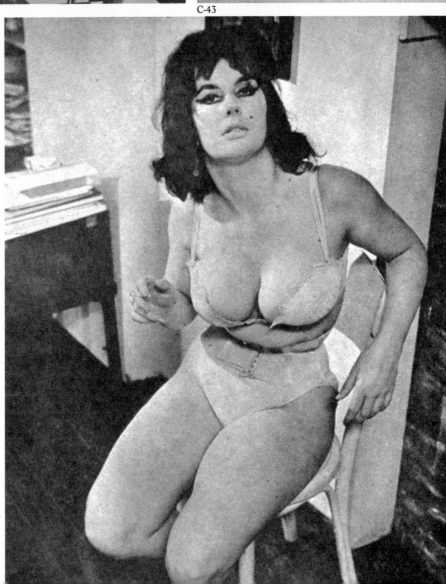

C-41. "Kim Foster proudly displaying her gift towel." *Pin-Up* (Padiham, Lancaster), c.1960. This British pocket-sized magazine's smiling models and liberal air-brushing technique created a happier pin-up experience for its viewers.

C-42. *Stocking Parade* (New York), c.1960. Not quite sophisticated enough to be a full-fledged fetish magazine, this digest-sized "aid to the artist, photographer, model, and physical culture student" simply presented suggestive pin-ups.

C-43. A "wistful little fistfull," posing satirically as a high fashion model, was part of a pictorial on the theme of "waiting for the right man to marry me." *Jem,* January 1961. *Jem* imitated *Playboy* with its variety of textual features, but its pin-ups were generally bolder than *Playboy's.*

C-44. This picture is notable for its direct sexual address to the viewer—a characteristic that became standard in most pin-up magazines of the 1960s. *Gala* (New York), November 1961. Primarily a girlie magazine, with no literary aspirations.

C-44

C-45. An almost touchable closeup of a reclining model, putting the viewer's eyes, as it were, in the head of the model's lover. *Topper* (Hollywood, Calif.), August 1962. *Topper* is one of the better-known *Playboy* followers but centers on erotic themes.

C-46. Marny Cella. *Parade* (London), March 27, 1965. *Parade*, the current incarnation of *Blighty*, the British magazine for the armed forces in World Wars I and II, regards itself as "The Man's Magazine Women Love to Read." Its pin-up style is provocative but not bold.

C-47. Ursula Blauth, star of the film *The Naked Countess*. *Continental Film Review* (London), December 1971.

C-48. Pin-ups suggesting auto-eroticism have existed for decades (see Kirchner postcards, *A-39*, page 51, for example), but only in the 1960s did this theme, like many others, become a specialized pin-up genre. Starting in poorer-quality magazines such as this—*Striperama* (New York), 1962—auto-eroticism has now become standard pictorial fare for quality magazines like *Penthouse*.

C-49. Part of a double-page spread from a digest-sized magazine, showing direct visual-sexual access—in this case oral (via phallic symbol) and frontal (via spread position). *Heels and Hose* (North Hollywood, Calif.), 1965.

C-45

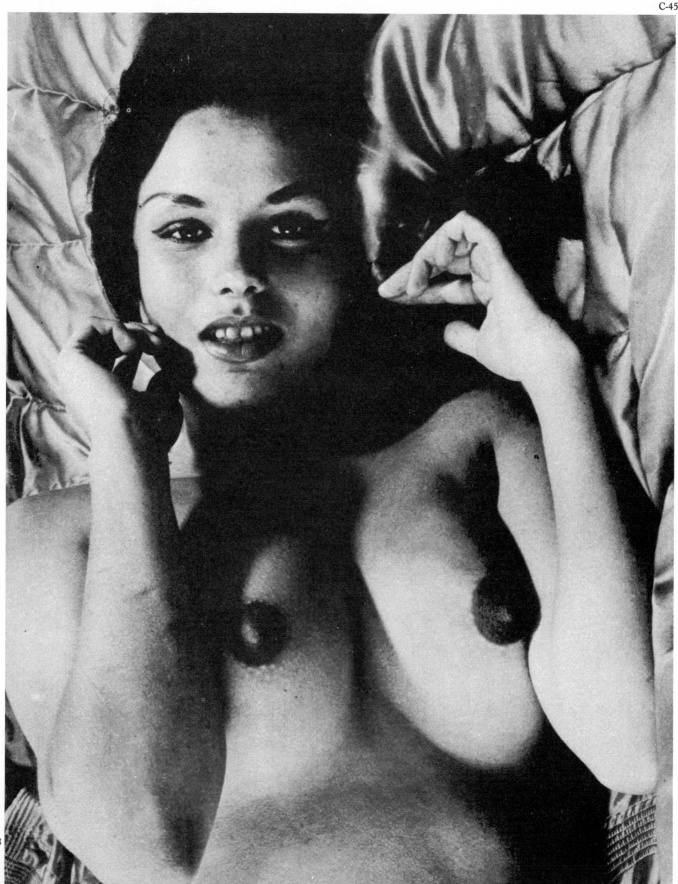

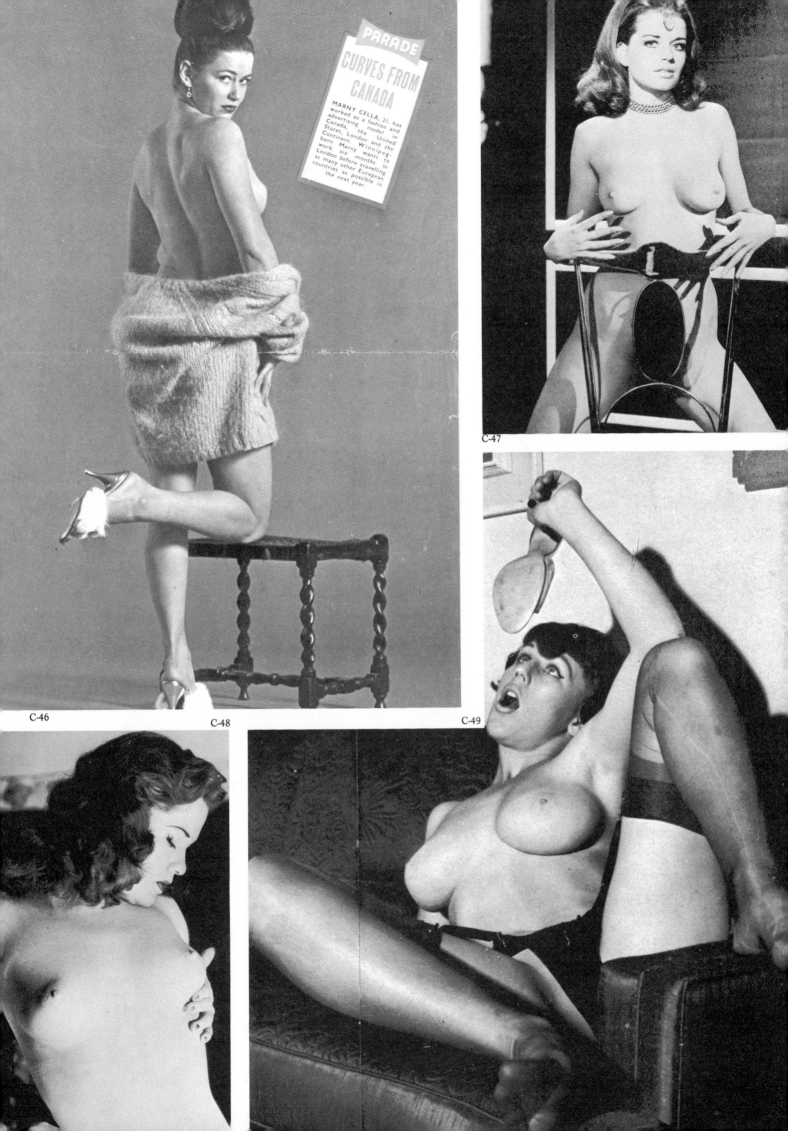

C-47

C-46

C-48

C-49

C-50

C-51

C-52

C-50. This picture, all that was shown on a full page of *Heels and Hose*, January-February-March 1966, illustrates the fetish theme as separate from pin-ups. Exclusive focus on a particular part of the anatomy, or on particular devices (hose and heels, for example), clearly violates the spirit of the pin-up in which a human being as an entity addresses the viewer.

C-51. A serious seductive pose. *French Follies* (North Hollywood, Calif.), 1964. Pubic hair still could not be shown in girlie magazines, so what was not hidden by the model's hand was evidently "whited out."

C-52. Retouching seems to have given a stiffening uplift to the breasts of this model; the panties—what can be seen of them—seem also to have been added through retouching. *Black Stocking Parade* (New York), 1963. Short of showing sexual devices, leather and rubber garments, and sadomasochistic teams, this digest-sized magazine comes as close as possible to fetishism.

Color Plate 15. This picture is noteworthy for its pin-up within a pin-up—the famous Monroe calendar pose, hanging on the wall. *Cabaret Quarterly* (Skokie, Ill.), 1956. An early imitator of *Playboy*, *Cabaret Quarterly* focused particularly on burlesque, stripping, and the night club scene.

Color Plate 16. Marguerite Empey, *Playboy's* Playmate of the Month, May 1955, where she was described as "only a part-time model . . . she's a receptionist for a Hollywood broadcasting company . . . also studying dramatics and . . . modern dance." (Graphic House, New York.) (See also *C30*, *C31*, *C32*, page 88.)

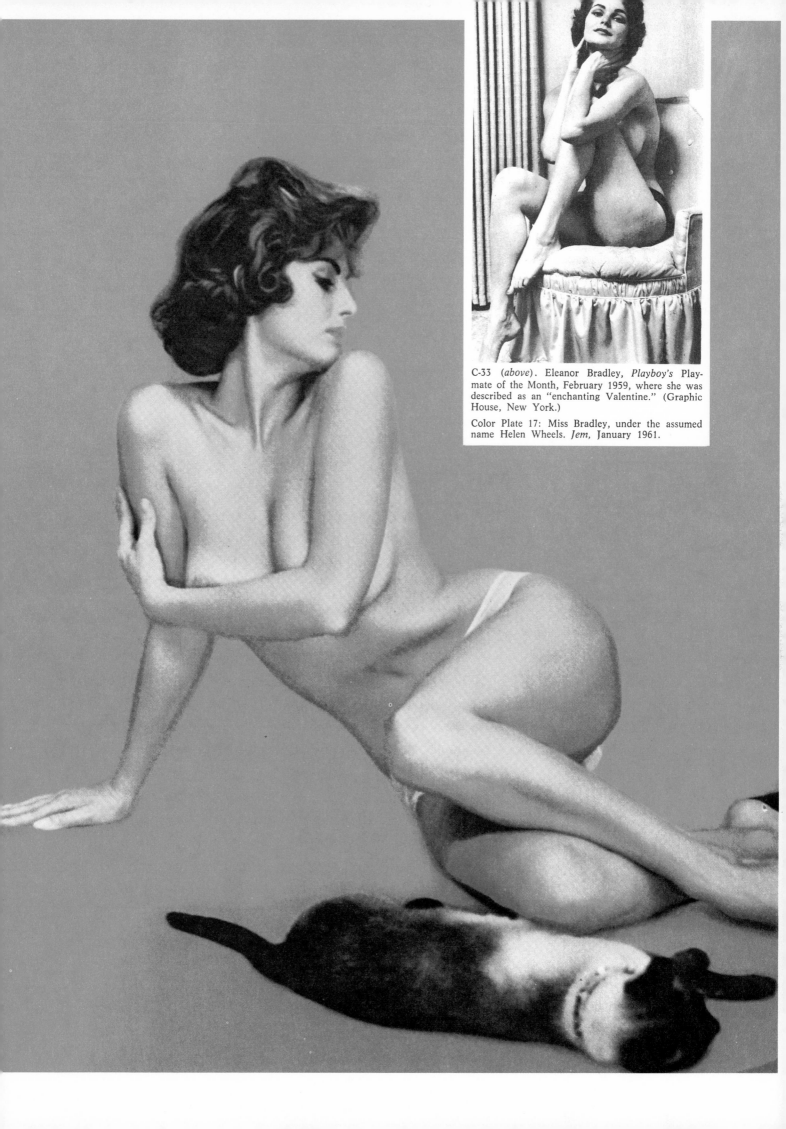

C-33 (*above*). Eleanor Bradley, *Playboy's* Play-mate of the Month, February 1959, where she was described as an "enchanting Valentine." (Graphic House, New York.)

Color Plate 17: Miss Bradley, under the assumed name Helen Wheels. *Jem*, January 1961.

Color Plate 18. Despite the suggestiveness of these pictures—the bedroom setting, the seductive expressions—careful attention— through garment placement, pose, and picture cropping—was given to what could and could not be exposed of this sultry, nymphlike model. *Jem* (New York), August 1964.

Color Plate 19. *La Femme* (Whyteleafe, Surrey), 1969. An English use of the modern "stockings" theme—following the American lead, with pretensions to French authenticity.

Color Plate 20. Lorna Nelson, in a delightfully awkward attempt to combine the cheesecake and the direct visual-sexual styles—to no avail. *Cavalcade* (New York), August 1968. One of *Playboy's* better-quality followers, *Cavalcade* contains good fiction and well-written articles of general interest.

Voulez-vous danser avec moi?

L A danse avait toujours été pour Martine l'un des buts de sa vie, son horizon, et sortie de là, elle ne voyait pas très bien ce que la vie pouvait avoir d'agréable. Il faut bien dire que Martine avait le rythme dans la peau. Que ce fût une valse, un tango, ou un jerk, tout lui était bon. Tout lui était bon pour onduler des fesses, montrer sa taille fine, lancer sa poitrine à droite ou à gauche et, avec de grands mouvements de bras, faire le simulacre d'implorer le dieu de l'amour.

Tout au moins, c'était bien l'image qui naissait dans l'esprit des garçons qui la regardaient et avaient parfois le plaisir de la prendre par la main : l'Amour ! Ils ne pensent donc qu'à ça ?

Son corps souple et harmonieux se transformait à leurs yeux en un délicieux appel à la sensualité, et les mouvements qu'elle exécutait n'étaient qu'une invite à de plus profondes voluptés.

Aussi, lorsque, au soir de ce circuit en Bretagne, Michel l'invita, ce n'était pas sans une petite idée derrière la tête. Ils avaient pourtant peu dormi la veille : malgré le car-couchette qu'avait loué la société pour son personnel, elle ne valait pas son lit. Et puis, le nombre d'arrêts en pleine nuit les avait toujours tenu éveillés. L'après-midi, championnat de chasse sous-marine : Michel avait été classé 4e. Ce qui n'était pas si mal et Martine avait applaudi plus fort à l'annonce des résultats.

— Vous dansez?

Tu parles, Martine avait bondi dans ses bras. Elle avait un peu le béguin pour ce grand blond dégingandé de Michel. Lui, n'avait pas le même amour qu'elle pour la danse et cela se voyait du premier coup. Ses mouvements étaient heurtés, saccadés, alors que Martine était tout souple, rythmée : quand on est jeune et qu'on se plaît, on passe sur beaucoup de détails. Et puis, les danses modernes permettent toutes les fantaisies.

Enfin, vint un slow. La piste se remplit de couples enlacés. Michel la serra contre lui. Il lui sembla qu'elle était nue sous sa robe, mais il ne dit rien.

Pourtant, au bout d'un moment, il s'écarta un peu et osa la regarder : elle souriait. Il jeta un simple coup d'œil dans son décolleté. On ne voyait pas l'ombre d'une étoffe... Elle le serra davantage. Il la sentit souple, féline, se couler contre lui.

Ses jambes s'infiltrèrent entre ses cuisses. Son odeur, forcément un peu forte, l'enivrait.

Michel ne sut pas très bien s'y prendre. C'était bien : malgré le chaleur du bruit, de la nuit toute proche. Elle prit sa main et ils se retrouvèrent sous les pins. Au loin on entendait la mer. Ils allèrent vers la plage.

Et, pendant qu'il goûtait le premier baiser, il glissa une main vers sa poitrine. C'était bien cela, elle était nue. Ce fut elle-même qui ouvrit tous les boutons et il put prendre à pleines mains ce qu'il désirait tant, avant d'y poser sa bouche.

Elle lui ouvrit aussi les boutons... et elle chercha vainement. Michel faisait des efforts, ça se voyait. Il crispait les mâchoires, retenait sa respiration, serrait les beaux seins offerts et sentait ses cuisses chaudes et déjà entrouvertes... rien n'y fit. Elle n'eut dans la main que le pâle reflet de ce qu'elle désirait.

Ils revinrent silencieux, sans comprendre. Michel était vexé. Martine avait envie de pleurer. Mais une idée lui vint pourtant. Elle avait remarqué qu'elle remarqué le regard fuyant de Bruno, tout à l'heure en dansant.

Elle ne s'avoue pas vaincue pour ce soir. Elle mise tout sur la danse :

— Bruno, tu danses?...

Color Plate 21. "Martine," *Folies de Paris et de Hollywood* (Paris), March 1972. Although its airbrushed pin-ups are not as bold or sensual as those of contemporary British or American pin-up magazines, *Folies* is banned from public display and must be requested by name for under-the-counter purchase.

Ironically, France, which was regarded for many years as the mecca of love and sex, is now one of the most conservative countries in the pin-up domain, and *Folies* represents the most daring approach taken by French magazines today.

Color Plate 23. This pin-up puts together many of the elements thus far observed. *Topper* (New York), December 1971. The model is standing (see panties hanging, not flat against body), but the photography makes her appear to be lying down.

Color Plate 22. A sultry model puffs a cigarette—a prop that goes as far back as postcards (see, for example, *A-43*, page 53, and *A-44*, page 54). *Man to Man* (Los Angeles), July 1971. This magazine is comparable to *Rogue* in its limited scope of general-interest features and emphasis on girlie pictorials.

Color Plate 24. Josee Troyat. *Penthouse*, June 1971. The text accompanying the nine-page pictorial on Miss Troyat, Pet of the Month, emphasizes her independence of spirit, self-sufficiency, and reflections on life: "In these days of Women's Liberation, when beauty contests get picketed and gibes of 'male chauvinism' are hurled at magazines for men, it takes a defiant spirit among females, and a mind not easily intimidated, to proclaim Petdom as a pinnacle of women's rights. It also takes the breath away when these sterling qualities are found in the persuasive person (35-23-36) of Miss Josee Troyat, who at 19 makes a delicious debut as Pet of the Month. Says Josee: 'Liberation for women is what I am doing now—posing like this for *Penthouse*. It would never have been possible in my mother's youth. She would have been condemned, instead of admired, for showing off all her beauty.' As Josee sees it—and she is reading philosophy with her eye on an eventual Ph.D.—the freedom to be herself as a woman is true women's liberation."

MISS JOSEE TROYAT/PENTHOUSE PET OF THE MONTH

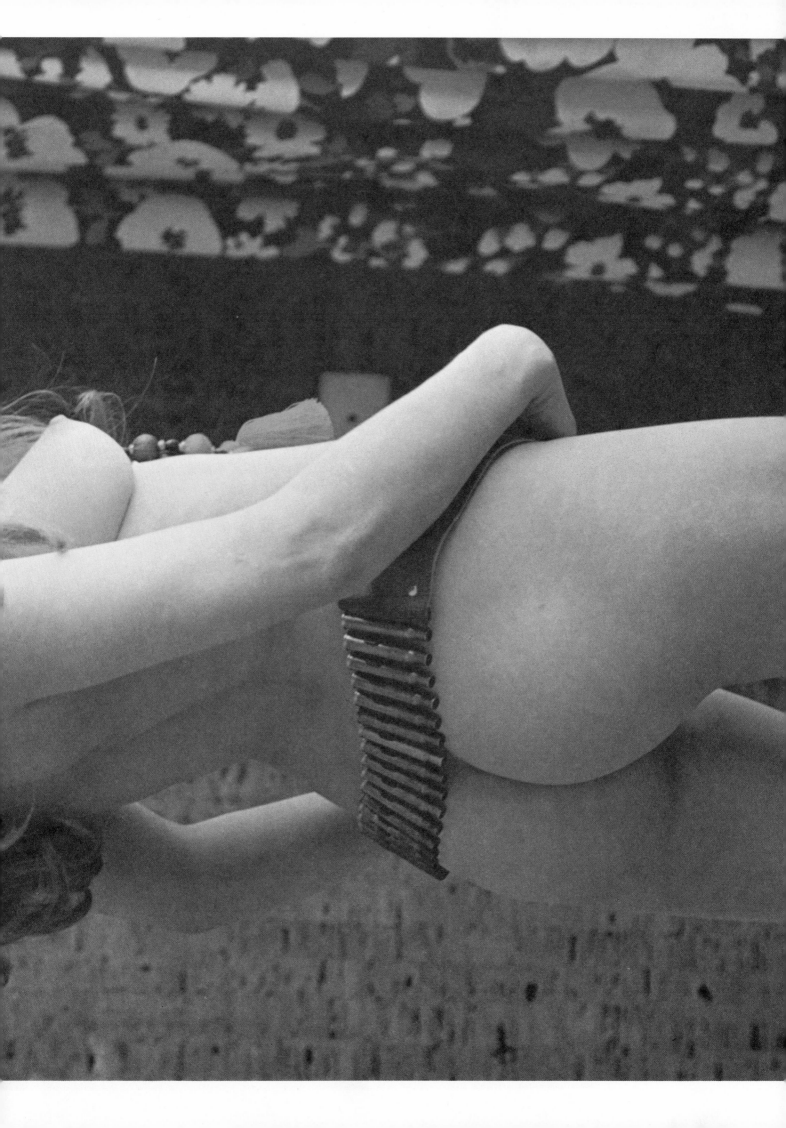

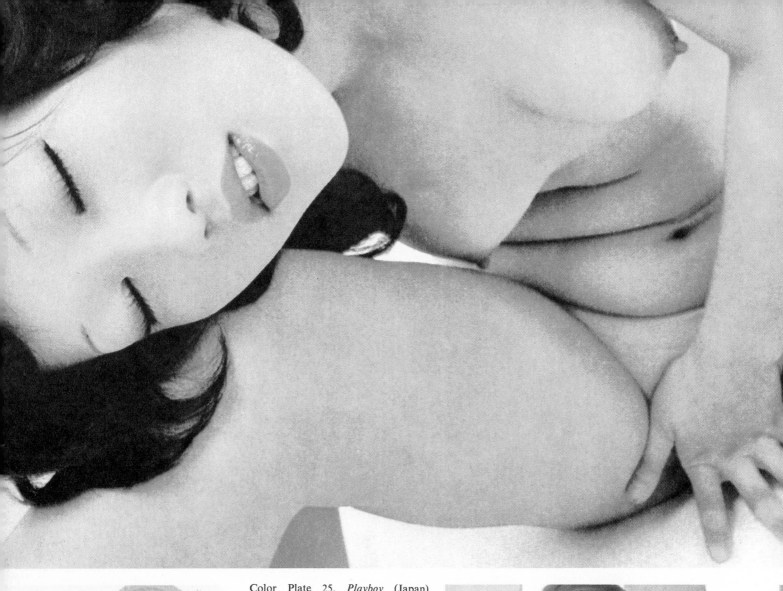

Color Plate 25. *Playboy* (Japan), December 14, 1971. A weekly general-interest magazine, not related to *Playboy* (Chicago). Only the advertisements and a few pin-ups are sophisticated. Esthetically, however, the latter show some of the most creative pin-up photography in any contemporary magazine: unusual camera angles, unexpected close-ups, expressive body positions—distorted, but beautifully so. These Japanese photographs add new depth to the esthetic of pin-ups.

Color Plate 28. *Men Only's* stylistic influence is evident in this centerfold photograph from *Penthouse*, June 1972. Having introduced pubic hair in its centerfold pictorials and nipple play in its girlie features, *Penthouse* has been challenged to move the models' hands toward the genital area. More cautious in this direction than *Men Only*, *Penthouse* has consequently dropped to second place, in circulation as well as in daring, among London's high-quality girlie magazines. The model for this centerfold feature was Nevenka Dundek, 20, described as Yugoslavia's "risingest" movie and television actress. The use of exotic models is part of *Penthouse's* stress on a cosmopolitan image.

Color Plate 29. Belinda Carson-Browne. *Mayfair*, May 1972. *Mayfair* includes general-interest articles, fashions, fiction, humor, and pin-up pictorials that are moving confidently toward full beaver poses. *Mayfair*, like *Penthouse* and other quality men's magazines competing for the same readership, is imitating *Men Only's* shift in auto-erotic emphasis from nipple play to genital play suggesting masturbation. Although auto-eroticism may symbolize modern Women's Liberation concepts of self-sufficient womanhood, such poses in men's magazines are intended primarily for the erotic arousal of male readers. Photo: Ed Alexander.

Color Plate 26. "Belinda." *ER* (Munich), April 1972. This German equivalent of *Playboy* carries the same high-quality, prestigious image.
Colour Plate 27 (*lower right*). "Sabine." *Lui* (Paris), May 1970. Although it highlights luscious *demoiselles* in inviting situations, and includes such *Playboy* features as centerfold pin-ups, *Lui* reflects current French conservatism towards the treatment of sex

in print. In fact, *Lui* and *Playboy* can now be considered equally modest in comparison with British girlie magazines. Of all the European *Playboy* counterparts, *Lui* maintains the most sophisticated image and is most ambitious in its non-pin-up features. It is one of a number of periodicals issued by Filipacchi Publications, a rapidly growing enterprise devoted to many aspects of sophisticated modern living.

Color Plate 30. "Studio Peeps—No. 1," from the first issue (digest-size) of *Men Only* (London), December 1935. For the 1930s, *Men Only* was fairly controversial. It was the first English magazine aimed at an all-male market, and besides artist-rendered pin-ups it had photos of "art" nudes and screen stars. By the early 1950s, it had absorbed two other popular British magazines, *London Opinion* and *Lilliput*. In the early 1960s, it went into the *Playboy* format; then, incorporating *Escort* in May 1971, it increased its size again, becoming the boldest and most "modern" of the high-quality pin-up magazines, and in 1972 achieved a record-breaking British circulation of 400,000.

Color Plate 31. Nearly four decades after "Studio Peeps," *Men Only* is again the talk of London for its daring treatment of sex. Even this auto-erotic pose (by Rita Reaumur, April 1972) is mild by comparison with some of the magazine's other pictorial explorations. *Men Only* focuses on quality color photographs of beautiful young models in masturbatory, beaver pin-up poses. Its pictorials also delve into Sapphic sensuality—for example, a clothed young maid lovingly lathering her mistress's nude body. Editorial emphasis is on short fiction and articles about night life, contemporary culture, politics, sports cars, fashions, and the like.

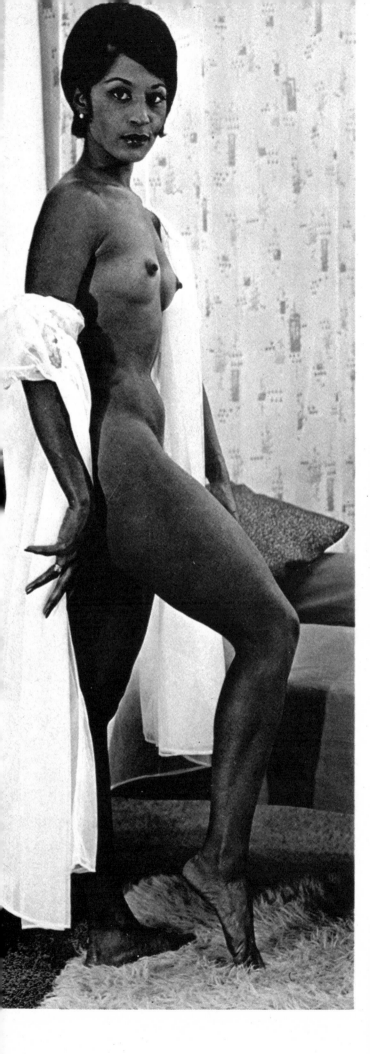

C-53. Black models appear infrequently in white magazines—possibly as a form of pin-up tokenism. This curvaceous black model is displayed in the standard repertory of pin-up poses. *Jaguar* (New York), March 1966. Like other lesser *Playboy* imitators, *Jaguar* contains fiction and nonfiction in each issue but emphasizes girlie pictorials.

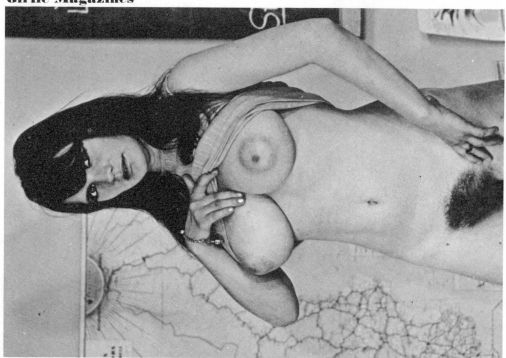

C-54 (*left*). "Lena." In the early-to-middle 1960s, pin-up models began to pose in overt sexual positions—and here is a prime example. *Ultra* (North Hollywood, Calif.), July 1965. This magazine and the dozens of others that have followed it should be regarded as publications treading on the borderline of fetishism—the distinction being one of degree, with respect to the model's bodily address to the viewer. If the whole pose, including the model's facial expression, is subordinated to the exposure of leather or rubber clothes, buttocks, vulva, or tongue, the picture is specifically fetishistic.

C-55. "Lena . . . a mere seventeen years old." *Gammla Blue* (Stockholm), 1969. A relatively tame picture from what was probably a one-time publication from Sweden, although the line "Printed in U.S.A." appears on the inside front cover. Most of the magazine depicts, in blaring color, models in "beaver" and "split-beaver" poses (that is, with pubic hair fully visible and with exposed vulva, respectively)—a logical extension of the direct visual-sexual style (see C-49, C-52). Subsequent plates show even the quality magazines moving cautiously in this direction.

C-56. Despite her faint smile and sideways glance toward the viewer, this freckled model seems almost formidable. *Rogue* (New York), August 1970. Another *Playboy*-style magazine, distinguished by its relentless emphasis on buxom models and de-emphasis of literary articles.

C-57. The model makes the most of her pendulous breasts by posing, almost animal-like, in a seductive trance. The dark area between her legs is the narrow end of a guitar. *Rogue*, August 1970.

C-57

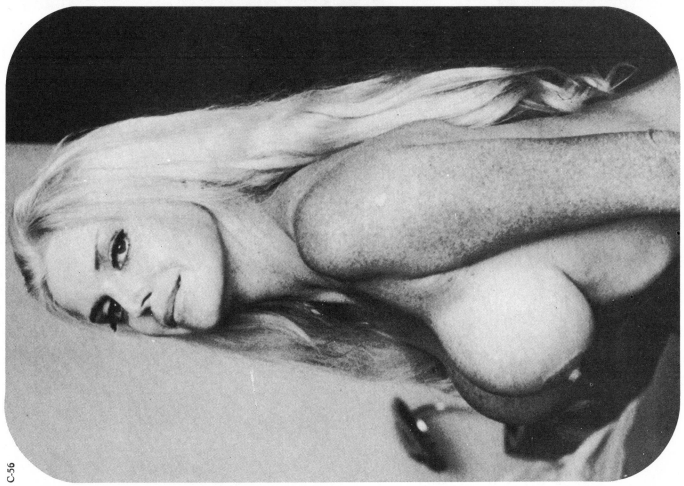

C-56

125

C-58. Following the Petty-Varga tradition, Aslan creates gorgeous, superrealistic pin-ups—bodies idealized beyond the usual photographic standards and rendered with astonishing skill. Typical of Aslan's artistic facility is this rear view of a modest, undeniably appealing young woman. *Lui* (Paris), May 1970.

C-59 (*right*). Two other Aslan pin-ups that reflect his elegance and versatility. Despite the models' direct, serious gaze and the presence of such contemporary devices or appurtenances as boots, undershirt, skin-tight pants, or eyeglasses dangling from mouth, Aslan infuses these pin-ups with an affection and tenderness that are reminiscent of Kirchner's delicate postcard girls.

C-60. *Humor Graph* (Japan), 1969. The magazine's subtitle is "Exciting Series IV—Erotic Eye." This popular magazine containing only pin-up photography emphasizes youthful sensuality and erotic playfulness. Not a *Playboy* counterpart, it may be regarded as a Japanese equivalent of *Frolic* or *Topper*.

C-61. Tin Chin Fei. *Hong Kong Movie News* (Hong Kong), March 1968. This magazine covers fashion, the contemporary scene, travel, and girlie pictorials, including foldouts, like this one, that are classy in pin-up style but somewhat conservative compared to Western counterparts from the same period. Chinese girlie magazines tend to show more Caucasian than Oriental models, possibly because—erotic woodcuts notwithstanding—the pin-up concept does not easily fit into the Oriental life style and tradition. Chinatowns of European and American cities provide the largest market for these magazines, hence the use of bilingual texts and titles.

C-62. This petite, doe-eyed young model—in contrast to the *Rogue* pin-ups—is featured for her very look of innocence. *Club* (London), October 1970.

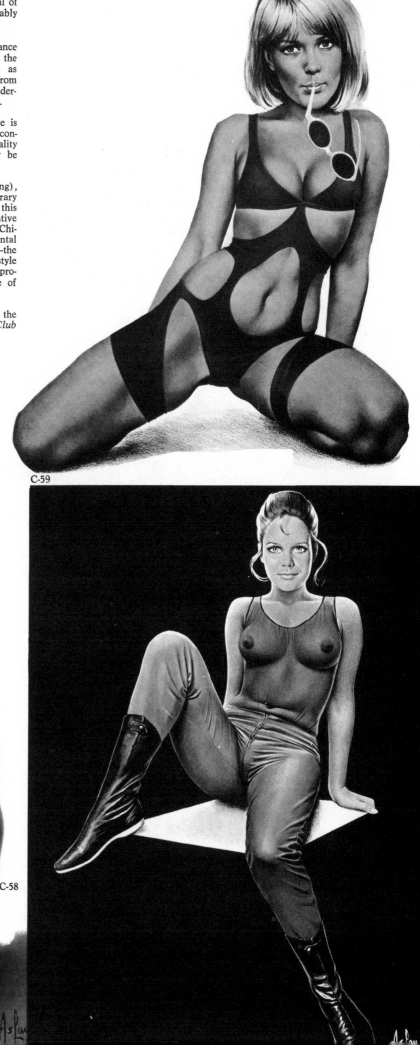

C-59

C-58

C-60

C-61

C-62

C-64

C-63. Centerfold. *Playmen* (Rome), July 1971. Like *Playboy* and *Penthouse, Playmen* subtly exposes the pubic hair of its centerfold subjects. The photography has the unmistakable stamp of a quality magazine.

C-64. Foldout. *Mini* (Hong Kong), Fall 1971. Not as conservative as *Hong Kong Movie News, Mini* focuses more extensively on pin-ups. It might be best compared with *Jem* or *Rogue* in America.

C-65. *Sin El Fil* (Beirut), c.1970. This popular Lebanese magazine resembles *Hong Kong Movie News* in content, offering a little of everything—movie gossip, fashion, the "scene," stories, sports, and personalities. The pin-ups, however, are of rather poor quality, with a 1950s cheesecake look about them. The cover shows by far the best pin-up in *Sin El Fil*. Note the retouched G-string and the dark circle covering the model's nipple, a pastie supplied by the magazine's art department.

C-63

C-65

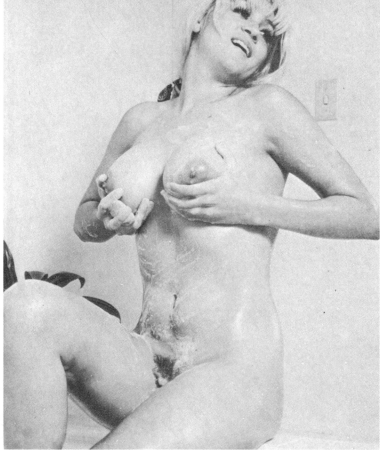

C-67

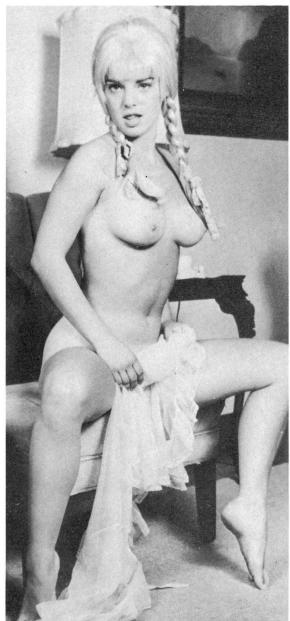

C-66

C-66 and C-67. *Pix* and *Adam* (Los Angeles), November 1971. These magazines are twin-sisters. From the same West Coast publisher, selling for the same price, and with similar pin-up pictorials and other features (mostly the former), *Pix* and *Adam* stay safely within the censorship boundaries observed by the higher-quality magazines. Their pin-ups tend to be more buxom and sexually direct than those of, say, *Penthouse*.

C-68. "Tough Tessie." *Rogue,* February 1972. The shadowy pubic hair, oral suggestion, and breast-tease combine to produce a startling image of sexuality in a young, rather hard-looking model.

C-68

C-71. Brenda Olsen. *Bachelor* (New York), December 1971. This awkward-looking position, with the intention clear, demonstrates that an ordinary pin-up pose could easily become a split-beaver.

C-69. *"Vorsicht, Radfahrer!"* ("Caution, bicyclist!") *Sexy* (Hamburg), February 26, 1972. Printed on pulp paper, this weekly tabloid is devoted almost entirely to material about sex and to pin-ups that are stylistically about five years behind those in America or British magazines. Banned from above-the-counter distribution in 1972, *Sexy* can now be obtained from newsdealers only by request.

C-70. A typical layout from *Die Nachrichten* (Hamburg), March 30, 1972. This weekly tabloid, from Hamburg's sex center St. Pauli, was originally issued as *St. Pauli Nachrichten*. It contains near-pornographic pictures of heterosexual and homosexual couples and trios intermingled with beaver poses and other bold modern pin-ups.

C-70

C-69

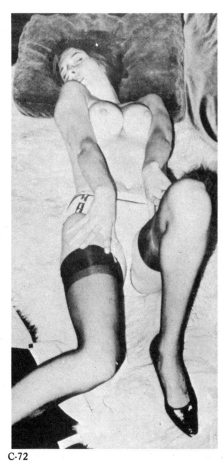

C-72. A characteristic example of the sexual approach of *Search* (London), Vol. 1, No. 12, 1971. *Search* and other monthly or quarterly digest-sized magazines like *Climax, Forum, Open,* and *Relate* are among the successful newer British publications featuring lively correspondence, in which readers' sexual problems, observations, and experiences are published. Boldly erotic pin-ups accompany articles on defloration, Sapphism, oral sex, fetishes, sexual techniques, and "deviate" experiments.

C-73. *Fringe* (London), No. 8 [March 1972]. A recent development in the British newspaper pin-up tradition, this London weekly tabloid, printed on pulp paper, prints bold pin-ups—beaver poses, hose and heels, borderline bondage, sadomasochism—and articles about sex.

C-74. Linda McDowell. *Knave* (London), April 1972. The first issues of *Knave* (1968-69), a British middle-level girlie magazine (equivalent to *Rogue* or *Topper* in America), focused on single themes—pornography, underground, Sapphism—but now each issue contains five or six pictorial features in which beaver poses predominate. *Knave's* publishers also issue *Fiesta* (founded 1966), a slightly less sophisticated all-girlie magazine with a wider distribution.

C-72

C-73

LINDA

C-74

C-75. The first appearance of "Jane," the best-known British pin-up comic strip. *Daily Mirror* (London), December 1932. She appeared for 27 years (1932-59) and was Britain's most popular World War II pin-up idol. "Jane" later became a feature in the U.S. armed forces paper *Stars and Stripes*.

C-76. A front page featuring Gwenyth Siddle, "Ideal Holiday Girl." *Daily Mirror* (London), June 25, 1959. This newspaper was the first in Great Britain to present pin-ups, mostly screen stars, as a daily feature (1936), and the first to publish a nude pin-up (1938). Its cover pin-ups still attract a huge readership. Somewhat more daringly than the *Mirror, The Sun*, another London tabloid, founded in 1969, also includes front-page pin-ups to boost circulation.

C-77. Betty Page. *Reveille* (London), November 12, 1956. In the mid-1940s, this weekly tabloid began putting pin-ups on its front pages, and by the mid-1950s, pin-ups dominated the make-up. The contents of *Reveille* include articles of popular general interest—adventure, sports, crime, scandal, stage and screen, and beauty contests. Cheesecake pin-ups also spice its inside pages.

C-75

C-77

Heroines of the Screen

Heroines of the Screen

As noted above (pages 37-39), pictures of dramatic and burlesque stage beauties were important in the development of pin-ups in the late 19th century. The appearance of such pictures in general-interest magazines—and on postcards from 1900 to about 1920—was also a major means of publicity for aspiring, as well as famous, stage actresses.

With the rise of motion pictures, however, and the establishment of Hollywood as the world's film capital, a new publishing phenomenon occurred. *Photoplay*, in 1911, became the first in a long parade of Hollywood fan magazines, which, over the next sixty years, were the principal publicity vehicles for film studios and performers. Their peak years were 1922-41—a period when silent films became a universally accepted art form and, after talking pictures were inaugurated, sound films provided millions of viewers throughout the world with at least temporary escape from the Great Depression and their forebodings about the oncoming World War II. Hollywood stars were the idols of the masses, and the screen magazines told about their personal as well as public lives.

The early fan magazines reviewed new films and carried "storizations" illustrated by photographs of the dramatic action. They contained society-type gossip columns; their reportage was romantic but discreet. They always included several pictorial features on the most attractive young stars of stage and screen—largely dignified portrait poses rather than, as later, exploitative pin-up shots. The image of the beautiful actress was, around 1915, akin to that of the Gibson Girl. Those farther down the Hollywood ladder—Keystone Comedy Girls and Mack Sennett Beauties (D-5), starlets or unknown actresses—were usually photographed, as burlesque stars had been previously, in the cheesecake style. By exception, a few stars like Theda Bara posed for more serious pin-ups (D-1).

After World War I and during the 1920s, fan magazines poured onto the newsstands: *Motion Picture Magazine, Picture Play, Screen Book, Screen Play, Screenland, Shadowland,* and *Silver Screen,* to mention only a few. Gone from their pages were the stage actresses who could not make the transition to the screen, for the fan magazines and their readers were now interested only in film stars—and in carrying the myths of their glamorous world, and of its fantasy and unattainable dreams, to the doorsteps of America and the rest of the world.

A nearly forgotten phenomenon of Hollywood's seamier side in the 1920s was the proliferation of sensational sex movies (somewhat like today's "skin flicks"). For every good movie with respected stars, there appears to have been a film that exploited the postwar looseness of morals. *Alimony,* released in 1924, advertised "beautiful jazz babies, champagne baths, midnight revels, petting parties in the purple dawn, all ending in one terrific smashing climax that makes you gasp."

What was true of movies and movie goers might well describe the pin-ups and pin-up viewers of that period as well:

> sex dramas continued to be turned out in profusion, and there was still a marked emphasis on

portrayals of the supposed fast life of high society. Even the news reel did not entirely escape post-war influences, with its inevitable picture of bathing beauties in one-piece suits.

There was no question that the public liked these pictures. Even greater crowds nightly packed the country's twenty thousand picture houses, from Roxy's to the cheapest second-run village hall. Men and women from every walk of life, but especially those in the working class, found here the vicarious excitement, the thrills, the heart interest, that for a time enabled them to escape the troubles and disappointments of their own lives. The man working all day on the assembly-line in an automobile factory, the tired homeworker leaving the children with a neighbor for her weekly night at the pictures, did not want their entertainment on any higher plane:

> Please don't uplift me when I go
> To see a moving picture show.*

From 1925 on, any film star with a semblance of personality or sex appeal was expected to pose for countless numbers of publicity stills—black-and-white glossy photographs released to agents, columnists, managers, newspapers, general-interest magazines, and fan magazines. These stills, whose use and distribution reached beyond fan magazines, became the basic medium of movie star pin-ups. Indeed, the fans could order photographs of their favorite stars directly from Hollywood studios, bypassing all intermediary publications. Every month, hundreds of thousands of fan letters—most of them requests for photographs of the stars—arrived at the film studios. Meanwhile, the fan magazines reached staggering circulations—at times, up to 4 million copies a month.

Hollywood "sex goddesses" or "sex symbols"—film stars whose faces, bodies, and personalities, whose very names, were synonymous with sex—emerged in the 1920s, and they remain an important film phenomenon to this day. Outstanding, at first, were such names as Clara Bow (D-9) and Louise Brooks (D-14); in the 1930s, Greta Garbo (D-22), Jean Harlow (D-15), and Marlene Dietrich (D-33).

The sense of craft and serious theater that had pervaded fan magazines through the mid-1920s was displaced by fun, humor, and the happy abandon of the Hollywood scene. Magazines like *Film Fun* (D-23), *Movie Humor* (D-27), and *Screen Fun* enjoyed great popularity. Each issue featured dozens of pictorial spreads on stars and starlets scantily clad in swimming suits, sexy costumes, feather boas, see-through gowns, and veil-like accoutrements. Those were the gayest years for Hollywood pin-up girls, partying starlets, and high-kicking chorus girls.

The 1940s began by imitating the frivolity of the previous decades, but World War II was too sobering an experience to permit the continuation of undiluted fun and glamor. Hollywood sex symbols soon became instruments of morale-boosting propaganda for the men in the armed services. With the diminishing in-

---

* Foster Rhea Dulles, *America Learns to Play* (New York and London: Appleton-Century, 1940).

terest in frolicking, laughing starlets, Hollywood producers placed even more emphasis on typecasting their star performers: Veronica Lake (*D-34*) and Gloria Grahame (*D-42*) were, each in her own way, seductresses. Ann Sheridan (*D-36*) was "The Oomph Girl," the personification of sex appeal; Rita Hayworth (*D-38*), the kept woman; Jane Russell (*Color Plate 14*), the earthly, buxom moll—and, on the wholesome side, Esther Williams (*D-37*) was the graceful beauty queen of the water. Betty Grable . . . was simply unique. Her "gams" heightened or bolstered the spirit of hundreds of thousands of soldiers during the war. The classic pose—the one-piece swimming suit, high heels, and delicate ankle bracelet—seemed to say, "Follow me home, boys, I'm what you're fighting for" (*Color Plate 3*; *D-39*).

After the war, fan magazines tended to become more sensational. Influenced in part by a rash of "invasion-of-privacy" magazines led by *Confidential,* screen magazines began to exploit the psychosexual and decadent aspects of Hollywood stardom. The appeal was to less mature, somewhat less educated, and much less sophisticated readers than in previous years.

Among the more popular American fan magazines of the 1940s and 1950s were *Movie Fan, Movie Pix, Movie Secrets, Movie Show, Screen Fun, Screen Life,* and *TV and Movie Screen.* Similar publications appeared in France, Germany, Great Britain, Italy, and Spain (*D-24*). In fact, almost every European country had screen magazines that were comparable in scope and style to the leading American fan magazines and that contained pin-up photographs of actresses and starlets. Screen magazines were also published in Australia (*D-43*), India, and Japan.

The affluence of the postwar years contributed most to the decline of fan magazines, especially in the United States. National prosperity allowed increasingly large numbers of people to realize their own dreams, thus rendering the Hollywood dream superfluous. With the rise of television, millions of movie goers, who regularly had attended film performances at least once a week, remained at home to watch television programs, and film attendance decreased disastrously.

During the 1950s, Marilyn Monroe was the undisputed queen of the Hollywood sex goddesses, and no other Hollywood actress could approach her as a sex symbol. Monroe typically projected herself—both in publicity and in films—as the dumb-blonde sexpot, the extreme exploitative image of femininity. Only later, in the course of her tragic personal life, was the myth exploded—conceivably by the very conflict that Women's Liberation confronts today: woman as sex object versus woman as person.

Yet the insatiable publicity agents of the film industry kept trying to duplicate the Monroe image. Jayne Mansfield looked and acted somewhat like Monroe and posed for dozens of calendars during the 1950s (*Color Plate 36*); she also posed in several issues of *Playboy*—always in the centerfold and once in the nude. Distinguished from Monroe chiefly by being a British export to Hollywood, Diana Dors, another "blonde bombshell," also posed for calendars (*Color Plate 37*). Mamie Van Doren (*D-46*) must be included in the same roster.

The most notable post-Monroe sex goddess, however, was neither a Hollywood product nor another dumb-blonde type. Brigitte Bardot projected the image of an individualistic, shameless sex kitten (*D-51* through *D-54*). Promoted heavily by the English magazine *Continental Film Review,* she appeared in its calendars from 1955 well into the 1960s. By 1959, Bardot was one of the world's most publicized stars, perhaps not as much through her films as through various printed media—calendars, magazines, and posters. Although acclaimed for her many outdoor bathing scenes in films, she is most strongly "imaged" in connection with motorcycles, leather, and the wildness of the open road (*G-28*). Tough, independent, wanton, and earthy, she stands opposed to the soft, servile plaything of screen world fantasies.

In the 1960s, and to the present, the exaggerated physical characteristics of the sex symbol have tended to diminish in favor of a more believable sexuality. Further, the dramatic talents or more rounded personalities of the newer sex goddesses have been brought to the fore, both in their publicity and in some of their films. Among these stars are Ann-Margret (*D-58*), Claudia Cardinale (*D-55*), Jane Fonda (*Color Plate 52*), Sophia Loren (*G-26*), and Raquel Welch (*G-27*), as well as Ursula Andress and Catherine Deneuve. A recent addition to the glamor roster is Julie Ege (*D-57*), who was described in *Gent,* June 1971, as

> a Norwegian cutie whose British movie studio hopes will be a sex symbol of the seventies. . . . At twenty-five and twice divorced, Julie has been a farmer's wife, a dentist's wife, a $4.80-a-week maid, and a Miss Norway.

In their publicity, more recent film stars tend to avoid the standard pin-up style and the pin-up mediums. They rarely pose for fan magazines, hardly ever for calendars. Certain superstars, in fact, seem to regard themselves, and are considered by their public, as "too beautiful," or too serious as dramatic actresses, to be mere pin-ups. Indeed, some beautiful film stars, like Julie Christie (*D-60*), are better known for dramatic versatility than for sexual allure. Some, like Audrey Hepburn or Grace Kelly, are not voluptuous enough to be pin-up types. Others, like Elizabeth Taylor (*D-59*) or Ava Gardner (*D-43*), are generally photographed as surpassingly beautiful women whose faces alone can convey their attractiveness, power, mystery, or fascination. The contemporary poster, which is becoming their main photographic vehicle, usually shows them not in studio poses but in scenes from their films. Other pin-up mediums replacing the fan magazines are the quality publications, such as *Playboy,* and the general-interest magazines, such as *Life,* which present articles in interview form or pictorial features about stars of the screen. Today, of course, there are still fan magazines, but they have become little more than illustrated gossip columns, publicity vehicles aimed at a diminishing audience of teen-agers, who are more interested in folk singers and rock musicians than in the Hollywood life-style. Fan magazines have had to reach beyond Movieland for their materials, with features, for example, on Jacqueline Kennedy Onassis, TV personalities, popular singers, and other manifestations of the celebrity world.

D-1. Theda Bara, "The Vampire." 1915. Hollywood's first sex-goddess, Miss Bara was famous for her long kisses, bare shoulders, revealing exotic costumes, and erotic intensity. In the course of Hollywood's first colossal publicity campaign, her agents claimed she "ruined 50 men, made 150 families suffer." Her high-paying contract forbade her to marry, to appear unveiled, or to enter a Turkish bath.

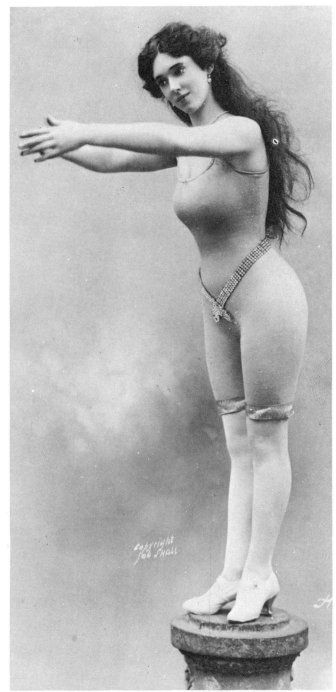

D-2

D-3

D-4

D-5

D-2. Lalla Selbini, vaudeville performer. 1909.

D-3. Annette Kellermann. A "still" from the scandalous skinny-dip scene in *Daughter of the Sun* (1917). Miss Kellermann, an Australian who started swimming to overcome infantile paralysis, began her celebrated glass-tank exhibits in 1906, and three years later invented the "revealing" one-piece bathing suit. She initiated the "swim star" tradition that culminated in the 1940s with Hollywood's best-known aquatic star, Esther Williams.

D-4. Mae Murray, during the 1920s, waltzed her way into a $7,500-a-week movie contract, surpassing the figure earned (and displayed) by the earlier *femme fatale*, Theda Bara.

D-5. Mabel Normand, "The Keystone Girl." c.1915. Mack Sennett's first pin-up queen, who appeared in many films with Charlie Chaplin.

D-6. Betty Compson. *Motion Picture Classic* (Brooklyn, N.Y.), March 1922.

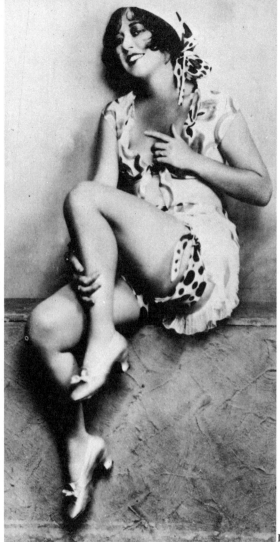

D-7

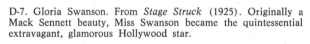

D-8

D-7. Gloria Swanson. From *Stage Struck* (1925). Originally a Mack Sennett beauty, Miss Swanson became the quintessential extravagant, glamorous Hollywood star.

D-8. Ann Pennington, a Ziegfeld star, famous for her "dimpled knees." 1925.

D-9. Clara Bow, c.1925, "The Hottest Jazz Baby in Films," symbolized the spirit of the Roaring Twenties. "It" was the word then used to describe that indefinable female charm, and Miss Bow became famous as "The It Girl."

D-9

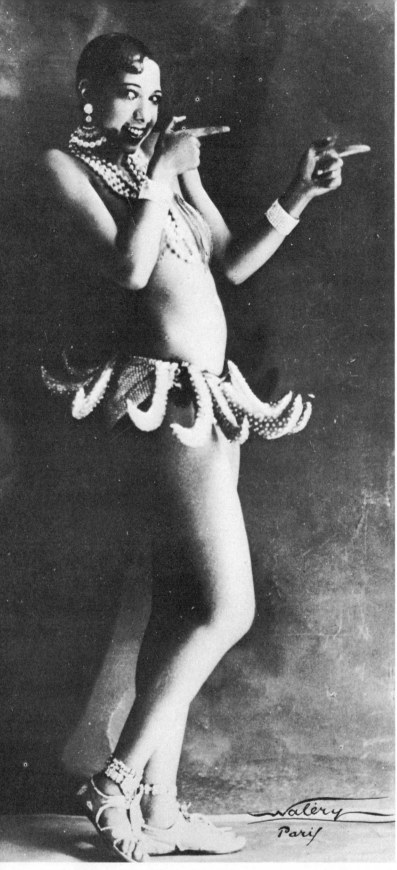

D-12. Mistinguett. c.1932. Famous as early as 1899, the French music hall star Jeanne Bourgeois (1873-1956), known as Mistinguett, appeared, with Maurice Chevalier and other leading actors, at the Casino de Paris, Folies Bergère, and Moulin Rouge, for more than 50 years. This vivacious entertainer rose to the very top as a pin-up queen during the flapper era, when breasts were noticeably de-emphasized.

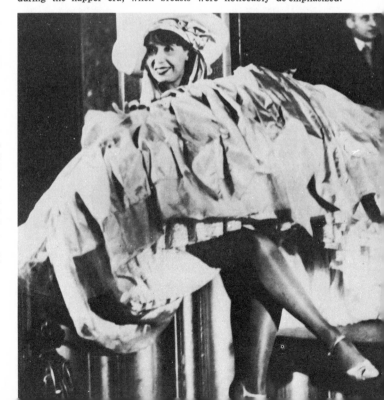

D-10. Josephine Baker. c.1926. American-born Miss Baker rose to stardom as an entertainer in Paris in 1925. There, in her engagement at the Folies Bergère, where she was billed as "The Dark Star," she made her most famous appearance. Wearing no clothes except for a girdle of rubber bananas, "La Baker" danced on a mirror, singing *Ave Maria*. This number caused such a sensation that shortly afterward, banana-clad black "Josephine dolls" were selling by the thousands to tourists and children, and Miss Baker was for some time called "The Banana Girl." Although she is not renowned as a film star, she did appear in films during the 1930s as well as in a German film in 1954. This photograph is not of the actual "Banana Girl" performance but is from a postcard issued soon thereafter. (Museum of the City of New York.)

D-14. Louise Brooks. 1929. Appearing first in the *Ziegfeld Follies* and *George White's Scandals,* Miss Brooks went on to Hollywood and was first known as a sex symbol, later as an actress in German films.

D-13. Billie Dove. From *An Affair of the Follies* (1927). Miss Dove, who epitomized the heyday of the flapper, was active in films from 1921 to 1932.

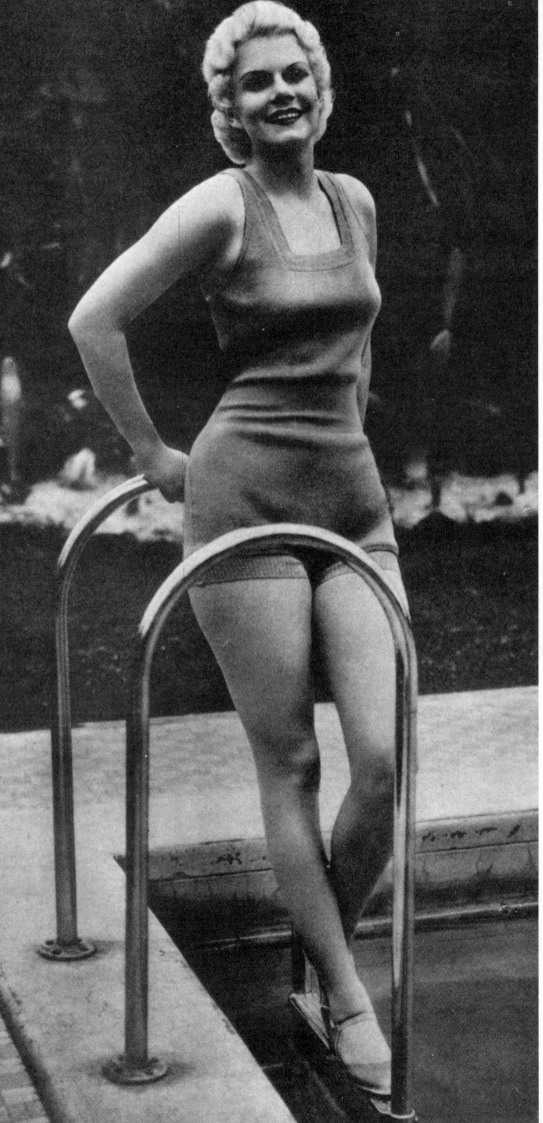

D-15

D-15. Jean Harlow. An early portrait, c.1930, of Hollywood's platinum blonde sex-goddess of the 1930s. In *Hell's Angels* (1930), she stirred millions of American men when she whispered to her lover the now famous line, "Pardon me while I change into something more comfortable."

D-16. Ginger Rogers. c.1931. A lovely, leggy portrait of Miss Rogers in her pre-Astaire years. The first Astaire-Rogers film was *Flying Down to Rio* (1933).

D-17. Olive Borden, who acted in films from 1925 to 1933. 1928.

D-18. Virginia Bruce. An early publicity still, 1929. Miss Bruce later appeared in *The Great Ziegfeld* (1936).

D-19. Mary Nolan, another Ziegfeld beauty, often mentioned in "scandal" sheets. 1929.

D-16

D-17

D-18

D-19

Heroines of the Screen

D-20. Mae West. From *She Done Him Wrong* (1933). Best remembered for her spoofs on sex, Mae West is celebrated today as the queen of camp. In 1927 a critic wrote, "Never has disgrace fallen so heavily as it did Monday night, when a nasty red-light district show opened and called itself *Sex.*" The "critic" was Mae West, the star of the show. A police raid later sent her off to ten days in the pokey.

D-21. Anna May Wong. From *Daughter of the Dragon* (1931). The only Oriental star of early Hollywood, Miss Wong was one of the most photographed actresses of the 1930s; typically, she played the role of a seductive villainess.

D-22. Greta Garbo. From *Mata Hari* (1932). Fostering an image of a sophisticated recluse, through the years "The Great Garbo" was publicized for being publicity shy.

D-21

D-20

D-22

FILM FUN

DECEMBER 20¢

"EXTRA"
SPECIAL!

D-23. *Film Fun* (New York), December 1933. Hollywood fan
magazines had come a long way in eleven years. (Compare *D-6.*)

Foby Wing

D-24

D-25

D-26

D-27

D-28. Joan Crawford. c.1933. A pin-up girl in the 1920s, Miss Crawford later became one of the most enduring film actresses.

D-29. Dolores Del Rio. From *In Caliente* (1934). Considered one of the all-time great film beauties, Miss Del Rio is shown here in the first two-piece bathing suit ever seen in movies.

D-24. "Foby" [i.e. Toby] Wing. *Cinegramas* (Madrid), September 1934. Miss Wing, the most famous Busby Berkeley chorus girl, was a popular pin-up figure featured in many movie magazine pictorials. Like American film magazines, *Cinegramas* carried articles on the leading Hollywood stars and included many cheesecake pictures of unknown starlets.

D-25. Marion Martin. 1935. A comedienne who made scores of films in the 1930s and 1940s, seen here in an irresistible pin-up pose.

D-26. Lucille Ball. From *Roman Scandals* (1933). Yes, Lucille Ball!

D-27. Lilli Palmer. *Movie Humor*, April 1937. From *Great Barrier* (1937), the publicity for which created the label "The New Screen Vamp" for Miss Palmer. Standard studio cheesecake of the time.

No one adjective describes Lana's personality—she can change it so easily, as illustrated by the pictures on these pages. Below, she is mysterious in a glamour shot suited to the title of her next film, "These Glamour Girls."

D-30. Lana Turner. This early photograph is from an article entitled "Hottest Thing on the Metro Lot," *Pic* (New York), August 1938, showing young Miss Turner as a brunette. Later, as a blonde, she was celebrated as "The Sweater Girl" in a series of well-known pin-up shots.

D-31. Carole Landis. 1940. On the Hollywood scene since 1937, by 1940 Miss Landis had come to be known as "The Ping Girl." She was the greatest delight to photographers since Harlow, and, before making films, had been used mainly for publicity stills, known technically at that time as "leg art." A critic is said to have described her as a "bureau with the top drawer pulled out."

"PIC"

COVERING THE ENTIRE FIELD OF ENTERTAINI

ARMY INTELLIGENCE TEST
CAN YOU PASS IT?
WORLD'S MOST DREAD DISEASE

GOBS AND GALS FROLIC IN GAY TUG-BOAT PARTY.

WHITE MEN IMPERSONATE INDIANS, BITE SNAKES.

10c 12 CENTS IN CANADA
AUG. 19, 1941

MARLENE DIETRICH

D-33. Marlene Dietrich. *Pic*, August 19, 1941. The paragon of the *femme fatale* during her prime years, German-born Marlene Dietrich was to maintain her exotic image—and her svelte figure—for several decades to follow.

D-32. Dorothy Lamour. From *Typhoon* (1940). *Real Screen Fun* (New York). November 1940. Symbol of both romance and sex, Miss Lamour was celebrated for her low-cut, side-slit sarongs.

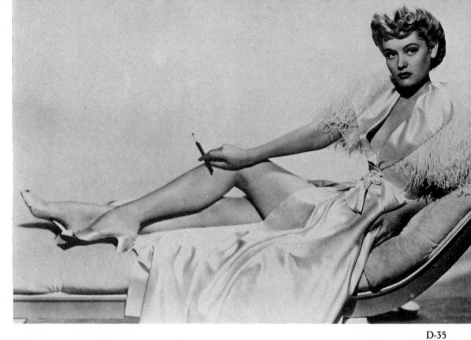

D-34

D-35

D-36

D-37

D-38

D-34. Veronica Lake. c.1945. Famous for hiding part of her wistful face behind flowing, silken hair, Miss Lake, "The Peekaboo Girl," projected the image of a sultry moll.

D-35. Alexis Smith. 1945. Having starred in *Conflict* in 1945, Miss Smith still looked good in her 1971 comeback in the stage production of *Follies*.

D-36. Ann Sheridan. From *Navy Blues* (1942). After Betty Grable and Rita Hayworth, Miss Sheridan, a comedienne and dramatic actress, was probably the most popular World War II pin-up. Known as "The Oomph Girl," she embodied a hard-boiled, no-nonsense approach to sex.

D-37. Esther Williams. 1943. A pin-up of the more "wholesome" variety, Miss Williams was not a sex symbol but was often photographed in a swim suit—for the many romantic roles she played as Hollywood's "movie mermaid."

D-38. Rita Hayworth. 1945. Miss Hayworth was second only to Betty Grable as a wartime pin-up favorite. Dressed in scanty negligée, perched on a bed, she had appeared in *Life*, August 11, 1941, which proclaimed her "The Goddess of Love of the Twentieth Century." It was reported that a pin-up of Rita Hayworth was stuck onto the atom bomb dropped on Hiroshima. At the outbreak of the Korean War in 1950, when Miss Hayworth's popularity with G.I.s was at another peak, she was receiving 2,500 requests per week for pin-up photos.

D-39. Betty Grable. 1942. The famous Grable pose—with the "million dollar legs"—that helped win World War II. The G.I. demand for this pin-up ran as high as 20,000 per week. It was printed in *Time's* overseas edition, as well as in *Yank*, the official G.I. magazine, and as late as the 1950s it appeared on material designed to teach Army recruits how to hit their mark. The original pin-up photograph, reproduced here, was black-and-white. A hand-colored version appears as *Color Plate 3*.

Bonnie Manville who hopped from Broadway to marriage with Tommy Manville to Hollywood.

Queen of all Pin-Ups is Jane Russell, glamorous Hollywood star who has never been in a motion picture. Jane's first cinematic vehicle the much-censored Outlaw, is soon to be released.

Red haired and Ooomphy Ann Sheridan

HEDY LA MARR

RITA HAYWORTH

KAY ALDRIDGE

SHOWGIRLS' PIN-UP PARADE

D-40. Double-page spread from *Show Girls*, March 1945. A typical "Pin-Up Parade," showing, among the six subjects, Rita Hayworth, Hedy Lamarr, Ann Sheridan, and Jane Russell. The caption for Miss Russell reads: "Queen of all pin-ups is Jane Russell [evidently in the process of succeeding Betty Grable], glamorous Hollywood star who has never been in a motion picture. Jane's first cinematic vehicle, the much-censored *Outlaw*, is soon to be released." (See *Color Plate 14*, page 94.)

D-41. Lena Horne, c.1946. Considered the first black sex image in Hollywood films, Miss Horne was, and still is, known for her great beauty. In her films of the 1940s, Lena Horne, performing in sleek, elegant gowns with sensuous vitality, characteristically sang in "specialty numbers." Today, in concert or on TV specials, she conveys the same excitement with convincing modernity.

D-42. Gloria Grahame. c.1949. The epitome of the "bad girl" in the early 1950s, Miss Grahame was one of the few Hollywood sexpots to win an Academy Award (1953), for her work in *The Bad and the Beautiful*.

D-43. Ava Gardner. *Movie Life* (West Melbourne, Australia), August 1, 1953. In the late 1950s and early 1960s, Miss Gardner came to be regarded as "the world's most beautiful animal"—too beautiful, or too much a superstar, evidently, to be a mere pin-up. Of these beauty goddesses—Elizabeth Taylor (*D-59*), Julie Christie (*D-60*), or Sophia Loren (*G-26*), and Miss Gardner—there is a surprising dearth of standard pin-up photos from the prime years of their careers.

D-42

D-41

D-43

153

CHARLES K. FELDMAN
GROUP PRODUCTIONS PRESENTS

the seven year itch

starring

Marilyn Monroe

and

Tom Ewell

A **CINEMASCOPE** PICTURE

Released by 20th CENTURY-FOX

COLOR BY DE LUXE

EVELYN KEYES · SONNY TUFTS · ROBERT STRAUSS · OSCAR HOMOLKA · MARGUERITE CHAPMAN · VICTOR MOORE · ROXANNE

BILLY WILDER · BILLY WILDER · GEORGE AXELROD

D-44

D-45

D-44. Marilyn Monroe. From *The Seven-Year Itch* (1955). The publicity for this film was based on a series of pin-up stills showing Miss Monroe's dress blown upward by a blast of air through a subway grating. This reproduction is from a "lobby card" for use in movie houses.

D-45. Anita Ekberg. c.1955. Swedish beauty queen, a sex goddess in the Monroe image.

D-46. Mamie Van Doren. c.1957. With Jayne Mansfield and Diana Dors, Miss Van Doren was another look-alike to Marilyn Monroe. Her public style, the type of publicity, and the kinds of roles she played were generally based on the image of the "Blonde Bombshell."

D-47. Gina Lollobrigida. c.1960. Miss Rome of 1947, Gina Lollobrigida starred in Italian and American films during the 1950s and 1960s, and proved she could act as well as flaunt, in her varied roles through the years.

D-48. Martine Carole. c.1957. French sex-bomb of the 1950s, Miss Carole never attained the international fame of Monroe or Bardot but was widely acclaimed in her native France.

D-49. Julie Newmar. c.1959. A later exemplar of the sex-symbol image established by Marilyn Monroe, Miss Newmar was played up for her height (5' 10½") as well as for other measurements.

D-50. Shirley Eaton. A publicity still from *Goldfinger* (1964) showing Miss Eaton not in the raw, but attired in a thin coat of gold paint. This role won the actress instant fame.

D-46

D-47

D-48

D-49

D-50

D-51

Brigitte Bardot, the most famous European pin-up girl of
the mid-20th century. Moodier, tougher, more independent
and adventurous than Marilyn Monroe, with whom she has
often been compared, Bardot has a unique identity and a
vast following. These pictures reflect her growth and variety
of mood. D-51, at the beginning of her career, in *Manina,
la fille sans voiles* (1952). D-52, hiking up her dress for a
scene in *La Femme et le pantin* (1958). D-53, from *Voulez-
vous danser avec moi?* (1959). D-54, a publicity still for
La Vérité (1961). (Photos from *Continental Film Review*,
London. For another image of Bardot, see *G-28*.)

D-5

Brigitte

in

"*MANINA, LA
FILLE SANS
VOILES*"

1952

D-52

D-53

D-56

D-57

D-58

D-55. Claudia Cardinale. From *The Professionals* (1966). Like Gina Lollobrigida, Silvana Mangano, Sophia Loren, Monica Vitti, and Virna Lisi, Miss Cardinale has acting talent as well as beauty and a sex image. The late 1960s witnessed, for the most part, the diminution of "canned," or posed, pin-up-type photography in favor of sexy stills from films with the actresses remaining "in character." It is in shots like these that we see Sophia Loren (*G-26*), Raquel Welch (*G-27*), and Brigitte Bardot (*opposite page*).

D-56. Kim Novak. c.1958. One of the first modern sex symbols to break away from the sexpot stereotype, Miss Novak, like Garbo, was publicized as a combination of mystery and sensuality.

D-57. Julie Ege. 1971. Exemplifying the "in-action" style of contemporary pin-ups, Miss Ege is shown here in her first film, *Creatures the World Forgot* (1971). Miss Ege also appears in contemporary posters.

D-58. Ann-Margret. c.1964. First projected as a teenage sex kitten, Ann-Margret contributes vitality, vivaciousness, and sensuality to her more recent work as a dramatic actress.

D-60. Julie Christie. An early pin-up studio · still, c.1962. After she attained stardom in *Darling* (1965), Miss Christie was seldom if ever seen in standard pin-up poses such as this, but rather, like Elizabeth Taylor, in more sophisticated, high fashion, glamor shots. (Photo: British Film Institute, London.)

D-59. Elizabeth Taylor. From *Cleopatra* (1963). A child star in *National Velvet* (1944), Miss Taylor achieved fame for her "perfect" face and huge exotic eyes and only later for her dramatic ability. Having achieved superstardom, she did not pose for standard pin-ups, but film afficionados regard her as transcending pin-up status.

Heroes of the Screen

E-1 (*opposite*). Rudolph Valentino, as *The Sheik* (1921). Beginning his career as a dancer, this Italian-American actor rose to stardom as a dark, exotic, passionate lover in *The Four Horsemen of the Apocalypse* (1921), *The Sheik,* and *Blood and Sand* (1922). When he died suddenly in 1926, several women committed suicide, 100,000 condolence telegrams were sent, and a monument dedicated to his memory was erected in Hollywood.

Heroes of the Screen

For sixty years, movie fan magazines and general magazines have described, discussed, or illustrated the lives and loves and the dramatic activities of Hollywood heroes. More recently, contemporary posters have depicted movie actors of the past and present, ranging in time from Rudolph Valentino to Peter Fonda and in personality from W. C. Fields, Buster Keaton, and the Marx Brothers to Humphrey Bogart, James Dean, and Marlon Brando. Although men may identify with these heroes of the screen, women tend to fantasize about them, and, in their eagerness to learn everything they can about their male idols, women have always read fan magazines more avidly than men. Yet, through nature or nurture, women generally are not inclined to isolate flesh—the nude male body—from the rest of their fantasies with men, as men do with their pin-up girls. It is likely that, for emotional excitation, women do not need to see the nude or semi-nude male pin-ups. Thus, most pin-ups of Hollywood film heroes are portraits or action shots of fully-dressed leading men rather than figure studies.

As pin-ups, the stars range from beefcake types (Johnny Weissmuller and Tab Hunter) to ultrasophisticates (John Gilbert and Charles Boyer). All have one thing in common: a huge following of young as well as older women fans, and a tremendous demand for photographs showing them in their most characteristic moods, roles, or styles. These quasi-pin-ups may not show sexually evocative body poses, but they do address the viewer with the characteristics best recalled as having aroused the emotion or admiration or adulation of their fans through the years.

The illustrations on the following pages—which therefore emphasize personality rather than beefcake (discussed on pages 250-54)—were selected from a wide spectrum of film stars whose popularity has endured through at least a decade. They depict screen actors who, over the years, have come to represent basic Hollywood types of leading men or heroes: the passionate Latin lover (E-1), the romantic ladies' man (E-2, E-8, E-13), the suave or debonair ladies' man (E-5, E-21), the he-man (E-4, E-19), the tough guy (E-9), the primitive brute (E-10), the adventurer (E-6, E-7, E-12), the silent warrior (E-15), the underdog (E-14), the athlete (E-11), the all-American boy (E-20), the kid brother (E-18). Superstars of the 1960s—men like Michael Caine, Sean Connery, Albert Finney, Steve McQueen, Lee Marvin, Paul Newman, Sidney Poitier, and Robert Redford—appear on contemporary posters, more as cult heroes than as objects of film studio publicity, and they have been omitted in favor of more traditional movie heroes, beginning with Rudolph Valentino.

Many well-known stars have not been included here if they were preceded by earlier screen heroes who established the particular Hollywood type with which they are most commonly identified—thus, George O'Brien is here, but not John Wayne—or if they were contemporary with a more famous star of the same general type. Other leading men have had to be omitted because of space limitations in a book devoted primarily to female pin-ups: Gary Cooper, Tony Curtis, Kirk Douglas, Charlton Heston, William Holden, Ray Milland, Robert Mitchum, Laurence Olivier,

Gregory Peck, William Powell, Anthony Quinn, Frank Sinatra; and such Continental idols as Jean-Paul Belmondo, Rossano Brazzi, Horst Bucholz, Jean Gabin, Vittorio Gassmann, and Marcello Mastroianni.

E-2. Maurice Chevalier. c.1930. Hollywood's first male musical star achieved fame in *Love Me Tonight* (1932), in which he sang "Mimi." A romantic ladies' man, French-born Chevalier was also an international favorite as an entertainer until his death in 1972.

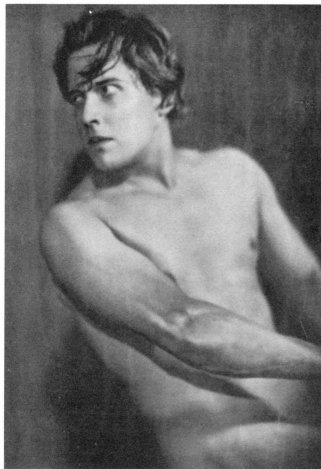

E-3. Ramon Novarro, from *Ben Hur* (1926)—an early example of Hollywood beefcake. Having starred in *Scaramouche* (1922) and *The Prisoner of Zenda* (1922), Mexican-born Novarro was at the peak of his early career when he was filmed in the nude in the galley scene from *Ben Hur*. He made a comeback as a character actor in 1958.

E-4. George O'Brien, from a physical-culture beefcake photo, c.1928. An avid health enthusiast who entered films as a stunt man, O'Brien was a big, robust Hollywood he-man for forty years (1924-64). Best-known films: *Sunrise* (1927) and *Noah's Ark* (1928).

E-5. John Gilbert, from *The Merry Widow* (1925). The silent screen's great lover was famous for his romance with Greta Garbo and for his appearances in films with her.

E-5

E-3

E-4

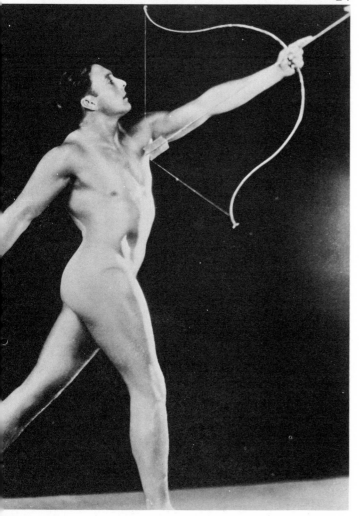

E-6. Douglas Fairbanks, from *The Private Life of Don Juan* (1934).
An athletic daredevil, acclaimed for his adventure roles, Fairbanks
appealed to both men and women, and was married to America's
Sweetheart, Mary Pickford. Best-known films: *Mark of Zorro* (1921),
Robin Hood (1922), *Thief of Bagdad* (1924), *The Black Pirate* (1927).

Ė-7. Douglas Fairbanks, Jr., from *Sinbad the Sailor* (1947). This picture and the one of the older Fairbanks show the close resemblance between father and son. Also a swashbuckler, the younger Fairbanks expanded his repertory to include suave, sophisticated characterizations somewhat like Ronald Colman's and David Niven's. Best-known films: *The Prisoner of Zenda* (1937) and *Gunga Din* (1939).

E-8. Tyrone Power. c.1938. Power became a star with *Lloyds of London* (1937) and *In Old Chicago* (1938), and he reached his dramatic peak in *Nightmare Alley* (1947). Like Robert Taylor, he was adored as a romantic leading man, especially by older women. Power died in 1958 during the filming of *Solomon and Sheba.*

E-9. Humphrey Bogart, from *High Sierra* (1944). James Cagney, George Raft, Edward G. Robinson, and other Hollywood tough guys never achieved "Bogey's" unique appeal to women. During the late 1960s, with the revival of many of his films and his appearance on contemporary posters, Bogart became a cult hero of the younger generation. Best-known films: *The Petrified Forest* (1936), *Dead End* (1937), *High Sierra* and *The Maltese Falcon* (both 1941), and *The African Queen* (1951), for which he was awarded an Oscar.

E-10. Johnny Weissmuller, from *Tarzan the Ape Man* (1932). A winner of three gold medals in swimming in the Olympic Games of 1924 and 1928, Weissmuller, in his Tarzan films, became the first of Hollywood's famous apemen—primitive, nonverbal, yet gentle with women and animals. His near-nude appearances in films and fan magazines provided a plethora of beefcake material for his fans.

E-8

E-9

E-10

E-11. Buster Crabbe. 1934. Like Weissmuller an Olympic gold medal winner (1932), Crabbe also portrayed Tarzan. His biggest film was *King of the Jungle* (1933), but he is best remembered for the lead roles in two serials, *Flash Gordon* (1936) and *Buck Rogers* (1939).

E-12. Errol Flynn, from *Santa Fe Trail* (1940). Regarded as a charming swashbuckler, Flynn was renowned for his devil-may-care attitude, his activities as a Don Juan, and his turbulent personal life. Best-known films: *Captain Blood* (1935) and *Robin Hood* (1937).

E-13. Charles Boyer. c.1942. *Savoir faire*, maturity, and a French accent contributed to Boyer's image as the premier Continental lover. His best-known role was Pepe le Moko in *Algiers* (1938), through which—although he never uttered the words—he came to be associated with the line, "Come with me to the Casbah."

E-12

E-13

E-11

E-14. John Garfield. c.1945. Hollywood's first big Method actor, Garfield portrayed a loner, a rebel, an underdog, an embittered, aggressive social outcast or criminal, fighting against odds for freedom, success, or romance. His first film, *Four Daughters* (1938), made him an instant star.

E-15. Alan Ladd, from *The Blue Dahlia* (1946). One of the few blonde-haired male stars who remained popular for many years, Ladd was generally silent, poker-faced, hard, and introspective. For a major male lead, he was surprisingly short—about 5' 6". Best-known films: *The Great Gatsby* (1948) and *Shane* (1953).

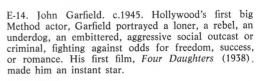

E-16. Clark Gable, at mid-career, c.1948. Gable's strength, intelligence, charm, romance, and roguery made him "The King" of Hollywood male stars. His far-reaching effect on women, over many years, can perhaps best be measured by listing his leading ladies: Greta Garbo, Joan Crawford, Jean Harlow, Myrna Loy, Norma Shearer, Jeanette MacDonald, Lana Turner, Loretta Young, Marion Davies, Constance Bennett, Helen Hayes, Rosalind Russell, Hedy Lamarr, Barbara Stanwyck, Ava Gardner, Gene Tierney, Jane Russell, Claudette Colbert (in *It Happened One Night;* Gable's Oscar-winning performance, 1934), Doris Day, Eleanor Parker, Yvonne de Carlo, Sophia Loren, and Marilyn Monroe.

Heroes of the Screen

E-17. Elvis Presley. c.1959. First celebrated as the swivel-hipped, guitar-wielding pop singer who revolutionized popular music in the 1950s, "Elvis the Pelvis" made his first film, *Love Me Tender,* in 1956. Millions of teenagers screamed with ecstasy at the sound of his voice or the movements of his hips. Although largely displaced by later pop stars such as the Beatles and Tom Jones, Presley still is highly popular.

E-18. Rock Hudson, from *Sea Devils* (1955). A "manufactured" star of the 1950s, groomed to be Cary Grant's successor, Hudson was regarded as a romantic lead of the boy-next-door variety. Best-known films: *Magnificent Obsession* (1954), *Giant* (1956), *Pillow Talk* (1959).

E-19. Burt Lancaster, from *Desert Fury* (1947). Before becoming a screen actor, Lancaster had been a circus acrobat, and after 25 years of Hollywood stardom, he is still a he-man whose body is an important feature of his image as an actor. Best-known films: *The Killers* (1946), *From Here to Eternity* (1952), *Elmer Gantry* (1960), for which he won an Oscar, and *Birdman of Alcatraz* (1962).

E-20. Tab Hunter, from a fan magazine, c.1955. Regarded as a pin-up boy by Hollywood fan magazines, this teenage rave of the 1950s sported a crew cut and was the quintessential all-American boy. Best-known films: *Battle Cry* (1955) and *Damn Yankees* (1958).

1933

1943

1950

1962

1946

Cary Grant. Although never quite as big a star as Gable, Grant has been the longest-lasting romantic lead in Hollywood history. These photographs span more than thirty years. Equally at ease in a Mae West comedy or a Hitchcock thriller, Grant has maintained a consistent image—that of a bright, debonair, British (but Americanized) ladies' man. Best-known films: *Holiday* (1938), *Gunga Din* (1939), *Philadelphia Story* (1940), *Arsenic and Old Lace* (1944), *To Catch a Thief* (1955), *That Touch of Mink* (1962).

1964

Calendar Pin-ups

F-1. The first known nude calendar girl. Millions of pirated copies of *Matinée Septembre,* an oil painting by Paul Chabas, appeared on calendars from about 1913. (Photo: Metropolitan Museum of Art, New York.)

Calendar Pin-ups

Girlie calendars have existed since the beginning of the 20th century. The earliest versions were usually based on art already available, or artists specializing in "girlie art" were paid high fees to create pin-ups especially for girlie calendars.

Until the 1940s, most calendars utilizing pin-up art carried advertising imprints (sometimes called "specialty advertising"), and this is still the dominant use of calendar pin-ups. In this field the major producers create "stock" calendars, imprinting them for gift use by insurance companies, banks, garages, manufacturers, laundries, and many other types of businesses large and small.

By now, total annual sales for the American calendar industry alone are estimated at more than $150 million, of which about $7.5 million is generated by the sales of girlie calendars.

Brown & Bigelow of Saint Paul, Minnesota, the world's largest calendar company, prints well over 100 million calendars a year and has worldwide distribution through licensees on all five continents. Of its many lines, girlie calendars account for about 2% of total annual sales and amount to over 2 million copies per year. In addition to calendars, Brown & Bigelow manufactures playing cards, greeting cards, ink blotters, posters, matchbook covers, pencils, pens, key cases, memo pads, key chains, letter openers, and other specialty items, many of which, at various times, have used pin-up images. Its calendar themes stem from a shrewd instinct for popular taste.

Since Brown & Bigelow is also the world's oldest calendar company, the history of girlie calendars can be conveniently traced through its development and policies. Around 1903, Brown & Bigelow published its first calendar with a female subject, "Colette" (from a painting by Angelo Asti), a charming but conservative portrait of a young beauty. In the ensuing years, "Colette" helped sell more than 1.5 million calendars. In 1904, the first pin-up on a Brown & Bigelow calendar (*Color Plate 32*) established beyond doubt that the manufacture of girlie calendars could be a lucrative business.

By 1910, other publishers were also issuing girlie calendars. In 1913, the first-known calendar nude, *September Morn,* appeared. It was a reproduction of an oil painting, *Matinée Septembre (Color Plate 4 and F-1),* by a French artist, Paul Chabas (1869-1937), which might have gone unnoticed in the United States if Anthony Comstock, of the New York Society for the Suppression of Vice, had not seen the work on display in a New York art gallery window. Comstock demanded that the painting be removed. When a salesman explained that the painting had recently won a Medal of Honor from the French Academy, Comstock cried, "There's too little morn and too much maid. Take her out." A lively dispute in the New York newspapers gave the painting national notoriety and this modest work became a national *cause célèbre.* The image was immediately pirated by a number of calendar companies and was distributed by hundreds of thousands throughout the United States, as well as in other countries. Reproductions appeared on window display cards, posters, cigar wrappers, candy boxes, postcards, and even suspenders (braces). The postcards were banned in Chicago. Although the painting, which Chabas had sold for $10,000, was valued at $30,000 when it was donated to the Metropolitan Museum of Art in 1957, Chabas never received a penny for the millions of pirated pictures.

Meanwhile, Brown & Bigelow proceeded with its own girlie calendars, showing provocative but clothed beauties in topical, allegorical, or exotic settings. Its first semi-nude and nude girlie calendars, produced in the 1920s, contained art work by Rolf Armstrong (*Color Plate 33; F-4, F-6*), a painter who might well have influenced George Petty. Armstrong's work paved the way for several generations of calendar artists—Earl Moran (*F10*), Gil Elvgren (*F-12, F-27*), Zoë Mozert (*F-14*), and Fritz Willis (*F-23*) among them. Outside the Brown & Bigelow sphere, other popular calendar artists thrived—Petty, Vargas, and Al Moore, to mention a few.

Until the 1940s, the calendar industry was almost entirely on a wholesale basis for advertising purposes. Girlie calendars accounted for only a small part of the overall distribution, and because they served the business community, they tended to be conservative in appearance and "in good taste." Art work was used rather than photography, because rendered art was considered a more appealing, timeless, and romantic medium than photography. The large calendar companies made some calendars available for retail sale, but these were mostly from their larger business-oriented lines, very few of which had pin-up themes.

It was not until the early 1940s that significant numbers of girlie calendars were produced excusively for a retail market—and these were *Esquire's* Varga calendars. So great was their success that small independent calendar companies and a few girlie magazine publishers followed suit. Taking their cue from *Esquire,* Brown & Bigelow began producing sexier pin-ups, particularly those by Gil Elvgren.

In the late 1940s, photographic pin-ups became very popular. The most publicized pin-up in history, that of Marilyn Monroe (*Color Plate 2*), appeared in a 1951 calendar published by John Baumgarth Co. The original picture had been taken in May 1949 by Tom Kelley, a California photographer. Miss Monroe had met Kelley by accident, when, having smashed up a friend's car on Sunset Boulevard in Hollywood, she needed taxi fare to get to a rehearsal on time. Kelley gave her five dollars—and his business card. Several years later, apparently in need of money, she came to Kelley's studio and posed, discreetly, in a swim suit for several photos. Before she left, Kelley mentioned that he had occasional assignments to create artistic nude color shots for calendars, but the aspiring actress was not interested. A few days later, however, she telephoned him and agreed to pose *au naturel.*

When Kelley saw Miss Monroe in the nude, he observed (according to a later interview), "This wasn't just another girl. This was a girl with instinct for drama and showmanship. Her lips parted provocatively, her body was arched and magnificent. There was a natural grace about her." At that moment, Marilyn

Monroe turned into Everyman's dream girl. She was paid $50.

Not long after that, she appeared briefly at the end of *The Asphalt Jungle* (1950) and again at the end of *All About Eve* (1950). She was beginning to be noticed in Hollywood. Then the calendar story broke. Her studio advised her to deny she was the nude girl on the calendar. Instead, she called Kelley, got twenty-five copies of the picture, and distributed them to friends, newspapermen, and other photographers. Soon her nude pose catapulted her name and image to national recognition. The calendar sold by the millions; and more people knew what year it was in 1951 than ever before—and perhaps ever since.

In 1958, *Playboy* began publishing its Playmate calendars. And from then on, nearly every established girlie magazine has published photographic pin-up calendars. (See, for example, *F-24, F-28, F-34.*) Thus, the calendar business took on another dimension in the 1950s. The sexier pin-up images were sold directly to the public through girlie magazines, and the same models then appeared in the calendars. The few exceptions are Jayne Mansfield (*Color Plate 36*) and Diana Dors (*Color Plate 37*).

In spite of the demand for photographic girlie calendars, Brown & Bigelow continued (even to the present day) to issue artist-rendered pin-up calendars, now admittedly bolder than in the Armstrong days, but still relatively conservative. In 1952, the firm published its first photographic pin-up calendar, featuring Hollywood starlet Elaine Stewart *(F-13)*.

Through the 1950s and 1960s—watching at a distance the mad scramble for the sexier photographic pin-up market, pursued by the magazines and smaller calendar companies—Brown & Bigelow concentrated its girlie interest on calendars by Gil Elvgren and Fritz Willis. In 1971, convinced that photographic pin-ups were not a passing fad, Brown & Bigelow made its first strong bid in the photographic girlie calendar market—see, for example, *This Is A Plain Brown Wrapper (F-30)*—with a mixture of nude and semi-nude models, from very sexy to very "artistic."

In recent years, the thematic range of the pin-up calendar has broadened in two directions. First, there are calendars in the vein of contemporary posters—hip, political, sophisticated. The *Soulmate 1971* calendar (*Color Plate 5*) features gorgeous models in poses that satirize twelve historical themes about blacks in America. Second, in modern calendars, the "girlies" have become women rather than sex objects. They are varied—complex, moody, lonely, dynamic, poetic, engaged in life—hence more beautiful and appealing.

F-2. A pin-up of the "beauties" variety, c.1915, using the mirror to achieve two views of the model. Artist: Allen Gilbert. Published by Brown & Bigelow, Saint Paul, Minn.

F-3. *A Princess of Egypt.* 1926. Exotic theme, starry night, translucent gown, low neckline, and contoured breasts combine to make a languorous calendar pin-up. Brown & Bigelow.

F-4. Untitled. 1931. Rolf Armstrong, worked with live models—not from photography, like many later pin-up artists. Brown & Bigelow.

F-5. *Greetings.* 1926. An elegant flapper of the Roaring Twenties steps out of the latest model roadster. Artist: Eggleston. Brown & Bigelow.

F-6. *Hurry Back.* 1934. Armstrong used pastels, a faster medium than oils, to capture quickly the models' poses. Brown & Bigelow.

F-7. Untitled. 1937. An early example of a popular theme in pin-up calendars—girl and horse—the horse sometimes serving as a male symbol and perhaps suggesting bestiality. Artist: Patten. Published by B.D.

F-8. Untitled. 1939. Reminiscent of Petty's work, this stylized pin-up is "softer," less photographic, than those that were being done in *Esquire* at the same time. Artist unknown. Published by C. Moss.

F-9. *Idleness.* 1934. From a charming French-style calendar, unusual for its sophisticated drawing technique. Artist Louis Icart. Brown & Bigelow.

F-11. *Varga Calendar.* 1946. Sharp as a color photo, but anatomically incredible, the Varga Girl was queen of the artist-rendered calendar pin-ups—with distribution exceeding the million mark as early as 1942. Published by *Esquire.*

F-10. *The Dancer.* 1941. The subjects of Earl Moran, who followed Armstrong as a Brown & Bigelow calendar artist, are moody or mysterious. Although Moran's technique was almost photographic, he relied on idealization and romanticism. Brown & Bigelow.

F-12 (*opposite*). *Aiming to Please.* 1948. Perhaps the best-known of Brown & Bigelow's pin-up artists, Gil Elvgren came closest to Varga in the overt sexual appeal of his subjects. The rosy-cheeked model blowing on the gun (just fired) takes this pin-up theme somewhat beyond the traditional "Western" imagery. Brown & Bigelow.

BUBBLES

F-14. *Bubbles.* 1949. Zoë Mozert was often her own model. Her style is soft and sensitive, more romantic than sexual. Brown & Bigelow.

F-13. *"First In."* 1952. Film actress Elaine Stewart was a guest at a Brown & Bigelow sales conference around 1950, and she inspired the company to initiate photographic pin-ups. Brown & Bigelow.

F-15 (*left*), "Girl Golfers," and F-16, "Sparkling Eyes," are good examples of the re-use of pin-up photography. The calendar they appeared in, *Hollywood Models*, was dated for the year 1972, but several of the pictures originated as early as the mid-1950s. They can be dated by the hair styles and makeup, as well as by the corny themes and styles of the poses.

F-18. *Pleasing to the Palate.* 1956. Almost a living Varga girl—the influence is unmistakable. Pure cheesecake, even to the wordplay (on palette). Photo: Katie and Burt Owen. Published by A. Fox.

F-17. *Good Friends.* 1957. The horse-and-girl theme again, without the suggestiveness of *F-7.* Conservative by girlie calendar standards, this picture tries to emphasize wholesome, rural life. Published by Brown & Bigelow.

F-19. *The Glamor Girl Proverb Calendar.* 1957. Caption: "Cold hands, warm heart." A poorish-quality calendar in the vein of *Playboy* imitators during the mid-1950s. Two of the twelve color pictures are "Posed by Jayne Mansfield"; the other models are unidentified. [No publisher given.]

F-20. *Esquire Girl Calendar.* 1957. Envelope for the calendar, showing seductive pin-up in hose-and-heels outfit. Artist: Mike Ludlow. Published by *Esquire.*

F-21. *American Artists Calendar.* 1959. Although the title and symbol suggest one thing, the pin-ups suggest quite another. Like "art" photography magazines of the time, this calendar presents pin-ups with no attention whatsoever to principles of true art photography. The cover model is unidentified, but appears to be the well-known stripper Tempest Storm. [No publisher given.]

Color Plate 32. An early girlie calendar (1904), in which alluring pose and long hair are curiously akin to today's "natural style." Artist unknown. Brown & Bigelow, 1904.

755   FROM PAINTING BY HONNEBRUCK   MEDITATION   COPYRIGHT, 1903, BY BROWN & BIGELOW, ST. PAUL

Compliments of

BELDING BROTHERS

Silk Manufacturers

CINCINNATI

1904		JANUARY			1904	
SUN	MON	TUE	WED	THU	FRI	SAT
Full Moon 2nd.	Last Quar. 9th.	New Moon 17th.	First Quar. 25th.	☽	1	2
3	4	5	6	7	8	9
10	11	12	13	14	15	16
17	18	19	20	21	22	23
24/31	25	26	27	28	29	30

Color Plate 33. One of the first in a long line of superb American pin-up artists, Rolf Armstrong built a fine reputation on calendar art. This calendar illustration (1928) pre-dates Petty and Varga, who may have been influenced by Armstrong. Brown & Bigelow.

Color Plate 34. A Renoiresque trip back to the Psyche theme (see *A-28*). Soft pastel tones render this 1940 work more an "art" than a pin-up calendar, intended to be saved beyond the duration of a year. Artist: Mabel Rollins Harris. Published by C. Moss.

Color Plate 35. Untitled. 1941. One of the earliest photographic nude calendars, in the spirit of the art photography magazines of the era. The open space at the top was reserved for the name and address of the business firm using the calendar for advertising purposes. Published by C. Moss.

Color Plate 36. Jayne Mansfield. 1957. One of the dozens of calendar pictures of Miss Mansfield—seeking to achieve the kind of sensational publicity achieved earlier by Marilyn Monroe. Published by A. Fox.

Color Plate 37. Diana Dors. 1960. Like Jayne Mansfield, Miss Dors posed for many pin-up calendars in an attempt to gain publicity à la Monroe. Published by A. Fox.

Color Plates 38 (*below*) and 39. The pin-up at right, unusual for its lack of humor and subtlety, is one of the few serious seductive black calendar pin-ups. Both photos from *Mayfair Calendar*, 1972, distributed by J. Hoover and Sons, Philadelphia.

PIRELLI

M T W T F S S M T W T F S S

January 1 2 3 4 5 6 7 8 9 10 11
12 13 14 15 16 17 18 19 20 21 22 23 24 25
26 27 28 29 30 31

Color Plate 40. *Pirelli Calendar.* 1970. This most famous modern European pin-up calendar, issued since 1964, has become a status symbol, since its distribution is intentionally limited to selected customers and business associates of Pirelli tire dealers. Although its yearly printing does not exceed 45,000, several hundred thousand could probably be sold. Its superb color photographic pin-ups consistently reach a high level of elegance and sophistication. Published by the Pirelli Tire Company, London.

F-23

F-22. *Best Magazine, International Edition.* 1961. Aimed at a decidedly different audience than the *Pirelli Calendar*. The models appear to be from various countries, and the calendar pad is in English, French, and Spanish. Published by Best Magazine Co., New York.

F-23. *Artists Sketchbook Calendar.* 1962. The art by Fritz Willis reflects the bolder style of the 1960s. Brown & Bigelow.

F-24. *Topper Calendar.* 1963. This girlie calendar, derived from the magazine of the same name (*C-45*), imitates the *Playboy* style.

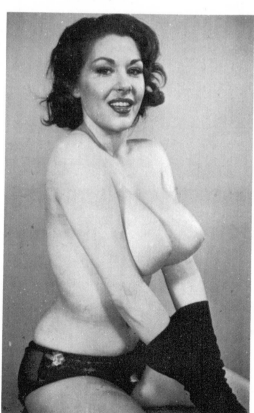

F-22

F-24

You've welcomed in the brand new year
And toasted it with cups of cheer
Now all you need is our girl here
To kiss you once and hold you near.

JANUARY

S	M	T	W	T	F	S
					1	2
3	4	5	6	7	8	9
10	11	12	13	14	15	16
17	18	19	20	21	22	23
24	25	26	27	28	29	30
31						

F-26

F-27

1969	AUGUST				1969
SUN	MON	TUE	WED	THU	FRI	SAT
					1	2
3	4	5	6	7	8	9
10	11	12	13	14	15	16
17	18	19	20	21	22	23
24 31	25	26	27	28	29	30

F-25. *Venus Calendar*. 1965. Reflects the increasing permissiveness of the 1960s, as well as the popularity of fetish themes. [No publisher given.]

F-26. *Superior Pin-up Calendar—"Busy Line."* 1966. Published by J. Hoover and Sons, Philadelphia. F-27. *Corinne.* 1967. Artist: Gil Elvgren. Brown & Bigelow.

Both calendar pin-ups are in the same spirit—smiling, teasing models, stress on hose-and-heels, with about the same degree of body exposure—but one is photographic, the other rendered.

F-28. *MR Calendar*. 1969. Derived from *MR* magazine and featuring "12 Big Beautiful Girls on 12 Separate Pin-up Sheets . . . For Your Year Long Pleasure," this calendar is blatantly sexual in its appeal and symbolism.

F-28

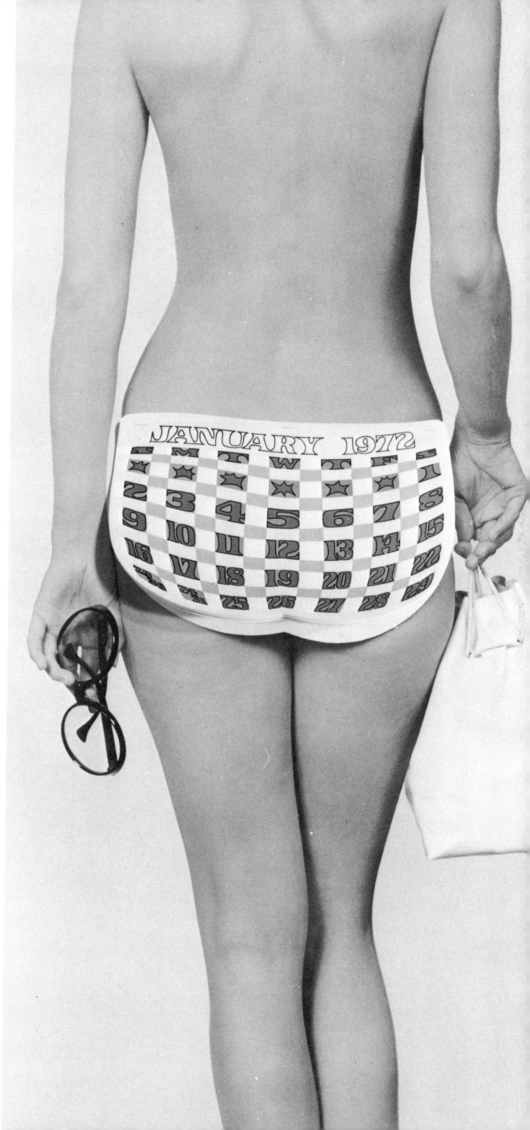

F-29. A contemporary poster-calendar (12″ x 60″). The pubic hair and full nudity are characteristic of pin-up art in the early 1970s. Published by Minerva Art Prints, Copenhagen, 1971.

F-30. *This Is A Plain Brown Wrapper.* 1973. This unusually titled photographic calendar contains nude pin-ups ranging in style and theme from fairly esthetic "art" photography to raunchy boudoir poses. Brown & Bigelow.

F-31. *Bikini Poster Calendar.* 1972. This huge poster-calendar (46″ x 22″) shows a life-size section of a model, whose bikini (stapled on) is actually a calendar, the leaves of which are peeled off each month—an innovative extension of the pin-up concept: the viewer can now literally undress the pin-up. Unfortunately, under "December" one finds only an advertisement. Brown & Bigelow.

F-31

Calendar Pin-ups

F-33. *Adam Calendar.* 1971. This offspring of *Adam* magazine offers both color and black-and-white pin-ups with a Spanish flavor and, in this picture, a subtle suggestion of the bondage theme. Published by Knight Publishing Corp., Los Angeles.

F-32. *Girls 1973.* This sophisticated pin-up calendar emphasizes natural beauty rather than assembly-line sexuality. Its tone of poetic moodiness is akin to that of the *Pirelli Calendar* (*Color Plate 40*). Published by Accidentia Druck, Düsseldorf, and by Universe Books, New York.

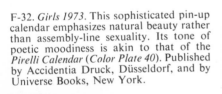

Poster
Pin-ups

Poster Pin-ups

Toward the end of the 19th century, poster artists in Paris used appealing images of women to attract attention to various products or forms of entertainment. Their models, in sexually evocative poses, were not depicted for their own sake but were presented to charm, delight, or fascinate the viewer so that his notice would be drawn to a product, service, or event.

Jules Chéret (1836-1932), the dominant figure during the great age of color lithography in Paris, began making posters in the 1870s and more than anyone else was responsible for the poster craze that enlivened the streets of that city and influenced much of the poster art of the Continent, Great Britain, and America for decades to come. Like the Japanese woodcut artists whose works did much to shape his style, Chéret did not try to give his figures three-dimensionality but presented them in flat forms and vitalized them through his brilliant use of color and rhythm (*Color Plates 41 and 42; G-2, G-3*). Through Japanese woodcuts also—for Oriental artists had depicted erotic images in their prints—Chéret and other French artists were freed from the respectability and sentimentality that had characterized much of the previous handling of female subjects in Europe and America. This new freedom led, in turn, to a more widespread use of women in advertising. Chéret's women—*toujours gaies, toujours riantes*—are the quintessence of sensuous, carefree carousal. The delicate outlines of limbs and torsos, beneath their garments, tease, provoke, and entice the viewer.

Chéret helped and influenced other French poster artists—most notably Henri de Toulouse-Lautrec (1864-1901). Lautrec's images of Parisian café life are not as festive as Chéret's. Their gaiety is intermingled with colors—jaundiced yellows, faded greens and browns—that seem tired or sullen, in contrast to the cheerful scenes they depict. Lautrec's women do not achieve the ecstatic allure of Chéret's pin-ups, but, even amid the *ennui* of their dancing or cavorting for the public, they demonstrate a unique sensuality *(G-1; Color Plate 43)*.

Other Parisian posterists whom Chéret influenced were Henri Boutet, Leonetto Cappiello *(G-13)*, H. Gray *(Color Plate 47)*, Jules Alexandre Grün *(G-14)*, Albert Guillaume, Lucien Métivet *(G-10)*, Georges Meunier, Misti *(G-16)*, and Pal *(Color Plate 45)*. Their poster subjects included theaters, music halls, cabarets, and celebrities, as well as commercial products such as liqueurs, oil lamps, and cigarette papers.

The most widely celebrated poster subject was Loie Fuller, an American-born actress who made her debut as a dancer in 1893, at the Folies Bergère in Paris. Miss Fuller was celebrated for her swirling dances, staged with stunning lighting effects in which colors shifted and changed according to the mood of her choreography.

> She is a spectacle that is scarcely equalled by rainbows, torchlight processions, Niagara Falls, or naval parades. She is apparently enveloped in weather . . . Through it all the young woman is as distinctly visible as though she were in her bath. Her garments are the merest atmosphere, which scatters and billows and bursts into opaline clouds as she agitates her round and supple body and flings her limbs powerfully in various directions.*

Her experiments in color, lighting, and motion may well qualify her for consideration as a progenitor of psychedelic art. Chéret designed the first poster of Loie Fuller (*Color Plate 42*) and later did two others. Lautrec also portrayed her, as did the posterists George de Feure, Orazi, and Pal.

After Chéret, Alphonse Mucha (1880-1939) was one of the strongest influences on poster art. Mucha's style is synonymous with Art Nouveau, and his mosaics created an impact on other poster artists as well as oil painters. Born in Bohemia, Mucha went to Paris in 1887 and built his reputation there. His florid, richly colored, highly textured treatments of subject matter are distinctive. Particularly noteworthy are his exotic "Byzantine" women *(G-4)*, best seen in the Job cigarette-paper advertisements (one of which appears as *Color Plate 44*) and a series of decorative panels done in 1897 and later *(G-5, G-6)*.

More stylized in his treatment of women is Aubrey Beardsley (1872-98), the most famous British practitioner of Art Nouveau. Beardsley's designs are decorative, but unlike Mucha's, spare and simple, yet his women evoke a sense of sophisticated decadence associated with high fashion *(G-12)*. Dudley Hardy (1867-1922), a contemporary of Beardsley, was clearly under Chéret's influence when he executed his celebrated covers for *To-Day* and *Gaiety* magazines. Hardy infused his poster art with a vitality and light touch—characteristics hitherto absent from English posters—and was particularly fond of displaying women in tutus and tights *(G-7)*.

As Art Nouveau gained momentum in European and American poster art early in the 20th century, fewer Chéret-inspired pin-ups appeared, and by 1910, the heyday of the French glorification of femininity was

---

* Hugh Morton, "Loie Fuller and Her Strange Art," *Metropolitan Magazine* (New York), May 1896, pp. 277-83.

past. In the Britain of the New Women and suffragettes, even the warmest of Beardsley's posters were austere. In Germany and Austria, there were Jugendstil posters, the Teutonic form of Art Nouveau (G-11), reminiscent of Mucha but without his special interest in female subjects. In Belgium (G-8, G-9), Italy (Color Plate 46; G-15), and even Japan (G-18), the styles of Chéret, Mucha, and Beardsley were variously felt and assimilated; but with an emphasis on form rather than subject, women were no longer emphasized in posters. In America (after an initial poster craze in 1894, when a revival of The Black Crook was advertised by several Chéret posters), posterists like Will Bradley, Maxfield Parrish (G-17), and Edward Penfield patterned their work on the decorative art of Mucha and Beardsley.

From 1914 until about 1960, the poster was no longer a major vehicle for pin-ups. During World War I, posters were given a new role: the glamorization of war, usually through heroic or allegorical themes, for propaganda, morale-boosting recruitment, and fund raising. (Even Charles Dana Gibson stopped depicting Gibson Girls in his wartime posters.) In World War II, although posters had become a less vital medium of communication and were more limited in production owing to paper shortages, they still served many of the same functions.

In the early 1920s, posters were widely used for product advertising in business and industry, but with the invention and spread of the radio, they diminished in value as advertising tools and their use was gradually limited to travel, the performing arts, and a few other specialized areas. Poster artists continued to depict attractive women, but with an emphasis on good looks, health, and cheerfulness, rather than on sexual appeal.

By the end of the Great Depression, posters had become a minor advertising medium. Advertising agencies preferred buying time on radio or space in newspapers and magazines. Posters on billboards were decried (as they are today) for defacing highways, landscapes, and urban architecture, and were considered inferior in status to murals, mosaics, or other forms of "lobby art." At about the time that television became the prime advertising medium, posters had been relegated to subways, buses, theater lobbies. A few advertising agencies began to employ photography in a wide range of advertising media, particularly in television commercials. Such use of photography gave rise to a new generation of posters, appealing, at least initially, to youth movements.

The contemporary poster first appeared non-photographically as the psychedelic poster—drawing on the decadence of Mucha and Beardsley. Rock music, in its first and still acknowledged association with drugs, inspired the first psychedelic posters. Characterized by day-glo colors, abstract design, and balloon-style lettering difficult to read, the psychedelic poster, with its dense texture, recalled the exemplars of Art Nouveau. Thus, many republications of those almost-forgotten artists were added to the catalogues of modern poster publishers. This style of poster gave way to the superslick ultrasophisticated photographic poster that today enlivens the environment of the young.

There are relatively few of the traditional pin-up poses in the wide spectrum of contemporary poster subjects. More prevalent are takeoffs on the pin-up linked with social, religious, racial, and patriotic themes—usually in the spirit of humorous iconoclasm or satire (G-23; Color Plate 49; Color Plate 51). As indicated earlier, four subjects never depicted sexually hitherto, are now frequently treated in sexual terms—old age, motherhood, interracial groups, and obesity (A-52). On some posters, the title, like a cartoon caption, is integral—for example, the boy-girl poster Pussyfoot (G-24); in others, the photography speaks for itself—for example, Lotus (G-25), which breaks the interracial sex barrier. Still other forbidden themes—homosexuality, fetishism, and soft-core pornography—are discussed in the final chapter.

Cult heroes—political and social revolutionaries, gurus, drug exponents, folk and rock musicians, and literary figures—are a popular theme of contemporary posters. So are certain superstars of the screen who prefer to bypass conventional studio pin-up stills: Sophia Loren (G-26), Raquel Welch (G-27), Brigitte Bardot (G-28), and Jane Fonda (Color Plate 52); Marlon Brando (G-29), a "revived" cult hero, as in the film The Wild One, and Peter Fonda (G-30) and Charles Bronson (G-31). Many older film stars—Theda Bara, Mae West, W. C. Fields, and Humphrey Bogart, to name a few—also appear on contemporary posters.

The modern poster has extended the range—and even the definition—of pin-ups. No longer limited to the cheesecake tradition, poster pin-ups now address us with many forms of sexual images—satirical, topical, ultrasophisticated, and sexually liberated. From peekaboo to orgy, eroticism for its own sake is much in evidence.

Departing from the escapist intention of earlier pin-ups, the new poster pin-ups emphasize goals sought by liberation-inspired youths—goals related not only to fashion and style, but also to sensory awareness, permissiveness, commune-ity, experimentation, and, above all, varieties of sexual experience.

Unlike its antecedents, the contemporary poster—in which the pin-up plays a significant part—is neither regarded nor treated as a limited, potentially rare collector's item. It is rather, like many other modern objects, mass produced and widely disseminated. Sold cheaply in poster shops, in book, campus, department, and other stores, and in "head shops" (along with psychedelia and other drug-related items), the contemporary poster may well be regarded as a medium of genuine popular art.

G-2. Chéret. *La Danse* (1891), 48″ x 32″, *premier panneau sans texte*. Not intended as an outdoor poster, this lithograph shows Chéret's stylistic buoyancy—skirts flying high, an infinite line of chorus girls swirl down from the heavens.

G-3. Chéret, *Saxoléine* (1892), 48″ x 32″. Characteristic use of provocative women to draw attention to a mundane product—lamp oil. The most prominent area is the large expanse of exposed flesh, from nose to breasts.

G-4. Mucha, *Salon des Cent* (1896), 25¼″ x 17¾″. Mucha was renowned for his florid handling of hair in his depictions of exotic "Byzantine" women.

G-5. Mucha, *The Iris* (1897), 42″ x 18¼″, *panneau décoratif,* from the series *Les Fleurs.* Mucha wove his favorite blossoms around beautiful women—flower goddesses.

G-6. Mucha, *Spring* (c.1900), 28″ x 12″, *panneau décoratif*. Besides the iris, Mucha made three more sensuous flower posters—of the rose, the lily, and the carnation. His fondness for series led him to do posters on many other themes, all revolving around images of women—Months of the Year, Four Precious Stones, Four Stars, Four Times of the Day—and two separate series (1896 and c.1900) on the Four Seasons.

G-9. Privat-Livemont, *Absinthe Robette* (1896). Strongly influenced by Mucha, Privat-Livemont was one of the best known and most successful Belgian posterists. The veiled nude, holding up a glass of absinthe, stands with provocatively arched spine.

G-8. Armand Rassenfosse, *Huile Russe* (1896), 38″ x 24″. The artist chose a chambermaid type to advertise his product (shoe polish) appropriately, in contrast to Mataloni's mismatch (*Color Plate 46*). The relaxed position of the model and her absorption in her work lend an intimate feeling to this successful poster.

G-7. Dudley Hardy, *A Gaiety Girl* (c.1894), 28″ x 20″. Hardy might well be called "the English Chéret," for his posters employ the same use of pin-up-type sex appeal for the purpose of advertising. This poster, designed for a play, *Gaiety Girl*, was used to decorate large wall areas of the theater.

G-10. Lucien Métivet, *Scala pour Vos Beaux Yeux* (c.1895). Very much in the spirit of the Gay Nineties, this poster shows the unabashed use of sexual allure as an advertising device.

G-11. Fritz Dannenberg, *Jugend* (1896), 25″ x 19″. Poster for *Die Jugend,* one of the earliest German magazines devoted to *Jugendstil.* Straddling a "popping" champagne bottle, the stylized elfin figure is early "soft-core"—used frequently in modern advertising.

Color Plate 41. Jules Chéret, *Olympia* (1892), 48″ × 32″. An example of Chéret's brilliant use of color. Chéret's women, like those in other great posters of the 1890s, were sensuous, provocative, enticing forerunners of pin-ups in other styles and mediums.

Color Plate 42. Chéret, *Loie Fuller* (1893). 48″ × 32″. The first poster announcing the debut of this sensational "psyche-delic" dancer. Beneath the rhythmic veils, Chéret delicately delineates the contours of Loie Fuller's swirling body.

G-1 (*facing page, inset*). Henri de Toulouse-Lautrec, *Jane Avril* (1893). 51″ × 37″. This first of several posters of the dancer shows Lautrec's brilliance as a designer. Although the model's leg is raised high, her face and general demeanor seem disen-

chanted, perhaps even sad. Lautrec's women nevertheless appeal to one's romantic notions about sordid cafe life. Chéret, whose posters by contrast were always deliciously pretty, regarded Toulouse-Lautrec as a master.

Color Plate 43. Toulouse-Lautrec, *Jane Avril* (1899). 22″ × 14″. In Lautrec's last poster of Avril, she seems to recoil from the serpent with which she is intertwined, yet the arch of her body and her sinuous entrapment inexplicably fascinate the viewer.

Color Plate 44. Alphonse Mucha, *Job* (1898), 57¼″ x 38½″. In this famous poster, the gracefully elegant model, fascinated with the burning cigarette, seems almost to be flirting with the cigarette paper being advertised. The near-psychedelic design and colors in combination with the cigarette paper make this a very popular contemporary poster.

Color Plate 45. Pal (Jean de Paléologue), *Cabourg* (1895), 60″ × 41″. Another artist whose work derived from Chéret, Pal (who signed the name Julius Price on his English posters) was more painterly than Chéret, "rounding", or modeling, his figures for three-dimensionality. Pal illustrated many magazines of the 1890s with cartoon-style pin-ups which were as well endowed as the delightful, delighted bather shown here.

Color Plate 46. Giovanni Mataloni, poster for *Auer Gas Lamps* (1895). The beauty of this teasing semi-nude (in a setting à la Mucha) transcends her incongruous role of promoting ordinary gas lamps. Published by Darien House, New York.

Color Plate 47. H. Gray, *Cycles Sirius* (1899). 54″ × 38″. An émigré to Paris, Gray made several outstanding posters for the Sirius company, showing free, festive nudes amusing themselves astride bicycles—then the rage. Published by Darien House, New York.

CYCLES Sirius

H. GRAY
99

14 & 16, Rue Duret, PARIS

Color Plate 48. *Mood in Deco*. 35″ × 24″. A contemporary poster in the post-Nouveau style called Art Deco. This poster is not actually from the Deco period but was made in the 1960s by artist Ed Robbins for Poster Prints, Norristown, Pa.

Color Plate 49. *Girl with the Nun's Habit* (1968), 42″ x 29″. A modern peekaboo pin-up, this poster satirizes the traditional celibacy of religious orders. Photo: George Adams. Personality Posters.

Color Plate 50. *Super Nova Girl* (c. 1971). An almost-life-size photo of a black beauty in a contemplative mood—a superb example of sophisticated contemporary poster conception and colour reproduction. Photo: Hans Feurer. Published by Post Verkerke Reprodukties NV, Bennekom, Holland.
Color Plate 52. *Barbarella* (Jane Fonda) (c. 1968). A publicity pose in the same satirical vein as the film

Color Plate 51. *Ultra Violet* (1968). 42″ × 30″. Themes abound in this poster. Above the pin-up of Andy Warhol's Superstar Ultra Violet, the pop art painting points the gun (violence) at YOU (victim) over the American flag. Photo: Oscar Abolafia. Personality Posters.

POSTER VERKLARING REPRODUKTIES NV. / BENNEKOM HOLLAND / 4522 / SUPER NOVA GIRL / PHOTOGRAPHY: LAENDERPRESS / PRINTED IN THE NETHERLANDS

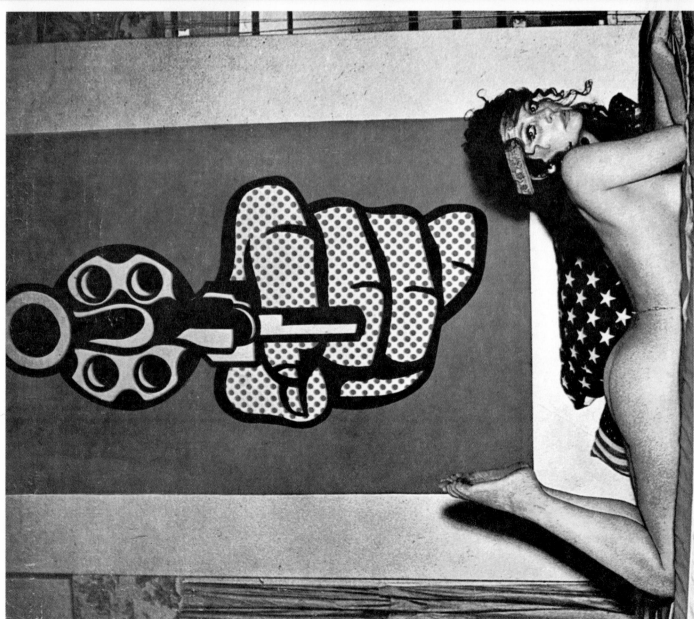

Color Plate 52. *Barbarella* (Jane Fonda) (c.1968). A publicity pose in the same satirical vein as the film *Barbarella* (1968). Miss Fonda, a crusader in the anti-Vietnam and Women's Liberation movements, has played many sexploitative roles in films and probably knows as well as anyone else the feeling of being regarded strictly as a sex object. Photo: David Hurn. Personality Posters.

G-12. Aubrey Beardsley, *The Stomach Dance* (1894), original approximately 9″ x 6″; revived as modern poster, 27″ x 20″. A leader of Art Nouveau in England, Beardsley was a book illustrator as well as posterist. Many of his drawings contained erotic images, particularly women with their breasts projecting from their corsets. His eroticism, however, usually bordered on the bizarre, and his stylized depictions of women make them seem cold and distant. In its original form, this poster was an illustration for Oscar Wilde's one-act tragedy *Salome*.

G-13

G-14

G-15

G-16

G-13. Leonetto Cappiello, *Le Frou Frou* (1899), 65" x 45". Born in Italy, Cappiello went to Paris as a young man and is considered a French posterist. Influenced by Chéret, his posters characteristically show pretty, smiling women playfully enjoying themselves.

G-14. Jules Alexandre Grün, *Scala* (1900), 48" x 35". There is little doubt of Chéret's influence—the jovial women, strong colors, and deliciously evocative position.

G-15. Marcello Dudovich, *Liquore Strega* (1906). An enchanting early-20th-century example of the pin-up in advertising.

G-16. Misti (pseudonym), *Le Petit Chat* (1899), 56" x 40". A typical French pin-up-type poster in which the treatment of the figure is similar to Cappiello's, the style to Chéret's.

G-17. Maxfield Parrish, *The Century* (1897), 20" x 13". Several of Parrish's posters and many of his book illustrations were variations on this wistful, knee-clasping nude, which he did as a poster for *Century Magazine*.

G-17

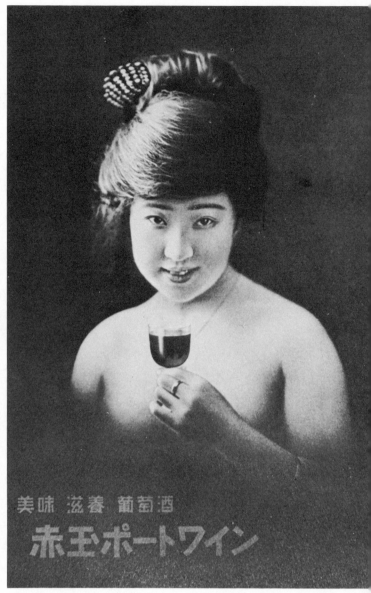

G-18. Tsunetomi Kitano, *Export Exhibition* (1911). This bilingual poster from the Orient combines traditional Japanese beauty with Art Nouveau style. The treatment of garment, hair, and flowers is unmistakably influenced by Mucha.

G-19. Japanese advertisement for port wine (1922). Toshiro Kataoka Agency. In this early Japanese photographic poster, a young model looks longingly at the viewer. A delicate and successful use of sex in advertising.

G-21. *High Boots* (1971). 41″ x 30″. Lovely body and pose combine with leather boots, elegantly suggesting the familiar boot fetish. Photo: Jerry Yulsman. Published by Personality Posters, New York.

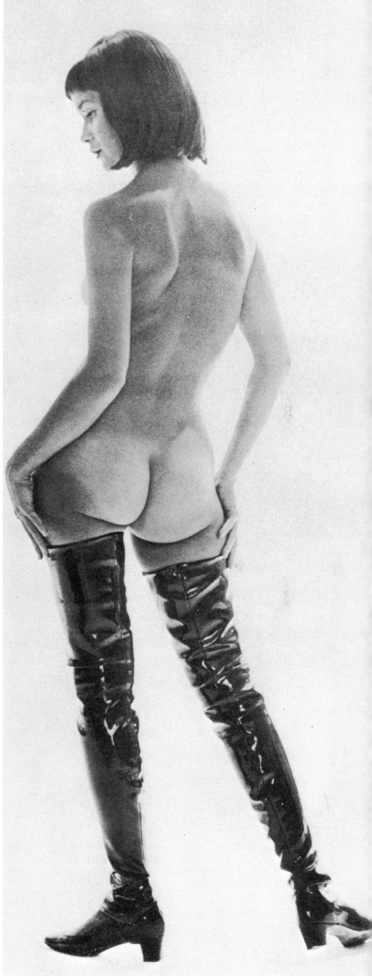

G-20. *Captive Bosom* (1969). 41″ x 29″. Dramatic closeup photo uses title and garment subtly to convey "bondage" theme. Photo: Mighty Mouse Studio, London. Published by Personality Posters, U.K., Ltd.

227

G-22. *Marie Three* (1969), 30″ x 43″. One of a series of pin-ups of the model Marie—here on a bed of "fluff," partly wrapped in cellophane. Photo: Isis Veleris. Personality Posters.

G-23. *Soul* (1970). 38″ x 25″. One of many posters on the emergence of black pride, or the "black-is-beautiful" theme. Here the smiling "Afro" model is identified with soul food: black-eyed peas, ham hocks, collards, yams, etc. Photo: Tony Currin. Personality Posters.

SOUL

G-24. *Pussyfoot* (1971). 41″ x 29″. Obvious sexual wordplay in a boy-girl pin-up poster, the boy in this case playing a small part in fulfilling the visual pun. Photo: Jerry Yulsman. Personality Posters.

G-25. *Lotus* (c.1970). 40″ x 29″. Nudity blends with the interracial theme in this exotic boy-girl poster. Iconoclastic rather than humorous, suggesting the profound beauty of an intimate relationship. Photo: Ruspoli-Rodriguez. Personality Posters.

G-26. *Sophia Loren* (1967). 42″ x 30″. The Italian actress and sex symbol in a scene from the film *Boy on a Dolphin* (1957). One of the earliest superstar posters. Miss Loren's pose is not in the traditional pin-up style, which is seldom seen in contemporary posters of movie stars. Poster Prints.

G-29. *Marlon Brando* (1967). 42″ x 30″. From the film *The Wild One* (1954), this is a "revival" poster issued in the late 1960's. Brando's earlier movies, such as *A Streetcar Named Desire* (1951), *On the Waterfront* (1954), and this one, generally showed him as a "brute"—tough on the outside, sometimes tender inside. Poster Prints.

G-27. *Raquel Welch* (1967). 42″ x 30″. A quasi-pin-up pose, in which presumably one sees a scene from the film *One Million Years B.C.* (1967). Miss Welch, a sex symbol, is the subject of at least half-a-dozen contemporary posters, some more "posed" than others. Poster Prints.

G-28. *Brigitte Bardot* (1967). 42″ x 30″. This well-known poster of the French sex-kitten shows Bardot's tough, independent spirit. The motorcycle, a phallic symbol, appears in several other famous posters (see also *G-29, G-30*). Poster Prints.

G-30. *Easy Rider* (Peter Fonda) (1969). 29″ x 52″. Fonda's role in *Easy Rider* propelled him to international fame. Radical, anti-war, anti-establishment, turned on to drugs, seeking Love and Peace—the character he portrayed greatly appealed to the hip generation. This prize-winning poster (*Newsfoto,* February 1969) shows Fonda on location. Poster Prints.

G-31. *Charles Bronson* (1970). 42″ x 29″. Hidden in supporting roles for many years, Bronson has only recently emerged as a film superstar—a silent, rugged stubbornly courageous man. Not glamorous or handsome in the traditional sense, Bronson portrays inner strength and conviction—characteristics prized by his growing number of young followers. Personality Posters.

Beyond the Cheesecake Tradition

Beyond the Cheesecake Tradition

This chapter deals with quasi-pin-ups and pseudo-pin-ups that derive from or exploit the pin-up idea. Some "true" pin-ups are included here for comparative purposes, particularly to illustrate the evolution of certain kinds of pin-ups into modern forms that formerly would have been called pornography but that now border on the respectable.

Introducing the chapter are four sequences of pin-up poses or situations as they have developed through the years. Certain poses, reappearing decade after decade, become familiar to, even expected by, the habitual pin-up viewer. Yet the sexual art of each decade has its distinctive spirit or character—for instance, the campy humor of the 1940s, or the serious, more direct sexuality of today. Not only are such comparative sequences entertaining, they also demonstrate graphically how the pin-up has come to its present state, how it may even be evolving beyond pin-up art in the original sense. Thus, where a model once touched her breast coyly, as an affectation, today she might fondle herself with undisguised pleasure. If today's generation of pin-up viewers is less shocked by open auto-eroticism than our grandparents were by coquettish suggestions, can we be far from the time when any sexual inclination or activity will be freely portrayed—in other words, the end of the need for peekaboo titillation that has always been the basis for pin-up art? The anti-pin-up may be coming of age.

Through these comparisons one can observe the patterns of shifting sexual focus: the early emphasis on the whole body; the shift to legs; the gradual emergence of the breast; the nipple in full view; the turn to the backside, buttocks becoming the dominant feature; the attempts to combine breasts and buttocks in one pose; the stocking-and-garterbelt motifs, first with, then without, panties; the gradual spreading of legs; the introduction of "beaver" poses, first with shadowy tufts of pubic hair, then the pubis in full view; the appearance of inner parts of the vulva in "split-beaver poses," with a de-emphasis of the rest of the model's body. The pattern is clear. Pin-ups, like so many other aspects of modern life, have become specialized. The whole is fragmented into areas of particular interest, even to the point of exploiting classic psychosexual hang-ups—fetishes.

With increasing knowledge, we have come to realize how wide a sexual latitude exists in every human being.

Psychoanalysis suggests that every person carries a seminal impulse of every emotion of which mankind is capable. Everyone has some Gandhi in him, some Hitler; generosity and selfishness; maleness and femaleness. These notions are now generally accepted and are being explored not only in theory but in reality—through various forms of psychotherapy, consciousness-raising groups, individual or collective experiments in living, and Women's Liberation (which in its broadest sense means men's liberation as well). All these movements, or directions, have at least one thing in common: expanding the range of personal experience to encompass the many feelings and predilections that depersonalized society has not previously encouraged.

Expanding sexuality is both prevalent and significant today. It is probed, brooded on, encouraged in literature, college and adult education courses, television, films, and a myriad of publications that cater to such specialized sexual interests as homosexuality, sapphism, nudism, fetishism. The concern here is mainly with such publications and especially with those "specialized" pictures that suggest, derive from, or otherwise relate to the pin-up style and purpose. Although many of the pictures selected depart radically from the cheesecake tradition, all of them retain at least one of its characteristics—address to the viewer of fantasy stimulation, for example.

Modern pictorial publications relying on specialized sexual interests should not be judged on a scale of "deviations" from the norm. As history makes clear, the norm inevitably changes. Thus the publications discussed here, if judged at all, should be considered in terms of their basic honesty or dishonesty in presenting their material—although it must be noted that much of the subterfuge of publishers is a direct consequence of censorship and of postal laws that have set arbitrary limits on what can and cannot be published legally.

Some of the pictures in this chapter are, without doubt, tasteless, and many defeat the spirit of the original cheesecake formula. But there is no disputing the ever-increasing demand for them. Circulations of "all-beaver" magazines are soaring. Homosexual pin-ups, addressed to the many sprouting Gay Liberation groups, are emerging in quantity. Presented pictorially, these developments serve further to document the evolution—and perhaps implicit downfall—of the pin-up.

H-1

H-2

H-3

H-4

H-5

H-6

H-1 through H-12. Comparative series on the theme of pin-ups in mirrors. Following a chorus girl of the 1860s are an "art" photograph (*Art Inspirations,* c.1920), a semi-nude show girl (c.1928), a burlesque star (1938), a burlesque dancer (c.1955), a French pin-up, and an assortment of mirrored models from the late 1960s to the present, ending with Marianne Gordon, a *Penthouse* Pet of the Month. (H-6, *Folies de Paris et de Hollywood,* 1962; H-8, *View.*)

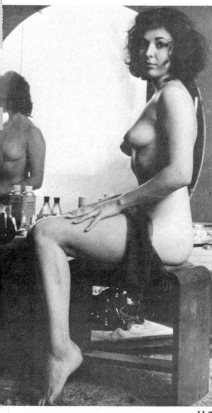

H-7

H-8

H-9

H-10

H-11

H-12

241

Beyond the Cheesecake Tradition

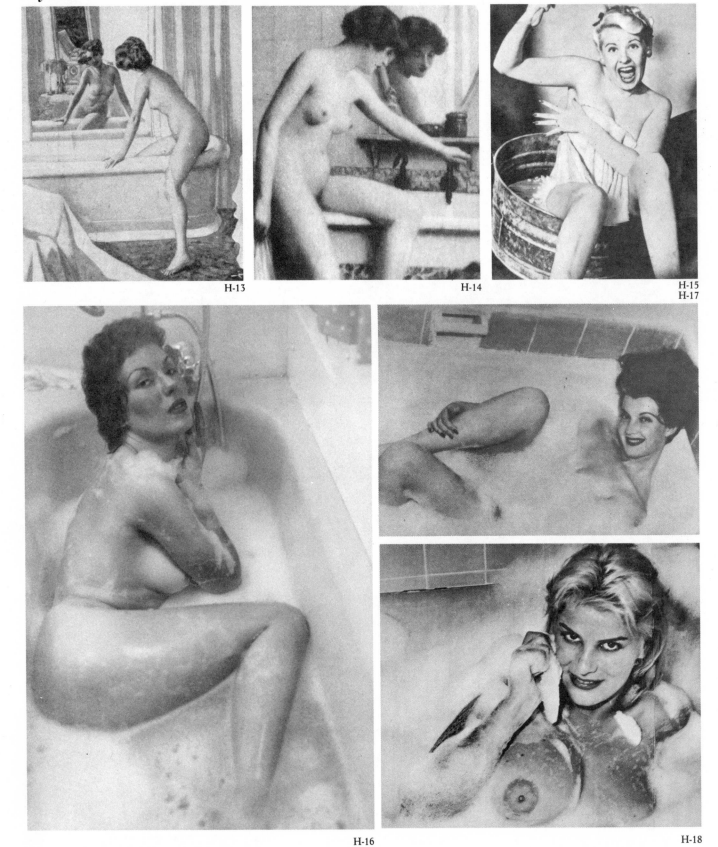

H-13   H-14   H-15
                                               H-17

H-16   H-18

H-13 through H-27. The bath motif, beginning with two early all-nude models daintily and naively preparing to bathe (c.1900 and c.1925). The remaining photographs show the progression of sexual allure from the humor of the 1940s to the more direct sexuality of the late 1960s to the present. H-15, H-17, two photos in which the model's sexual parts are completely covered. In the remaining photos there is a gradual emergence of breasts, nipples, the pubic area, buttocks, and finally a conservative beaver pose (*Knave*, September 1971). (H-16, *Topper*; H-25, *Parade*, London.)

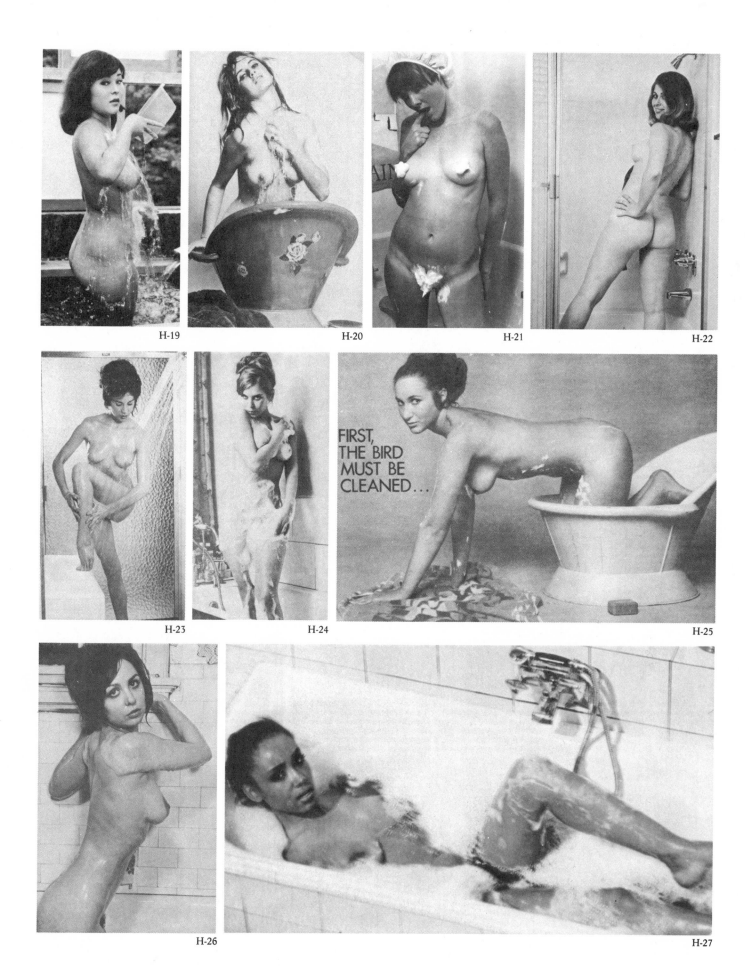

H-19

H-20

H-21

H-22

H-23

H-24

FIRST,
THE BIRD
MUST BE
CLEANED...

H-25

H-26

H-27

Beyond the Cheesecake Tradition

H-28

H-29

H-30

H-31

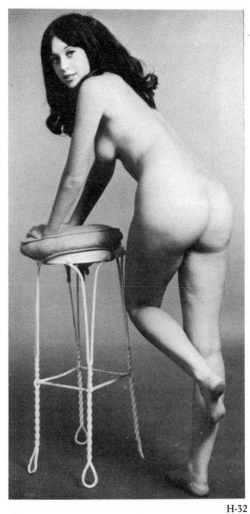

H-32

H-33

H-28 through H-34. A sequence based on bare behinds—sometimes regarded as the "buttocks fetish"—starts with a naive "art" photograph from c.1930 and shows a progression of posterior views, with an increasing emphasis on erotic suggestiveness. As the pictures become more modern, the innocence is replaced by a bold sexuality. The black model, from a contemporary poster, "Coppertone" (Personality Posters), is somewhat out of context, since the poster is an obvious spoof on tanning cream and thus divides its content between sexuality and its satirical message. (H-29 and H-30, *Folies de Paris et de Hollywood;* H-31, *Ultra;* H-32 and H-34, *Rogue.*)

H-34

H-35

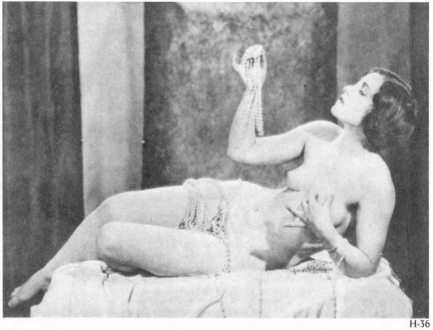

H-36

H-37

H-38

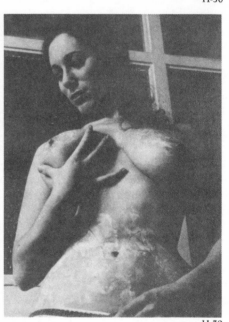

H-39

H-40

H-41

H-42

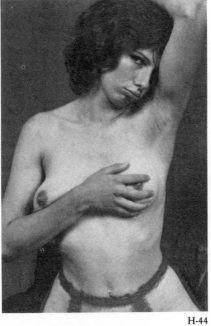

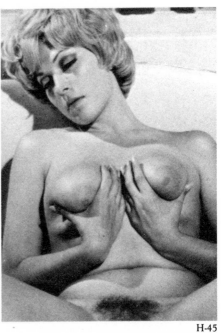

H-43

H-44

H-45

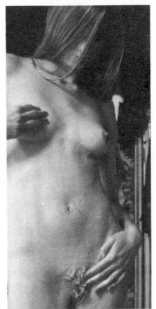

H-35 through H-48. Breast- and nipple-play. The first two pictures, "art" photographs from c.1925, show remarkable candor for their day. They are followed by two "cupping" pictures from the early and mid-1950s. The remaining photos, from the 1960s and 1970s, show a progression of increasing seriousness. Note also the distinction between those models who appear to be pleasing themselves and those who are using breast-play as a lure to the viewer. Some of the pictures show, or try to show, unabashed ecstasy in auto-eroticism. (H-47, *Men Only*, April 1972; H-48, *Mayfair*, May 1972.)

H-46

H-47

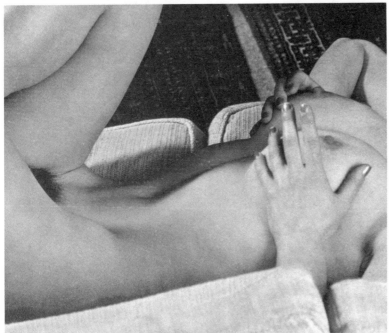

H-48

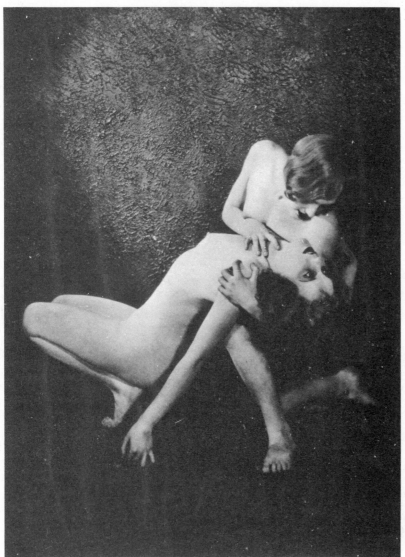

H-49

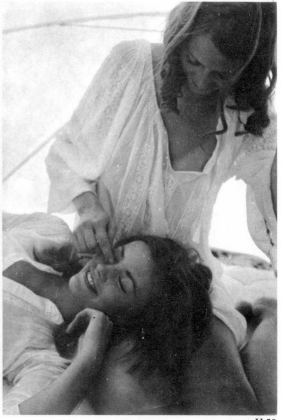

H-50

H-49 through H-55. Sapphic pin-ups, going by degrees towards the suggestion of lesbianism. For whom are they intended? H-49, a theatrical pose by the Philbin Sisters, c.1930, in which eroticism is evident but not sexually explicit. H-50, from a 1973 calendar published by Accidentia Druck, Düsseldorf, and Universe Books, New York. H-51, "Sisters" embracing in a photo-poem (*Men Only*, April 1972). H-53 "Parisiennes" in a London erotic stage review (*Men Only*, April 1972). H-55, a contemporary poster portrait, *Les Girls*, showing models in explicit lesbian roles of "masculine" dominance and femininity (Personality Posters, New York).

H-51

Sapphic pin-ups

As early as the 1920s, Sapphic pictures (illustrations of women interacting with women) appeared occasionally in pseudo-art magazines. Now, some girlie magazines (*Men Only,* for example) and calendars contain highly suggestive pictures—but within the borders of legality—of women together in erotic or potentially erotic situations. Are these women performing for lesbian readers or for male titillation? (Although men have not traditionally been inclined to advertise any interest in lesbianism, such interest has always been evident. In some brothels, prostitutes have put on shows—often using dildoes, false male organs, to simulate copulation.) In their poses, the models are often addressing the viewer, not each other; so it is likely that these pictures are intended mainly for men. Frequently they utilize garterbelts, high heels, silk stockings, and other gear that, as seen on page 258, is associated with fetish art.

H-56. The suggestion of lesbianism, intentional or otherwise, appears frequently in women's lingerie and clothing advertisements in magazines of the highest quality. This ad for brand-name lingerie ran in *Cosmopolitan* (New York), May 1972.

H-53

H-55

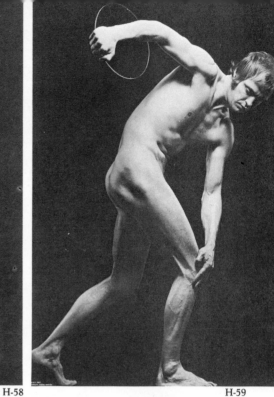

H-57   H-58   H-59

H-57 through H-62. "Art," physical culture, and musclemen. H-57, Terrel Kennedy, dancer, c.1928. H-58 and H-59, an amusing pair of discus throwers, one from c.1930, the other a contemporary poster, c.1970 (Personality Posters U.K. Ltd.). H-60, W. Balmus, c.1930, "all-round athlete from Australia, in one of the effective poses that make his act an artistic success in Keith vaudeville." H-61, a black model, 1936—not uncommon in "art" photography magazines. H-62, Anthony J. Sansone, c.1935—"Not a Greek god in bronze, but . . . deep-tanned and powerful."

H-60   H-61

W. BALMUS, all-round athlete from Australia, in one of the effective poses that make his act an artistic success in Keith vaudeville.

H-62

H-63

H-64

H-65

H-63 through H-66. Modern beefcake. H-63, John Decola in standard pose, for article on body-building food. H-64, highly oiled skin surface exaggerates still further overdeveloped muscles of this model—from an advertisement for gymnasium equipment. H-65, prize-winning muscleman captioned: "an amazing study in combined bulk and streamlined symmetry. Yvon Brunet's bone structure is ideally constructed to accommodate this optimum of muscle massiveness." H-66, Ernie Phillips (described as "big, powerfully-built, supremely-chiseled") and Betty Weider, from *Young Mr. America*, Union City, N.J., 1965.

H-66

Male pin-ups

As observed earlier, pin-ups of male screen stars and superstars are mostly for women. Their appeal generally consists in more than physical attributes—romance, adventure, charm, and so on (see pages 161-73). Here, we are concerned with male pin-ups intended primarily for men.

From the 1920s on, pseudo-art magazines presented male dancers and lithe athletic types; the models became more muscular as the years went by. Musclemen evolved from widespread interest in physical culture in Great Britain and the United States during the 1920s. They seem to suggest a heroic carryover from the Greek gods, but with an emphasis on virility and potency, and with overdeveloped musculature as the indicator. Typical was Charles Atlas, who began as a "97-pound weakling" and whose developed body in the advertisements has not changed since 1921. Some musclemen have developed their bodies to what many people consider a grotesque degree.

The advertisements in the "straight" musclemen magazines are for body-building equipment, vitamin products, and other musclemen publications. Feature articles and illustrations stress physical fitness, competition, growing from weakling to superman, and attracting women. The principal readers are young men, from the age of puberty

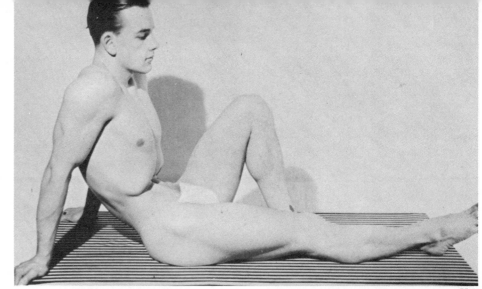

H-67

H-68

H-69

H-70

H-71

H-72

H-67 through H-72. Transitional pin-ups, from magazines with titles that are ambiguous in relation to their content. H-67, smooth-skinned model sucks in stomach to emphasize chest structure. H-68, a well-oiled model with G-string jock and fishnet backdrop accompanied by a caption telling how the reader may build the same muscles. (From *Judo-Muscleman World*, a magazine whose inside cover reads:

> All Physique reproductions herein are published in order to aid the artist, sculpture, photographer and model, also the physical culturist and enable them to further pursue their studies of the basic human figure the fundamental basis of all art. It is the purpose of this publication to capture the fixed lines, contour lighting and definite shadows, in order to enable the artist and photographer to make more authentic reproductions. The model to observe the various poses and the physical culturist to gain incentive and perhaps be inspired by the many fine physiques appearing here.)

H-69, unmistakable homosexual suggestion. H-70, a picture from *Boys in Leather* (Los Angeles), 1964, all of whose illustrations show men in various states of undress (but never nude), wearing leather clothes associated with motorcycles and "chopper" clubs. H-71, artist's rendering of male counterpart of female fetish prototypes—in this case, modern telephone-line workers in skin-tight jeans and "engineer" boots—supermasculine he-man types. H-72, caption gives model's name, age, height, weight, and body dimensions—waist, calf, arms, neck, chest—plus address from which photographs may be ordered. (H-67, H-69, H-71, *Physique World*, Ridgefield, N.J., c.1962; H-68 and H-72, *Judo-Muscleman World*, New York, c.1960.)

H-73 and H-74. Two contemporary posters, Michelangelo's *David* and a model, *"Herbie."* Both are clearly intended for the gay market—the former by virtue of its selection as a contemporary poster and its boyish erotic suggestiveness, the latter by virtue of its "tough" style and soft-core use of pneumatic drill as erection-substitute. *"Herbie"* may also be regarded as a spoof on the male-physique magazine style. (Both published by Personality Posters, New York.)

H-75 and H-76. From an openly homosexual magazine, *Him* (Hamburg), October 1971. Becoming increasingly popular in the 1970s, gay magazines do not attempt to hide behind physique or fetish themes and do not treat homosexuality as a psychological or social ill. The new gay magazines—stylish, often artistic—generally depict young or boyish models in nude, semi-nude, or erotic poses. They also crusade for social and political (legal) acceptance of homosexuality. There is a paradox here: Logically, women's magazines should be presenting male pin-ups as counterparts of Playmates or Pets, but up to now, male pin-ups of the beefcake variety are presented more for homosexual men than for heterosexual women. (Photos: Wolfgang Selitsch.)

H-73   H-74   H-75   H-76

to the mid-thirties, interested mainly in building their bodies in a quest for self-confidence and admiration by their buddies and girl friends.

Next in the progression are transitional publications—homosexual physique magazines—in which the poses, type of models, settings, and garments suggest bisexual, homosexual, and/or sadomasochistic intentions. In these magazines, which began in America around 1950, one senses subterfuge: They are ambiguously titled; references are made to the "philosophy" of the physical culturist; the editors feel called upon to state such purposes as "aiding the artist, sculptor, photographer, and model"; no copyright is claimed; sets of photographs are offered for sale; one or two dull, poorly illustrated articles may appear on judo or karate, evidently so the magazine can claim another "instructional" function.

Other magazines—*Boys in Leather,* for example—are quite open in their intention. Some strive for quality status as homosexual magazines espousing the cause of Gay Liberation. Such publications are relatively new;

they try to establish with candor and style the modern recognition of homosexuality.

In many homosexual magazines, the reader is awed by the consistently large size of the models' penises. According to one model (whose explanation was corroborated by several others), the exaggerated sizes are created by partial masturbation just prior to the photographic shooting. Often a thin gut string is tied around the erect penis, fed between the model's legs, and pulled down from behind to make a full erection appear to be "soft," in a natural hanging position. Frequently, in such poses, one of the model's hands is behind his buttocks, and when that is the case he is most likely holding a gut string. So much for inferiority complexes due to penis envy!

Homosexual physique magazines feature two basic body types—the supermasculine, often hairy-chested, muscleman; and the sensitive, lean-limbed, streamlined youth. Both types are frequently semi-nude, in association with leather jackets, "stomper" boots, and "chopper" motorcycles.

H-77. Paul de Feu. *Cosmopolitan* (London), April 1972. All of London buzzed when this full-color double-page spread appeared. Mr. de Feu, aged 36, was married to, but separated from, Germaine Greer, celebrated champion of Women's Liberation. A construction worker by trade and a college graduate in English literature, he described his posing as the first nude male pin-up in a major British women's magazine as "striking a blow for male servitude." According to an item on "Female chauvinist sexploitation" in *Time,* February 14, 1972, Mr. de Feu stated: "I'm a guy who likes birds. Normally, I'd spend a lot of time, chat and money taking a girl out in the hopes of getting somewhere with her. This way—being a pinup—I've got to the clothes-off stage with thousands of birds straightaway." During that same month, *Cosmopolitan* (New York) printed a centerfold nude photograph of the American actor Burt Reynolds.

H-78. "Mark—Soho Newsletter Spring '72 Pin-up." *Soho Newsletter* (New York), Spring 1972. Published in a bimonthly community newsletter, this counterpart of the female beaver pose, "posed for women, in the context of sexual liberation," represents the newest development in the "sexist exploitation of the male body." (Photo: Jeanne Black.)

Nudist magazines

Much like the muscleman magazines, nudist magazines range from genuine espousal of the nudist way of life to unmistakable exploitation of nudist photography simply as a guise to picture nude men and women legally. In both real and "pseudo" nudist magazines, the text espouses the principles of free, healthy living. Many of the magazines carry both genuine and pseudo-nudist pictures: the viewer can distinguish one from the other by the backgrounds, props, and pose, posture, and attitudes of the subjects. Nudist magazines are usually available through the same retail outlets that sell pin-up magazines. Many originate in Scandinavia but are published internationally. Sample titles are *Sun & Health* (international), *Gymnos, Helios, Hellas, Sauna,* and *Tidlösa;* and, in the United States, *INS* (*International Nudist Sun*), *Nude Living, Nude Look, Nudism Today, Nudist Adventure, Nudist Week,* and *Sundial.* American magazines emphasize sun worship; European magazines focus more on nudist living in conjunction with physical culture.

H-79

H-80

H-79 through H-87. The pictures on this and the following page are from magazines that espouse the principles of nudist living, health, sunshine, shamelessness of body, and beauty of the "natural" state. The viewer will sense which pictures are of genuine nudists and which are printed as a legal means of distributing nudity despite otherwise unpermissive postal laws. H-79, H-80 and H-82 date from 1946, H-81 from 1965. The photos on the following page date from the 1960s or from 1970. (H-81 and H-83, *INS;* H-84, H-85, H-87, *Nude Living;* H-86, *Tidlösa,* Sweden.)

H-81

H-82

Beyond the Cheesecake Tradition

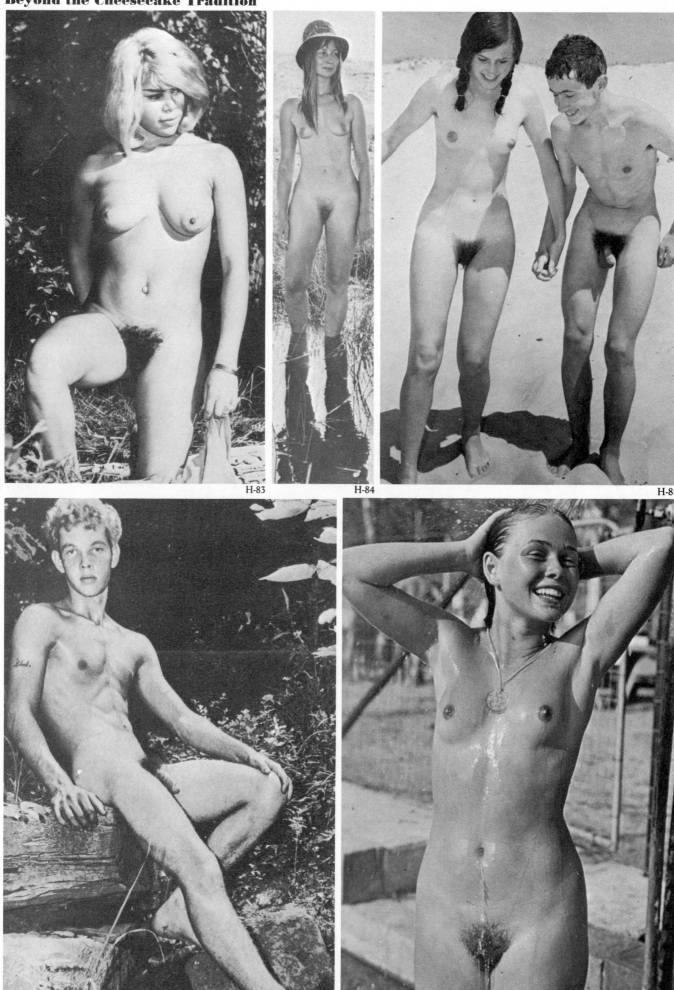

H-83

H-84

H-85

H-86

H-87

Bondage themes

Usually coupled with flagellation and sadomasochism, bondage photography, like some fetish themes, originated in pseudo-art magazines. Bondage photographs tend to show the models in action with each other, and not directly addressing the viewer. Most of the "action" shots, however, are static, with the models really holding their positions for the camera—hence, indirectly for the reader.

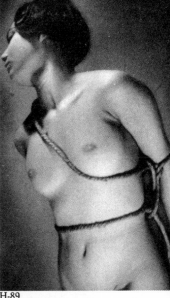

H-88 through H-92. In both style and appeal, the bondage theme is evidently far afield from pin-ups. The first two pictures, from "art" photography magazines (c.1930 and c.1940, respectively), typically only hint at sexual intent, while the more recent three (from the British publication *Humiliation in Bondage*, c.1965) make their messages quite clear.

H-88

H-89

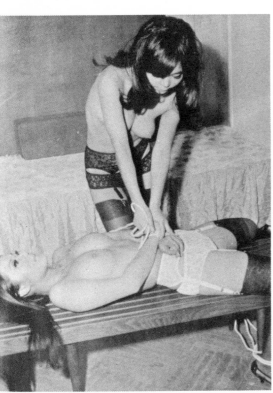

H-90

H-91

H-92

Beaver poses

Since about 1970, quality magazines like *Penthouse, Men Only,* and *Playmen*—at first subtly, then quite obviously—have exposed the pubic hair of their centerfold subjects. Somewhat earlier, however, other girlie magazines, appealing to another kind of audience, had been depicting models in "beaver" poses—in which nude or semi-nude models deliberately assumed positions that unmistakably called the viewer's attention to their exposed pubic area. (More recently and more daringly, some of these lesser-quality magazines and some underground newspapers and newer "radical" magazines have been publishing pictures of models in "split-beaver" poses—with vulvas as well as pubic hair fully exposed. The models not only spread their legs, but use their hands to hold their hips apart, or use their fingers to separate the vulvar lips, and/or contort their bodies so that the viewer cannot help but gaze at the models' vaginas. Whole issues of some magazines are given over to such pictures, which are so specialized as to belong to the fetish category. The pictorial emphasis is so much on those angles, positions, and closeups that reveal the female genitalia that the rest of the model is out of focus or out of proportion—or simply secondary to her pubic area. This emphasis violates the spirit of the traditional pin-up, in which at least a major portion of the model's body is intended to be viewed as an entity. Elsewhere in this volume there are pinups in which pubic hair is treated as a natural feature, deserving of neither banishment nor worship.

257

H-93   H-96   H-97

Fetish themes

Clothing related to fetishistic activity is the most common fetish theme. Indeed, the clothes—separate, unique fetishes—and not the models, are the subjects of the photographs. The models in fetish photographs, in fact, are usually not "well built" enough to be properly encased in the rubber and leather waist-pinching gear that accompanies the closely related bondage fetish. As a consequence, many fetish pin-ups are artist-rendered rather than photographed—as for example, Allen Jones's well-known double poster, *What do you mean?/ What do I mean?*—a black-skinned blonde-haired woman with sharply pointed nipples, shiny leather legs, and lethal-looking spiked heels (*H-96*).

Numerous fetish pin-ups show models wearing garter-belts, even full corsets, made of leather and designed to squeeze the model's waist to suggest bondage. Leather brassieres either squeeze breasts upward so that they pop out of the bra, or have holes of various sizes through which nipples and part of the breasts protrude. Other items in the wardrobe include spiked heels, black stockings, gloves. The range is immense, as are the various kinds of activities.

H-93 through H-97. Five quite different artist-rendered fetish pin-ups, from various sources. Magazines specializing in this theme have titles like *Bizarre*, *Black Stocking Parade* (*H-95*), *Bound*, *Exotique*, *High Heels* (*H-93*, *H-97*, *H-106*, *H-108*), *Nutrix*, *Secret Pleasures* (*H-94*, *H-104*, *H-105*), and *Unique* (*H-103*). The women share traits of hardness, exaggerated sexual parts, "pointiness"—always in association with bondage (pinched waists) and sadomasochism (spiked heels). H-96, Allen Jones, *What do you mean?/What do I mean?*, 1968, is a two-part contemporary poster published by Personality Posters, New York, and Motif Editions, London.

H-98 through H-100. Hose and heels, seen here in three standard forms. (H-98 and H-100, *Sextet*.)

H-98   H-99

H-100

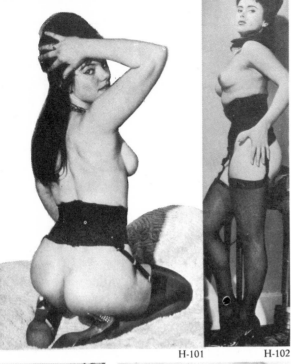

H-101   H-102

H-103   H-104

H-105   H-106   H-107   H-108

H-101 through H-110. Fetish clothes —a progressive sequence from small waist-belt to total leather. Selected from a variety of sources (most not claiming copyright, some not naming the publisher, some naming publishers who cannot be traced), these pictures are not true pin-ups because their emphasis and intention are tied primarily to the clothes and other fetish accoutrements instead of the model's natural charm or physical attributes. The selections, however, do stress the model's address to the viewer (via eyes or body) and therefore represent fetish poses that approach the pin-up style.

H-109   H-110

Soft-core

Soft-core pornography—pictorial punning on erotic themes —is frequently overlooked because it has been around for so long. Often seen in advertising, it is frequently put into play with pin-ups, and attains its most sophisticated form in the contemporary poster. In television commercials, soft-core can be subliminal or farcical. On the one hand, for example, a gasoline commercial shows a "winning" automobile (phallic symbol) tearing through (penetrating) a large hoop with paper stretched across (hymen), which suggests that anyone using the advertiser's product will be both virile and potent. On the other hand, the message of a celebrated shaving cream commercial is blatant. Against a sizzling burlesque song as background, a moist-lipped, thickly accented Scandinavian seductress throatily commands, "Take it off . . . take it all off!" while the man strips his face of shaving cream and whiskers.

Sometimes products themselves take on sexual symbolism and thereby become ideal for soft-core techniques. The Chrysler 300 automobile was designed and advertised as a big car for men only. Long and powerful, it had a prominent front grill. When the Edsel automobile came along, with its vertical, oval, somewhat bifurcated front grill, some observers postulated that a head-on collision of the two cars would be tantamount to an automotive orgasm.

In pictorial soft-core, the erotic overtones are usually not so cataclysmic or far-fetched. For years, magazine covers, space advertisements, and posters have made use of soft-core themes (see *G-11* for an early example in a poster). The contemporary poster is the first medium to utilize soft-core as a distinctive art. The visual pun is still present, but there is greater emphasis on the erotic suggestion than on the symbolic vehicles. All in all, soft-core in contemporary posters is no longer merely humorous or seemingly accidental. Presented for its own sake, it now has its own esthetic.

H-111 through H-118. A selection of soft-core subjects, showing the visual pun at first disguised on a magazine cover (May 1935); H-112, a topless model in "candid" photo with caption "Picture Yourself Playing Your Favorite Instrument" (c.1960); H-113, a touch of autoeroticism (c.1953); H-114, topless model kissing dog with raised head (c.1970); H-115, Japanese advertisement for cigarette lighters (1971); H-116, French advertisement for chocolate-covered biscuits (c.1965). The final two subjects, contemporary posters, turn soft-core into an art of its own. H-117, *Egg in Elbow* (c.1970) suggests erotic penetration—or, to some viewers, birth. (Photograph: Alain de Garsmeur. Published by Personality Posters.) H-118, *Cream* (1970), has obvious oral-genital implications, achieved innocently enough through the use of lips and ice cream in a Pop Art rendering. (Artist: Michael English. Published by Poster Prints, Norristown, Pa.)

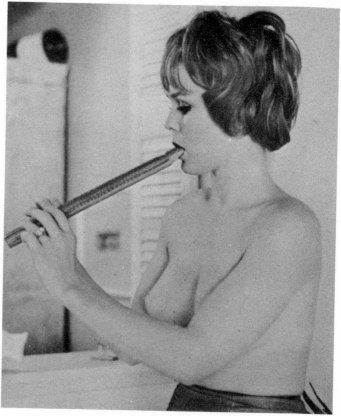

H-111

H-112

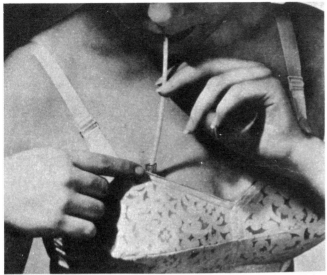

H-113

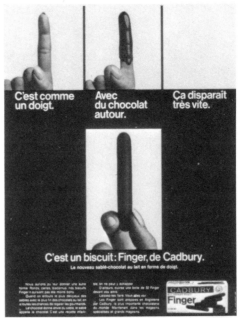

C'est comme un doigt. Avec du chocolat autour. Ça disparaît très vite.

C'est un biscuit: Finger, de Cadbury.

Le nouveau sablé-chocolat au lait en forme de doigt.

CADBURY
Finger

H-116

H-114

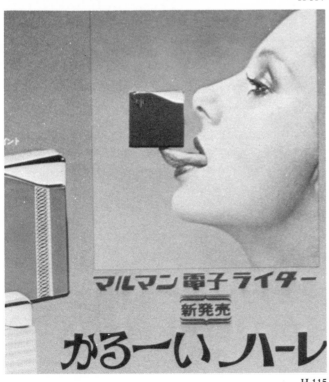

マルマン電子ライター
新発売
かるーい ハーレ

H-115

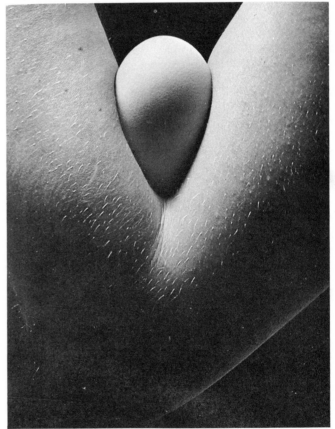

H-117

H-118

Bibliography

Abdy, Jane. *The French Poster: Chéret to Cappiello.* London: Studio Vista, 1969.

Bauwens, M., et al. *Les Affiches étrangères illustrées.* Paris: Boudet, 1897.

Buscaroli, Piero. *Le seduttrici.* Milan: Borghese [n.d., c.1960].

Carline, Richard. *Pictures in the Post: The Story of the Picture Postcard.* 2d ed. Bedford: Fraser, 1971.

Chellas, Allen (ed.). *Cheesecake: An American Phenomenon.* N.J.: Hillman, 1953.

Cruse, Alfred J. *All About Cigarette Cards.* London: Perry Colour Books [n.d., c.1940].

Dulles, Foster Rhea. *America Learns to Play.* New York and London: Appleton-Century, 1940.

Evans, I. O. *Cigarette Cards and How to Collect Them.* London: Jenkins, 1937.

Hillier, Bevis. *Posters.* London: Weidenfeld & Nicolson; New York: Stein & Day, 1969.

Ivins, William M., Jr. *Prints and Visual Communication.* Cambridge, Mass.: Harvard University Press, 1953.

Kyrou, Ado. *L'Age d'or de la carte postale.* Paris: Balland, 1966.

Lange, Ed. *The Shameless Nude.* Los Angeles: Elysium, 1963.

Lauterbach, Carl, and Anatole Jakovsky. *A Picture Postcard Album: A Mirror of the Times.* London: Thames and Hudson, 1961. Also issued as *Postcard Album: Also a Cultural Art.* New York: Universe, 1961.

Levin, Martin (ed.). *Hollywood and the Great Fan Magazines.* New York: Arbor House, 1970.

Maindron, Ernest. *Les Affiches illustrées, 1886-1895.* Paris: Boudet, 1896.

Marcus, Steven. *The Other Victorians: A Study of Sexuality and Pornography in Mid-nineteenth-century England.* New York: Basic Books, 1966; London: Weidenfeld & Nicolson, 1967.

Marx, Roger. *Les Maîtres de l'affiche.* Paris: Chaix, 1896-1900. 5 vols.

Mayor, A. Hyatt. *Prints & People: A Social History of Printed Pictures.* New York: Metropolitan Museum of Art, distributed by the New York Graphic Society, 1971.

Metzl, Ervine. *The Poster: Its History and Its Art.* New York: Watson-Guptill, 1963.

Mott, Frank Luther. *A History of American Magazines.* Cambridge, Mass.: Harvard University Press, 1930-68. 5 vols.

Mucha, Jiri. *Alphonse Mucha: His Life and Art.* London: Heinemann, 1966.

Mucha, Jiri. *Alphonse Mucha: The Master of Art Nouveau.* Feltham, Middlesex: Hamlyn, 1966.

Mucha, Jiri, et al. *Alphonse Mucha: Posters and Photographs.* London: Academy Editions, 1971.

Peterson, Theodore. *Magazines in the Twentieth Century.* Urbana, Ill.: University of Illinois Press, 1964.

Saltpeter, Harry. "Nice Nellie, the Gibson Girl." *Esquire,* February 1943, pp. 47ff.

Schardt, Hermann. *Paris 1900: Französische Plakatkunst.* Stuttgart: Belser, 1968.

Sobel, Bernard. *Burleycue: An Underground History of Burlesque Days.* New York: Farrar & Rinehart, 1931.

Staff, Frank. *The Picture Postcard and Its Origins.* London: Lutterworth; New York: Praeger, 1966.

Sternberg, Jacques, and Pierre Chapelot. *Un Siècle de pin up.* Paris: Planète, 1971.

Sullivan, Mark. *Our Times: The United States, 1900-1925.* New York: Scribner, 1926-35. 6 vols.

Van Every, Edward. *Sins of America: As Exposed by the Police Gazette.* New York: Stokes, 1931.

Wember, Paul. *Die Jugend der Plakats, 1887-1917.* Krefeld: Scherpe, 1966.

Wortley, Richard. *Pin-ups Progress: An Illustrated History of the Immodest Art.* London: Panther, 1971.

Numbers with letter prefixes refer to pictures. Pictures are grouped in the volume as follows:

Numbers with the prefix CP refer to Color Plates.

The Author

Mark Gabor was born in New York in 1939. After receiving a B.A. in literature from Reed College and an M.A. in education from New York University, he worked in book publishing for ten years, principally as managing editor for publishers of art books. Strong interest in contemporary art led him to organize Flatsfixed Gallery/Events (in Soho, New York's latest art center, south of Houston Street), which emphasized the integration of art works with dance, electronic music, and new theater. Mr. Gabor has designed and executed experimental theater sets, installed trapezes in studios and lofts for private use, and performed in happenings and avant-garde dance events. He plays conga drums professionally as well as in workshops for actors, dancers, and children. Currently he earns money as a carpenter and handyman. He plans to move to Amsterdam to explore living in another culture and to pursue street theater, emphasizing circus techniques as a means of easier communication.

He and his wife Nancy, an actress and teacher of improvisational theatrical techniques, have a four-year-old daughter, Julia.

His study of pin-ups as a popular art form was inspired by his participation in a Men's Liberation group growing out of empathy with the precepts and philosophy of Women's Liberation.